PRAISE FOR

HANGDOG DAYS

"Well-researched and fun with flashes of neon—Smoot's *Hangdog Days* captures all the wild color of climbing in the late '70s through the '80s."

—Lynn Hill

"In *Hangdog Days*, Jeff Smoot offers an enlightening behind-the-scenes perspective on this fantastic era and its memorable characters. I was climbing in the areas he describes where and while these scenes were playing out. He captures them vividly."

—Hans Florine

"*Hangdog Days* recalls the colorful personalities and ethical struggles that spurred a revolution in rock climbing. This fun trip back in time will motivate you to climb harder."

—Paul Piana

"Powerful, moving, compelling, outrageous, fascinating—*Hangdog Days* captures eighties climbing perfectly. If you're a climber and you can read, this book's for you."

—Cam Burns

"Full of Homeric characters, epic struggles, heroes and heartbreaks, all played out on an international stage—fans of adventure narratives can't do much better than *Hangdog Days*."

—John Long

HANGDOG DAYS

CONFLICT, CHANGE, AND THE RACE FOR 5.14

JEFF SMOOT

MOUNTAINEERS
BOOKS

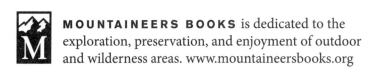 **MOUNTAINEERS BOOKS** is dedicated to the exploration, preservation, and enjoyment of outdoor and wilderness areas. www.mountaineersbooks.org

1001 SW Klickitat Way, Suite 201, Seattle, WA 98134
800.553.4453, www.mountaineersbooks.org

Printed in the United States of America
Distributed in the United Kingdom by Cordee, www.cordee.co.uk
22 21 20 19   1 2 3 4 5

Mountaineers Books and its colophon are registered trademarks of The Mountaineers organization.

Copyeditor: Laura Case Larson
Design and layout: Jen Grable
Photographs: Front cover, upper right: *Todd Skinner and Robin Jones resting between attempts on* Never Never, *Icicle Creek Canyon, 1983*; front cover, lower left: *Alan Watts contemplating* Rude Boys *(5.13c), Smith Rock, 1985*; back cover: *Todd Skinner and crew, including Geoff Weigand and Kim Carrigan, at the base of* The Stigma, *Yosemite, 1985* (Photo by Bill Hatcher); frontispiece: *Alan Watts hiking in to Crooked River Gorge, Smith Rock, 1985*; p. 268: *Todd Skinner and Paul Piana on the* Free Salathé *(VI, 5.13b), Yosemite Valley, 1988* (Photo by Bill Hatcher)
All photos by author, unless otherwise indicated.

Library of Congress Cataloging-in-Publication Data is on file for this title.

Mountaineers Books titles may be purchased for corporate, educational, or other promotional sales, and our authors are available for a wide range of events. For information on special discounts or booking an author, contact our customer service at 800-553-4453 or mbooks@mountaineersbooks.org.

♻ Printed on recycled paper

ISBN (paperback): 978-1-68051-232-8
ISBN (ebook): 978-1-68051-233-5

An independent nonprofit publisher since 1960

For Todd

CONTENTS

Hey Pilgrim!

. . . Allow me to sway you with this plan of a trip down the road of fame, glory and the pursuit of the American dollar: I have just taken a few steps toward the goal at the end of that road and will extend to you now an invitation to come along on the tour of the season. . . . I think that you are going to dissolve if you have to spend another winter in Washington and so why don't you join me on <u>all</u> or at least part of the tour? No money? Absurd! No time? This is the only time of our lives when we dare spend all of our time. . . . What I'm trying to say is I need a partner for this rash tour and I want to know if you can leave your wife, children, dog, home, lawn and job for this short period on a quest for glory? . . . I'm on my way to Tucson in 2 weeks and hope to hear from you before then on your plans. Keep dreamin', stay hungry and remember that there is no finish line!

—Todd Skinner

PROLOGUE

At its heart, rock climbing is simply movement on rock. It is a balance of holding on and letting go, of pushing, pulling, and swinging your way upward, downward, or sideways as the features of the rock and your strength and skill allow. If you have ever climbed a tree, you understand the basics: grab a limb, throw your leg over, pull yourself up, repeat, and climb as high as you dare. Our prehensile limbs make us well suited to climbing. We can hang on to and toe in on edges; jam fingers, hands, and feet into cracks; and hook heels on flakes to pull ourselves skyward up a rock face. We can ascend to absurd heights, to our sheer delight or utter terror, depending on our particular disposition and what there is to hang onto.

Rock climbing is joyous, meditative motion, a sort of gravitational yoga on a vertical scale. Those able to master their innate fear of heights and rational aversion to falling great distances and being smashed into the talus come to enjoy a perverse sense of pleasure in dangling far above the ground. They push harder and higher in search of their physical and mental limits, hoping to survive, of course, but also to have fun.

While simple in theory, in practice rock climbing can be complicated. The climbing medium, the rock itself, is varied and defines the experience. Each type of rock has distinct features; each route is unique and may require specific combinations of athletic strength, gymnastic skill, and mental discipline. On a given route you might encounter cracks so thin that your fingertips barely fit in, or so wide that your fists, elbows, or knees scrape against the rock to maintain purchase; slabs so polished that your feet ooze off if you don't keep moving; or knife-edge flakes and glass-sharp crystals that rip fingertips to shreds if pulled on too hard. It is the flaws in the rock that give the climber something to hang on to and make climbing possible—the cracks, flakes, and imperfect edges resulting from exfoliation, erosion, the freeze-thaw cycle, and other geologic forces, or from man-made defects caused by quarrying or mis-adventures with dynamite. The steeper or more flawless a rock wall, the more physically difficult it is to climb. The higher or less protected a climb is, the more mentally challenging it becomes. What you might climb readily a few feet off the forest duff can become a desperate affair with a thousand feet of open air beneath you, when your muscles are tired, your nerves are frayed, and every move upward is a push into the unknown.

In those moments, the urge to retreat can be strong. Every climber eventually faces such a situation, a pivotal moment between success and failure—that thin line between life and death, triumph and utter humiliation that lurks everywhere in the mountains. Some climbers rush headlong toward these moments while others shy away after their first encounter with the void. These are the moments that define a climber.

What do you do when faced with such a moment? Go for it despite the risk of taking repeated long falls? Climb carefully down, train like mad, and try again another day? Practice the moves on toprope until you have them wired, then return to lead the pitch, confident that you won't fall? Rappel down with a power drill and place a half dozen protection bolts to make the route safe for you to lead? "Improve" a hold to make an "impossible" move easier? Or just chisel some edges into the rock to create big, fat holds up the wall so you and every other climber can do it?

A debate erupted in American rock climbing during the 1980s around these very considerations. It was fueled by the rules climbers had imposed, or tried to impose, on themselves and others over the course of the history of the sport, rules intended to maintain or even increase the challenge and adventure of climbing, but which more often just stirred up trouble.

You might wonder how an activity as straightforward as climbing on rocks could generate bitter controversy. After all, except when viewed through an evolutionary survival-of-the-fittest lens, climbing is not an inherently competitive pursuit. We no longer climb trees to avoid being eaten by predators, unless we're unlucky. Children climb fences, trees, and playground equipment as mindlessly as birds fly, without consideration of how or why. For most aspiring young climbers, conflict arises only when parents, teachers, playground monitors, camp counselors, and other overly concerned adult figures tell them to get down before they fall and hurt themselves. But watch a playground game of "king of the hill" for long enough, and you can see how dissention could arise.

This is a story about the sport of rock climbing during what I call the "hangdog days," that incomparable era of tricksters and traditionalists, great debates and bolt wars that erupted during the late 1970s and early 1980s. It was a period of revolution against the traditional ideals of free climbing as a purist, moralistic pursuit, and its resulting devolution into what became known as "sport climbing." The story is especially about the people involved, those I traveled and climbed with, revered and disliked, or merely crossed paths with once or twice along the way. These major and minor characters, from the great free soloists and traditional climbers of their generation to the lowliest of dirtbagging SOBs the sport has ever known, influenced my thinking about climbing, and ultimately life. This story explores what happened and why it mattered, not only to me but to the people involved and those who have followed.

I have always thought that by turning over these moss-covered stones I might dredge up something of value. I started writing this book several times during the ensuing decades, but it sat unfinished. It was always something I put aside for another day because, unlike other projects and responsibilities, I could come back to it. It could wait. I had time. Then Todd Skinner died.

Todd was one of my good friends and frequent climbing companions during the 1980s. In the letters he wrote to me each winter, in which he tried to cajole me out of rainy Seattle to the sunnier climes of Hueco Tanks or Joshua Tree, he liked to remind me that there is only so much time: "Time is the wind that blows down the corridor of opportunity slamming the doors," Todd wrote in one of those letters. I don't know if this is something Todd made up, quoted from a Louis L'Amour novel, or had read in a freshman philosophy course at the University of Wyoming (assuming finance majors even take philosophy classes). Perhaps it was a little of all three, since Todd was known to mangle a half-plagiarized, hackneyed quote. But it resonated with the news of his death, a reminder from an old friend: "If you're ever going to do anything that's important to you, do it now. This is the only time you have to do everything you ever wanted to do. Don't save anything for the future. The future is now." And, so, I started writing again.

The story is based on actual events, recounted from my faulty memory, haphazard notes, misplaced correspondence, various historical journals and climbing magazines of the era, and, later, by many online articles, social media posts, and discussion forum debates. I have changed or omitted a few names, either because certain people might be unhappy to find their real names attached to a portrayal of how they behaved back then, or because frankly, I don't remember the name of every person I met on the road thirty or more years ago. Aside from that, I have tried to faithfully portray personalities and events, perhaps more kindly than I might have if I'd really wanted to stir things up. Given the passage of years, I may have remembered some details and conversations differently than others might. If on occasion I present a name or historical fact inaccurately, it is unintentional and only through frailty of memory.

The book is part memoir, an account of what I remember, the places I went, the people I met, the stories we told, the slander we spewed around the campfire or during a road trip, and the events that transpired along the way. But mostly it is the story of a generation of climbers who had differing ideas of what climbing was or should be and who argued and acted out in some-times inappropriate ways. It is a story of how, in the end, their squabbles didn't change what is most essential and enduring about the sport.

The sport is still evolving, as it has always done and always will do—with each generation surpassing the next and advancing the game beyond the wild-est dreams of those who came before.

PART ONE

THE HANG-DOG DAYS

It took me an age to realize that with most stories worth a damn, the play of opposites was the force that set the story in motion, and in that motion loomed a question, often a very simple one.

—John Long

1 PHOENIX STYLE

Fred Beckey was sitting on a wooden bench in the book section at the REI Co-op on Seattle's Capitol Hill one afternoon in 1979, his right leg crossed over his left, a stack of books and magazines beside him. He was studying a Green Trails map and taking notes. Beckey, one of the preeminent American mountaineers of his day, was my hero.

In 1942, at age nineteen, Beckey and his brother, Helmy, just seventeen, made the second ascent of Mount Waddington, a remote 13,186-foot peak in the Coast Range of British Columbia. It was a major mountaineering feat that shook the climbing world. He had done more first ascents than almost anybody, ever, and was the author of the *Cascade Alpine Guide*, making him the closest thing there was to a Northwest climbing legend. And here he sat, in the flesh. I'd never seen Beckey in person before, but there was no doubt it was him. He looked just like in the pictures: tall and slim, with dark eyes set deep beneath a prominent bushy brow, his face weathered and craggy. He was a little scruffy, like he had come straight to REI from a week of climbing. He looked old, at least to me. Born in 1923, he would have been fifty-six years old that day, as old as I am as I write this. To a sixteen-year-old kid, he looked every bit of it.

Given the stack of materials beside him, I imagined Beckey was planning a first ascent somewhere in the North Cascades. Either that, or he was doing research for the third volume of his *Cascade Alpine Guide*, which he was rumored to be working on. I admit I was a little starstruck. Being shy by nature, instead of introducing myself, I walked past him and kept going, past the books, the freeze-dried food section, down the squeaky wooden ramp toward the clothing department, and then down the stairs that led steeply to the basement where they hid the shoe department.

The regulars at the University of Washington practice rock, which passed for our local bouldering area, had suggested I get a pair of EBs. My stiff boots worked well on easy routes, like the Tooth and Chair Peak, but they just weren't cutting it on the boulder problems at the practice rock, which required the finesse of a flexible rubber sole.

The clerk measured my foot and brought me a pair of size 9 EBs, a size smaller than my usual shoe size. "They'll stretch out," he assured me. I laced them up and tried them out on the ten-foot-high stone masonry wall they had in the basement for that purpose, an indoor climbing wall the likes of which I had never seen before.

"How are they?" he asked me.

"Kind of tight," I said. "They hurt. Maybe I should get a larger size."

"They're perfect," he said. "You want them tight, the tighter the better. If they don't hurt, they're too big."

BECKEY WAS GONE BY THE TIME I came back upstairs with my new pair of EBs, but he'd left a couple of magazines behind. I sat down and looked through them, curious to see what he had been reading. On top was the current issue of *Off Belay*, a local mountain rag full of articles on backcountry skiing, something of no interest to me. But underneath was the latest *Climbing* magazine, an issue devoted entirely to rock climbing, the one thing I was absolutely crazy about. The cover photo of a climber muscling up a 5.11+ route in the Shawangunks in upstate New York was arousing, but inside it got better, a virtual orgasm of rock climbing delight: reports of hard new rock climbs across America, including first ascents of 5.10, 5.11, and even 5.12 routes in Oregon, Wyoming, Utah, Colorado, and my home state of Washington; feature articles about even harder free climbing in the Gunks; the story of an ascent of *Astroman*, a long 5.11+ free climb in Yosemite, by two best friends; and compelling photos of athletic climbers powering up impossible-looking routes, clinging to imaginary edges, airing it out miles above the ground. Enthralled, I absorbed every word, photo, and letter to the editor.

What was most remarkable about *Climbing* No. 54 was that from the first page to the last, it told the story of a sport in a state of conflict. According to the articles and correspondence, certain rock climbers relied on controversial tactics: they hung on protection or didn't pull the rope down after falling, practiced a route on toprope before leading, preplaced chocks or pitons (or even bolts) for protection, and used gymnastics chalk for improved grip on the rock. In the view of the authors, those sorts of climbers were a bunch of good-for-nothing cheaters.

In the article about the Gunks, "Pox in Vulgaria: The Profit of Impurism," author Mark Robinson described the many problems associated with a new generation of climbers who, in trying to make a reputation for themselves, diverged from the accepted styles employed by the prior generation—by the likes of Steve Wunsch, John Bragg, Henry Barber, and John Stannard, pristinely ethical climbers who had "scrupulously adhered to the principles of clean and free climbing" while advancing the discipline during the early 1970s. Robinson complained that the new generation of Gunks climbers had begun to "cheat" to reach a higher standard of difficulty. Following the establishment of the last wave of hard climbs in the area—including *Supercrack*, at the time rated 5.12+ (then the top of the scale)—Gunks climbers had drifted into "the doldrums," a period of complacency where few new hard routes were climbed and repeating the established hard routes was considered good enough. Then some outsiders came in and shook things up. They climbed all of the old desperate testpieces faster and in better style, including a repeat ascent of *Supercrack* by Yosemite hotshot Ron Kauk. The Gunks locals were stunned. "Complacency gave way to insecurity," Robinson proclaimed, "and *something had to be done.*"

What had to be done, apparently, was to rehabilitate their shattered egos. Eager to prove themselves, this new wave of aspiring hardmen "got pressed into trying new climbs for which they weren't ready," while others resorted to controversial tactics, even drilling bolts on aid and chipping holds into the rock to allow "impossible" routes to "go."

According to Robinson, a line had been crossed. "In the Gunks we seem to have reached the point at which the present people cannot make gains in [difficulty] without a loss in [style]." Robinson envisioned a new breed of climber, one who could return to the old ways and advance both difficulty and style simultaneously. He pointed to recent ascents by "hotshot visitors" from Yosemite Valley, who had once again blown the Gunks away with their superior ability. But, Robinson noted, they had done so in "Phoenix style"—"hanging onto nuts after a fall in order to rest, figure out moves, practice sections of a pitch, and locate the next protection." Even these hotshot Valley climbers, Robinson complained, had given up on purity of style for gain in difficulty, "for the sake of making a name."

Being from the Pacific Northwest, I had been brought up in "the leader must not fall" school of climbing, where you were turned away at the trailhead if you forgot even one of the Ten Essentials, where if you failed to maintain three points of contact at all times you would certainly fall and plunge to your death. Despite my indoctrination into this cult of overbearing safety, I had managed to lead a couple of routes rated 5.9, and I had followed a 5.10 without always maintaining three points of contact and hadn't died. Still, the concept of climbing "Phoenix style" had never occurred to me. I had taken a couple of thirty-foot leader falls, and the only thing I wanted to do was lower off and go throw up in the bushes. I had stepped on a piton once, though, and now I felt bad about it. I felt like one of the cheaters. I wanted to go back and climb the route again without stepping on the piton, if only to clear my conscience.

At the time the only climbers I had heard much about were Beckey and Jim Whittaker, who in 1963 was the first American to summit Mount Everest. As I saw it, to become a well-known climber, you had to be prolific or climb something big. How hanging on a rope or preplacing a protection bolt on a rock climb could lead to fame and fortune was beyond me.

The best article in that issue of *Climbing* was the one about *Astroman*. Two friends, Mark Hudon and Max Jones, had teamed up to climb one of the longest hard free routes in Yosemite Valley. There was no hint of controversy in the article, no complaints about hanging on protection or cheating by using chalk or preplaced gear or any of that. Hudon and Jones simply went climbing. They challenged themselves against one of the most amazing free climbs in America, experienced spectacular technical climbing on perfect, steep granite, overcame the route's many difficulties through sheer tenacity, and had a blast. Damn! That was what climbing was about: the challenge, the camaraderie, the thrill of a day out on a big wall with your best friend. All the rest of that controversy crap, what was that even about? Hanging on the rope, putting in a bolt, trying to make a name for yourself as a climber by engaging in cheater tactics—who did that? And, really, who cared?

I was blissfully ignorant of the roots of the controversies described in *Climbing* No. 54. To me, climbing was still new and fun and frightening and absolutely irresistible. After reading that magazine a hundred times, I knew what I was going to do: I was going to train like mad until I could climb 5.12. I was going to go to Yosemite and climb *Astroman* as soon as humanly possible.

2 THOU SHALT NOT BOLT!

If you want to understand the business of rock climbing, and what sometimes makes it such a touchy subject, a good place to start is 1914, the year Italian climber Guido Rey published *Alpinismo Acrobatico*. In it he revealed the latest in climbing techniques employed in the Dolomites—artificial aid methods such as pounding in a piton, clipping in the rope, and being pulled up the wall with rope tension, all of which contrasted starkly with the English "fair means" approach to mountaineering. Adherents of the fair means school, particularly members of that bastion of snobbery the Alpine Club of London, dismissed ascents made using these "acrobatique" techniques as aberrations and derisively referred to those who employed them as "ironmongers." Such judgments did not stop the ironmongers, who pioneered many long, difficult routes in the Dolomites and elsewhere in the Alps. They pounded away at their iron pitons and dangled guiltlessly from their ropes and rope ladders, unconcerned with what a bunch of silly Englishmen thought of them and their unconventional yet effective methods of climbing "unclimbable" rock.

For whatever reason, the English fair means philosophy appealed to many early American rock climbers. Those who embraced it with puritanical fervor were persuaded that pitons and artificial aid offered an unfair advantage, threatening to make climbers too reliant on equipment. This likely had much to do with the influence of two men: John Muir and Robert Underhill.

John Muir, regarded as the original Yosemite climbing bum, the seminal "dirtbag" climber if ever there was one, had long waxed poetic about his Sierra adventures, which included many an idyllic rock scramble and terrifying mountain ascent, all made without such hindrances as ropes or partners. "No mountaineer is truly free," Muir wrote in 1878, "who is trammeled with friend or servant, who has the care of more than two legs." He rhapsodized about the freedom and sublimity of experiencing wild nature on its own terms. Embodying a pure ideal, he was just as apt to climb a fir tree during a windstorm to feel firsthand the fury of untamed nature as he was to scramble up a granite spire for the view or to discover a rare species of wildflower. The legions of climbers inspired by Muir's writings approached ascent as a means of self-discovery through unadulterated wilderness adventure.

Where Muir was the apostle, Robert Underhill was the evangelist. As editor of *Appalachia*, the journal of the Appalachian Mountain Club, in the early 1930s, Underhill preached to climbers about the evils of piton use and direct aid. He sermonized that mountains "must be surmounted by one's own unaided abilities," lest one destroy "the value of the climb." Underhill advocated that "no pitch has really been climbed where the direct aid of the rope has been resorted to." For decades, Underhill's disciples and their adherents defined the "rules" of how all climbers should climb. One such disciple declared that the rope was "intended for safety and not as a physical aid." Another referred to pitons as "crutches for incompetents." Taking this to a fundamentalist extreme, Hermann Ulrichs, a pioneering climber in the North Cascades during the 1930s, went so far as to reject the use of pitons completely. He refused to carry them even as anchors for an emergency retreat, feeling that "the tussle between the peak and me should both be entirely on our resources—not outside aids."

Still, the majority of climbers were not as concerned with what constituted "fair means"; they embraced pitons and artificial aid as tools for climbing mountains, and used whatever means necessary to win the summit and get down safely. In 1934, a trio of Bay Area climbers succeeded in climbing both Cathedral Spires in Yosemite with the direct aid of pitons and rope tension, boosting each other to reach holds, and even chipping the edge of an "impossible" flake with a hammer to create a good handhold. In 1937, members of the Colorado Mountain Club attempted to climb Shiprock, a desert spire in New Mexico; they failed spectacularly when their leader took a near-fatal fall on a difficult pitch, a single bent piton famously saving him from certain disaster. Two years later, the first-ascent party placed fifty-four pitons—and four expansion bolts—along their route up Shiprock.

Even as early as 1939, bolts were nothing new on the American climbing scene. They had been placed in Yosemite granite as early as 1875, when George Anderson made the first ascent of Half Dome by drilling holes in the side of the otherwise pristine impregnable granite, hammering in eyebolts, and standing on each progressively higher bolt to place the next. In that way, he eventually fixed a rope from bolt to bolt all the way to the summit. Muir was enthusiastic about and quickly repeated Anderson's route up the side of Half Dome. He didn't view the bolts as an abomination; he used them. But then, Muir wasn't a climber as such, just a sojourner.

Modern climbers first used bolts to surmount short, blank walls where no other equipment would work and the route would otherwise not "go." David Brower, a California climber and staunch environmentalist who became the first executive director of the Sierra Club, placed the occasional bolt during the 1930s, including the four used for aid during the 1939 first ascent of Shiprock. It was a feat he and his climbing partners referred to as "rock engineering," but which the prevailing moral authority chastised as "blasphemous."

During his 1946 solo attempt of the Lost Arrow Spire in Yosemite, John Salathé, a Swiss immigrant who invented the modern piton, encountered an impassable section high on the route. Being a blacksmith by trade, he forged a solution: by drilling holes in the rock and pounding in bolts he could clip in to and ascend, one after the other, he was able to engineer his way upward, just as Anderson had done on his ascent of Half Dome seventy years earlier. This short series of bolts was the first modern "bolt ladder" to be installed on American rock, and it eventually got him to within forty feet of the top. Ultra-conservative climbers in the Underhill camp remained critical of such a use of direct aid; to them, Salathé's bolts were a transgression.

Climbers also used various "rope tricks" to make first ascents. A group of climbers beat Salathé to the first "ascent" of the Lost Arrow Spire in 1946 by throwing a weighted line over the top, using it to fix another rope between the spire and the adjacent cliff, and traversing the rope rather than climbing the rock to reach the summit. Fred Beckey lassoed a rocky horn to reach the summit of Prusik Peak in Washington during the first ascent in 1948, and the summit of Shiprock was reached with the aid of a lasso as well. In 1967, inventive climbers at Smith Rock, an obscure volcanic climbing area in central Oregon, similarly ascended an "insurmountable" pinnacle by shooting a wire over the top with a bow and arrow, then pulling a rope over the pinnacle and climbing the rope to reach the summit. In a modern rendition, a party of climbers made the first "ascent" of a pinnacle in Colorado by flying a rope over the summit using a drone and then jumaring the rope to reach the top. For many climbers, using the rope and equipment in clever or inventive ways was—and still is—part of the game. There was no such thing as "fair means"; the means justified the end, particularly if the end was the summit of a hitherto unclimbed peak.

Although Underhill and Muir influenced generations of climbers, they had vastly differing views on the use of artificial aids when climbing mountains. So, too, did Royal Robbins and Warren Harding. Robbins, pioneer of such routes as the *Regular Northwest Face* of Half Dome and the *Salathé Wall* of El Capitan, believed drilling bolts was odious, morally degrading work that sometimes had to be tolerated, sparingly, to link blank sections of otherwise unclimbable rock. Harding, pioneer of the *Nose* and *Dawn Wall* routes on El Capitan, embraced the hard, manly work of bolting as integral to climbing big walls. Their differing views on bolting would play out in a decades-long battle on the granite walls of Yosemite.

IN 1957, WARREN HARDING ARRIVED in Yosemite intending to climb a new route up the northwest face of Half Dome. To his disappointment, he found a team including Royal Robbins already well on its way to success. Lacking a better plan, Harding picked a new route: the unclimbed 3,000-foot-high face of El Capitan. A ruggedly handsome blue-collar climber, short in stature but endowed with a large dose of self-confidence and an indomitable work ethic, Harding naturally chose the highest, most spectacular line: the Nose, the massive prow in the center of the monolithic wall. Harding and his rotating cast of partners spent some forty-seven days of climbing spread out over sixteen months on the route, fixing rope from ledge to ledge and ferrying food and equipment up the fixed ropes, laboriously forcing their way up the wall. Employed by expeditions to Mount Everest, this "siege style" tactic was mandated by the National Park Service on El Capitan, out of fear that climbers would get stuck high on the wall without the possibility of rescue. It practically ensured success; with enough climbers, rope, pitons, bolts, and supplies, a route could be, and was, pushed to the top. On the morning of November 12, 1958, after spending a long night drilling bolts up the final overhanging pitch, a delirious Harding pulled over the rim of El Capitan.

His ascent of the *Nose* generated significant publicity, largely because of the prominence of El Capitan, its high visibility to passing tourists, and the time it took to complete the climb. A feature article in *Argosy* magazine heralded the climb as "mountain-climbing history" and "the adventure of the year." Harding was able and perfectly willing to make a little money selling his story and photos of the El Capitan climb. This publicity, however, did not sit well with the Park Service, which was already unhappy that Harding's fixed ropes had hung on the wall for over a year—an eyesore. Shortly after the ascent received national media attention, the Park Service proposed a new policy: "We want to cut out the stunt and daring trick climbing that people go into hoping to be able to commercialize on what they accomplish," wrote NPS Director Conrad L. Wirth in support of the proposed ban. "The spikes or pegs that are driven into the cliffs and steep mountain sides deface and damage property," Wirth added. This was not the first time the Park Service had taken such a stand. In 1952, the Yosemite superintendent had threatened to ban "stunt or spectacle climbing" because of the crowds of tourists these climbs attracted and the Park Service's poor rescue capabilities. This time, in 1959, the Park Service was serious.

After effective lobbying by the Sierra Club and others, who foresaw that the intended ban on climbing with pitons would effectively ban *any* climbing in Yosemite, the Park Service backed down. If the ban had remained in effect, Yosemite climbing would have stagnated. Instead, it flourished.

In 1960, Robbins, Chuck Pratt, Joe Fitschen, and Tom Frost repeated the *Nose* in "alpine style"—in a single push from the bottom to the top, without fixing ropes as Harding had done—in six days. The following year, determined to see if a new route up El Capitan could be climbed from the ground up without fixed ropes, Robbins, again with Pratt and Frost, climbed a new line, the *Salathé Wall*. They abandoned their fixed ropes at a ledge partway up the wall and climbed alpine style into terra incognita. It was a daring ascent; the upper half of the *Salathé Wall* was steeper and more committing than the *Nose*, and without fixed ropes, a retreat or rescue would have been daunting, if not impossible. Theirs was a bold statement, and a challenge to all who would follow.

Yosemite became the leading rock climbing area in the world over the course of the 1960s, with early Yosemite big wall climbs following recurring themes. Rival climbers would vie to outdo each other, climbing progressively longer and more difficult routes up bigger, steeper walls. First ascents of breakthrough routes might be done in somewhat poor style, such as with fixed ropes and excessive bolts; repeat ascents would then be done faster or in better style. After a team climbed an El Capitan route using siege tactics, another team would climb it in alpine style, after which it was invariably climbed solo. Climbers of this era were not always overtly competitive, but the undercurrent of competition was never far below the surface. This spirit of one-upmanship pushed climbers to attempt harder routes using better style and technique, and the sport progressed rapidly. But in some cases it also led to charges of lying, cheating, and other dastardly deeds, real and imagined.

PITONS WERE THE EQUIPMENT of choice in the early years of Yosemite climbing. These metal spikes could be hammered into cracks as protection or aid placements, giving a climber the confidence of a secure anchor for the rope to hold him should he fall, and permitting ascent of steep cracks on the high granite walls. While placing a piton is satisfying, removing one is a brutish exercise requiring repeated hammering of the piton up and down or back and forth until it is knocked loose enough to be pulled or levered out. Unsurprisingly, each time a piton is placed and removed, a bit of rock is chipped away from the edge of the crack. On a high alpine face deep in the mountains, where only a few climbers might pass in any given year, the cumulative effect of piton placement and removal is negligible. But on popular lowland crags and particularly the granite walls of Yosemite, where dozens of climbers might pass during a single month, week, or even day, the effect became troubling. As Director Wirth had expressed in his denouncement of climbing with "spikes and pegs," pitons actually *did* deface and damage the rock—a natural resource under federal protection in Yosemite National Park.

After a route is climbed many times with pitons—"nailed," in the climber's vernacular—"pin scars" are left behind, which irreversibly alter the rock. By the late 1960s, some of Yosemite's most popular routes looked like "worn pegboards," as one Valley climber put it. One such climb that epitomized the ugliness of pin scarring was *Serenity Crack*, a thin crack on the Royal Arches formation, a slabby granite wall above the Majestic Yosemite Hotel (formerly the Ahwahnee). By virtue of its location and accessibility, the crack became a go-to line for climbers practicing piton craft before heading up the big walls. After years of nailing, the formerly wafer-thin crack looked as if someone had taken a jackhammer to it. *Serenity Crack* soon became the poster child for the evils of piton abuse.

In his climbing instruction book *Basic Rockcraft*, published in 1971, Robbins urged climbers to reconsider the use of pitons. "If we are to retain the beauties of the sport, the fine edge, the challenge," he wrote, "we must consider our style of climbing; and if we are not to mutilate and destroy the routes, we must eliminate the heavy-handed use of pitons and bolts." In an article published in the 1972 *American Alpine Journal* titled "Preserving the Cracks!," Frost joined Robbins in pressing climbers to change their ways before the rock was destroyed.

Ecologically minded climbers were horrified by the damage they and others were doing to the rock with pitons, and in the early 1970s they began to practice in earnest what they called "clean" climbing. They limited their use of hammer-placed pitons to only those climbs where pitons were an absolute necessity, and they began instead to use passive protection devices—artificial chocks, hand-placed pitons, and hooks over flakes, all of which could be set and removed without scarring the rock.

In the mid-1960s, commercially manufactured metal chocks—aluminum nuts and blocks tied to cord and cable—became available in Europe, replacing the machine-nut chocks English climbers had already been using for two decades. One of the most forward-thinking American climbers of his day, Robbins began using chocks in earnest in the mid-1960s, after seeing them used in Britain. Robbins recognized their advantages: chocks were lighter in weight, easier to place and remove, and less damaging to the rock than pitons. He eagerly showed other climbers how chocks worked, even establishing new free climbs in Yosemite and elsewhere without pitons to demonstrate that chocks were viable as protection for free climbing.

Despite Robbins's early advocacy for chocks, most climbers in the United States initially stuck with pitons, partly because they were more reliable and familiar, and also because chocks were not readily available. Colorado climber Pat Ament didn't know what to think of chocks when Robbins placed one in Eldorado Canyon's *Supremacy Crack* in 1966 during an attempted free ascent. Lacking confidence in this new technology, Ament led the severely overhanging thin crack while placing pitons instead, which made the climb much more difficult and strenuous.

In 1972, Doug Robinson's essay "The Whole Natural Art of Protection" appeared in the Chouinard Equipment catalog—alongside a new line of artificial chocks. Yvon Chouinard, a frequent climbing partner of Robbins and one of the leading Yosemite climbers of the late 1960s, was also one of the world's leading climbing equipment innovators. He had started forging pitons and selling them out of the back of his truck in the early 1960s; a decade later, he and his partner Tom Frost practically owned the piton market in America.

Concerned about the damage his pitons were doing to the rock, and sensing a paradigm about to shift, Chouinard, with Frost, Robinson, and John Stannard, started sketching out designs for prototype chocks in 1971, which he soon put into full production and offered for sale. The Chouinard Equipment line of chocks featured a wide array of aluminum wedges and hexagonal nuts threaded with cable or thin rope that could be slotted into a crack and clipped in to the leader's rope to provide protection or direct aid. Some of the smaller wired stoppers could be placed in existing pin scars and thus spare a crack from further scarring. Robinson's article explained how chocks worked and how they protected a precious, limited resource—the rock—from abuse. "Clean is climbing the rock without changing it," Robinson wrote, "a step closer to organic climbing for the natural man." Around the same time, Frost published his *AAJ* article highlighting the damage done by pitons—an astute and highly successful marketing ploy.

In the back-to-nature era of the early 1970s, the concept of climbing without damaging the rock or altering the landscape appealed to many American climbers, who envisioned themselves as enlightened mountaineers in tune with the earth. Almost overnight, a majority of climbers in the United States abandoned pitons in favor of clean, natural chocks. Galen Rowell's 1974 *National Geographic* article "Climbing Half Dome the Hard Way," about his first clean ascent of the *Northwest Face* of Half Dome with Robinson and Dennis Henneck, was also widely influential. It sealed the deal, inspiring a new generation of climbers to limit—if not entirely give up—the use of pitons. And, in the fine tradition of climbing, they became competitive about it.

Climbers now had a new "first" to vie for: the first "clean" or natural ascent. Climbing big wall and difficult free routes with chocks was a whole new game. If a route went "clean," you heard about it. Keep in mind that clean climbing was often possible only because a given route had been nailed so often that chocks could fit in the damaged cracks where pitons previously had been required. Even so, after a route had been climbed clean, the proponents of clean climbing felt strongly that it should always be climbed that way, to preserve the sacred rock from the assault of further piton use.

AND THEN THERE WERE BOLTS. By the 1970s, bolts had become accepted tools in the climber's arsenal, allowing climbers to push a route through otherwise impassable sections of rock. Bolting wasn't something any climber really wanted to do, mind you. Drilling bolts for hours up a sunbaked wall was unpleasant and exhausting. As Harding put it, "Screwing is more enjoyable than drilling bolt holes." Also, given the growing concern over rock damage caused by piton scarring and the shift toward clean climbing, many climbers had strong reservations about placing bolts. Discriminate bolting was generally tolerated, and for the most part climbers who placed bolts did so only out of necessity. But not always.

In 1961, Warren Harding climbed the *West Face* of Leaning Tower, a 1,500-foot overhanging Yosemite wall, in a siege-style ascent accomplished with the liberal aid of 110 bolts. It seemed Harding had gone out of his way to climb a line that required bolts—an excessive number of them. The next year, American climber Ed Cooper and Canadian climber Jim Baldwin set to work on a new route up El Capitan, also employing siege tactics and drilling bolt ladders to link a series of crack systems left of the *Salathé Wall*. Their route, the *Dihedral Wall* (completed with Glen Denny), took thirty-eight days over eight months, and 110 bolts, to complete.

These episodes of indiscriminate bolting caused some climbers to become unglued. Chouinard published an article in *Summit* magazine in 1961 questioning whether too many bolts were being placed by "unqualified" climbers, suggesting that only "expert" climbers had the right to use bolts, and that these "experts" had a right to remove offending bolts. When another climber proposed doing a new route on El Capitan in similar style, he was derided as a "maniac [who] must be stopped before he rapes El Cap and its significance to the world of rock climbing." In the face of such vehement opposition, the climber abandoned his project.

Harding, however, was seemingly immune to criticism of his style of climbing. He continued his iconoclastic ways, apparently enjoying going against the grain of the Yosemite climbing establishment—the "Valley Christians," as he called them. Amid all the controversy over bolting, Harding made two brash ascents in 1970 that escalated the conflict. First, with Rowell, he made the first ascent of the *South Face* of Half Dome, a blank, water-worn sheet of granite rising over 2,000 feet, with almost no cracks on the upper thousand feet. They drilled a reported 180 holes on the ascent, most of which they used to place "bat hooks," specialized hooks Harding invented that were tapered to fit into shallow bolt holes. Harding's critics decried his ascent of the *South Face* as an act of vandalism on a hallowed granite shrine, not what they would call "climbing." Harding and Rowell had not climbed the rock, these critics charged, but the holes they had drilled in it. It was a fair position; the pair had manufactured a route up the mountain where no natural line existed.

Unrepentant, Harding broke the bolting controversy wide open that winter with his ascent of the *Wall of Early Morning Light* (a.k.a. the *Dawn Wall*) on El Capitan, a direct line to the right of the *Nose* that was considered one of Yosemite's last great problems. With Dean Caldwell, Harding climbed the route from the ground up, taking twenty-seven consecutive days to complete the ascent. At the time, it was the longest continuous span climbers had spent climbing on El Capitan. Although they climbed in a single push to the top—in alpine style, more or less—Harding armed himself with a drill, hammer, and a big bag of bolts and tirelessly drilled his way up the wall, day after day, linking the discontinuous crack systems with bolt and rivet ladders and bat hook holes. He and Caldwell drilled an unprecedented 330 holes in the rock during the climb (roughly a drilled hole every ten feet), for which he drew the considerable ire of his antagonists—chiefly Robbins. It was a slap in the face to those who opposed bolts on moral grounds. Yet as far as Harding was concerned, Robbins and his ilk were "ideological fanatics," as he later put it in his book *Downward Bound*, veritable rock Nazis who treated climbing "as though it were some profound religious or political entity" they were in charge of because of their supposedly superior views. Harding would have none of this ethical zealotry. He climbed his way and didn't give a rat's ass what Royal Robbins thought.

What Robbins thought, of course, was that Harding's route was a travesty that needed to be erased. Taking up Chouinard's clarion call, Robbins repeated the *Dawn Wall* the following year with Don Lauria with the intention of "chopping" the entire route. He removed all of Harding's bolts on the first four pitches, then stopped. The route was not the bolt-up atrocity he had expected it to be. Robbins did not discuss his reasons, but Lauria observed that "it was actually gnawing at him as we proceeded." After their first bivouac, they "just climbed on despite the folly of the first day . . . without discussion," other than Robbins saying he felt the climbing was harder than he had given Harding credit for. Realizing he had made a mistake, Robbins left the remaining bolts in place. He even went so far as to eventually praise Harding as a "magnificent maverick" for not giving a damn about what the establishment thought.

3 CLIMB FREE OR DIE

Rock climbing continued to evolve rapidly during the 1970s, when free climbing became the rage. "Free climbing"—the fusion of natural man and organic motion on rock, as Doug Robinson put it, the purest manifestation of climbing—was superior to any form of aid climbing, pitons or no pitons. American rock climbers of this post-Beat generation discovered a powerful expression of freedom on rock. With a climbing-first lifestyle, focused mental and physical training, and a balls-out mentality, fueled partly by Vietnam War–era rebellion and sometimes by marijuana and other psychotropic "inspiration," they were soon able to visualize and free climb routes that were bolder and more difficult than their predecessors had ever imagined possible. This new generation found free climbs everywhere—steep cracks and faces overlooked by the previous generation whose gaze had been fixed on the big walls. They discovered that many of the old aid climbs could be climbed free, sometimes because of piton scarring that allowed fingers to fit into cracks that once accepted only the thinnest of pitons, and also because chocks were easier and faster to place than pitons, opening up steep cracks that could not have been led free if the leader had to repeatedly hang on with one arm to place pitons for protection. And, quite simply, these young guns were becoming better climbers than their elders.

The objective of free climbing, then as now, is to climb a given route using only the features of the rock to ascend; you grab the rock and climb, without using the rope or any equipment as an aid. To that end, free climbing is somewhat like a gymnastic performance, where the athlete tries to complete the entire routine, executing all of the compulsory moves, without falling off the apparatus. This is an apt comparison with respect to the hardest free climbs, since they truly require the training, fitness, and skill of a gymnast. The trouble was that some climbers started approaching climbing as a gymnastic exercise and treating the rock as an apparatus. Those who took a purely gymnastic approach to climbing were often maligned by those who viewed it as a spiritual pursuit. In part, this was because the rock gymnasts seemed to be disrespecting the traditions of the sport, which placed a higher value on adventure than pure ascendancy. That, and the rock gymnasts were outperforming their maligners.

In the mid-1970s, during this shift in the climbing paradigm, American free climbers still largely adhered to a traditional approach to free climbing. Routes were done from the ground up, with the climber starting at the bottom and finishing at the top. The leader would head up the route, placing protection as he climbed, and if he fell, he would lower back to the ground or a ledge, rest, then start again from there. Eventually, after several attempts in this "yo-yo" style, a climber might succeed in free climbing all of the moves, which would constitute a free ascent. As long as the climber started from the ground, placed all protection on lead, lowered back to a no-hands position after falling, and finally did all of the moves without hanging on the rope, grabbing gear, or stepping on a piton, it was considered a successful free ascent, at least back then.

More extreme proponents of the traditional style viewed yo-yoing as a form of cheating. They insisted on lowering all the way to the ground and pulling down their rope before trying again. Some even removed their protection before a fresh attempt. By their logic, if they had fallen off without a rope, they would have ended up on the ground, dead, so that is where they should start again. It was practically a religious ritual, this pulling of the rope and starting over.

One of the practitioners of this strict approach to free climbing was Jim Erickson, a Colorado climber who, over the course of his climbing career, developed some of the most extreme ethical convictions among any climbers of the era. In 1971, with Duncan Ferguson, Erickson made the first free ascent of *The Naked Edge*, an Eldorado Canyon classic ascending a prominent arête on Redgarden Wall. Despite the significance of their free ascent of the most visible and prized hard free climb in Colorado, Erickson felt a strong sense of guilt. He had fallen several times during the climb, and he and Ferguson had used pitons for protection—irredeemable transgressions in Erickson's view. To absolve himself of his guilt, he adopted a new philosophy: "You fall, you fail." Erickson believed that if you fell off, hung on the rope, or grabbed protection, you could not say you had free climbed the route, even if you later did all of the moves free, because the very act of hanging on the rope or pulling on gear, even once, was artificial aid. His approach was uncompromising: you get one try to free climb a route, and if you blow it, you don't get a second chance.

Erickson's was a thoughtful and philosophical approach to free climbing, especially when compared with his generation's increasingly athletic and gymnastic approach. To Erickson, the rock was not merely a gymnastic apparatus but an equal opponent that had to be respected. After his free ascent of *The Naked Edge*, he avowed not to use artificial protection to protect free climbing, not even pitons. He climbed the rock as he found it, placing protection as the natural form of the rock allowed, climbing boldly or not at all. In Erickson's view, the point of climbing was not to master the rock but to master oneself, on both the physical and mental planes.

Steve Wunsch, another Colorado climber, took a different approach. Although equally preoccupied with ethics, Wunsch believed Erickson's fall/fail approach was too strict and prevented discovery of a climber's ultimate potential. He thought it was acceptable to make as many attempts as required to climb a route, as long as you lowered to the ground and pulled the rope after each fall. "If ropes cost so much," Wunsch once quipped, "why not use them?" Using this style of climbing, Wunsch established many of the hardest free climbs in Colorado, as well as several hard first ascents in Yosemite. In 1974 he nabbed the first ascent of a route at the Shawangunks called *Supercrack*, an overhanging thin crack that he rated 5.12+. At the time—and for some time after—*Supercrack* was considered to be the hardest free climb in the world.

Although Erickson and Wunsch disagreed ethically, each respected the other's style. If Wunsch wanted to take repeated falls, that was fine with Erickson as long as he didn't spoil the route for others; and if Erickson was trying to make a first ascent of a route using his fall/fail approach, Wunsch would try it that way, too. In 1975, Wunsch made the first ascent of an Eldorado Canyon route named *Jules Verne*. By then, the hardest technical climbing on the route (5.11) had already been done, but one section, a steep face on the fourth pitch several hundred feet above the canyon floor, had so far resisted all attempts—not because it was too difficult but because it was too runout. Erickson and Ferguson had tried it and retreated. Because of their strict no-pitons ethic, they had been unwilling to place any to protect the thin, exposed face moves giving passage to the top of the wall. Respecting Erickson and Ferguson's decision to eschew pitons, Wunsch tried the pitch as they had, with only the smallest of chocks for protection—all that would fit into the available cracks. After several tenuous attempts that involved leading out twenty-five feet on thin, intricate face moves, risking a fifty-foot fall onto micro-size chocks slotted into a tiny crack, Wunsch finally succeeded in climbing the pitch. A fall on this pitch would have resulted in serious injury, if not death. Although the pitch was only 5.10c in difficulty, the mental challenge of leading it on-sight with illusory protection made it one of the most respected and least repeated pitches in Colorado.

Despite their differences of opinion as to acceptable free-climbing style, Wunsch, Erickson, and most of their fellow Colorado climbers agreed that hanging on the rope or pulling on gear tainted the ascent. If equipment held or assisted you at all during your climb, you could not claim a free ascent. They were not out to establish boulder problems on the walls of Eldorado Canyon or elsewhere; they climbed rocks to challenge themselves physically, mentally, and spiritually against what nature had to offer. Their holistic approach to climbing was popularized by the publication of several magazine articles and later a book, *Climb!*, which included riveting photographs depicting these prophets of purity on their most inspiring climbs.

For the most part, though, these ethical considerations made little to no impression on the average climber, who could not be expected to climb in highfalutin style just because some purist in Colorado or Yosemite did. They would climb as they pleased. As long as they weren't damaging the rock or hurting anybody in the process, why, they wondered, would it matter whether they hung on the rope or pulled on a piton?

The problem was, of course, that climbers can be egotistical and competitive. The leading climbers of the day, wanting to enhance their reputations, increasingly vied with each other for first ascents of hard free climbs. For some, climbing hard routes was merely for personal challenge or spiritual satisfaction. For others, it was about the status gained by climbing something harder than they or their peers had climbed before—a form of one-upmanship reminiscent of the Robbins versus Harding episodes in Yosemite. And for others, it was all about fame. This latter group often cared deeply about how a route was climbed, since first ascents of hard new free climbs were a precious, limited commodity. For example, a climber who used the yo-yo technique rather than pulling the rope every time was going to free climb a given route faster, bag more first ascents, and get his name in the magazines more often. And a climber who was willing to hangdog and chisel his way up routes was going to establish an even greater number of difficult free routes than a climber who refused to do either of those things.

Those who climbed for personal reasons hardly cared what the titans did or why they clashed. But with reputations and egos on the line, some climbers became obsessively concerned with the climbing styles employed by others, and even angry and combative when first ascents were done in inferior style and then reported in the magazines as breakthrough climbs.

For example, in 1979, a Colorado climber named Jim Collins free climbed *Genesis*, an old aid pitch on Redgarden Wall in Eldorado Canyon. *Mountain*, a British climbing magazine, obsessively chronicled Collins's progress on the route over several issues. When he finally pulled it off after months of effort, he rated the route 5.12+, hinted that it might be 5.13, and proposed renaming the pitch *God's Golden Hour of Power*.

Some climbers were upset that *Mountain* wasn't reporting the facts: that instead of lowering after a fall and pulling his rope, Collins was hanging on the rope and practicing the moves, thus completely disrespecting the accepted local style. In their view, Collins wasn't good enough to do the route, which should have been left for a better climber to do properly in the future.

In a 2003 article about his free ascent of *Genesis*, Collins, who went on to become a motivational speaker, explained that he had played a trick on himself in 1979: he thought about how climbers fifteen years in the future might climb the route, then projected himself psychologically forward to 1994 to mentally overcome the challenge of climbing such a futuristic route. Foreseeing that climbers of the future would approach climbing differently, he adopted futuristic tactics to make his ascent.

"Climbing teaches that the biggest barriers are not on the rock," Collins wrote, "but in our minds."

4 AS FREE AS CAN BE

One afternoon in September 1981, I noticed a mimeographed poster taped to a light pole at the University of Washington practice rock. Mark Hudon and Max Jones were coming to Seattle to give a slide show. Hot damn! All the rock rats agreed it was an event not to be missed. If you had given us backstage passes to a Circle Jerks concert that same day, we still would have gone to see Hudon and Jones. They were, in our view, gods. On the appointed day, a herd of gangly young men migrated from the practice rock to Kane Hall, sweaty T-shirts, chalk-dusted hands, and all, to see the show.

The Hudon and Jones slide show was a live version of their *Mountain* magazine features "States of the Art" and "Long, Hard, and Free," two of the most influential articles of the day. They opened with a montage showing the dynamic duo on various hard climbs, set to the Rolling Stones' "Gimme Shelter." Next came a sequence of spectacular images from one hard free climb after another, starting with some of their 5.11 and 5.12 climbs in the Lake Tahoe area, progressing into Yosemite Valley, then eastward to Colorado and on to upstate New York. Taking turns narrating, they described short, hard routes they had climbed in Yosemite, including early repeats of *Hangdog Flyer* and *The Phoenix*. Then they transitioned to some of their long, hard free ascents: the fifth ascent of *Astroman*; their "as free as can be" ascent of the *Salathé Wall* in 1979; the second free ascent of the *West Face* of El Capitan; and their climb of the *Regular Northwest Face* of Half Dome, all free except the bolt ladders—all with multiple pitches of 5.11 and up to 5.12, even a few bordering on the mythical 5.13.

We absorbed the whole spectacle, not only the stunning images of Hudon and Jones at grips with so many spectacular climbs—desperately steep, impossibly thin cracks hundreds even thousands of feet off the ground—but also their improbable tales: the gripping runouts and near failures; Hudon miraculously holding an iron cross between two flakes as his feet cut loose beneath him; Jones eking out a crux move twenty feet out from his last protection. They shared their theories about route difficulty, and how body size and genetics play a role in determining how hard a given climber can climb. They described what it was like to climb 5.12, how it meant being just at the edge of control, constantly about to fall off. They speculated about the coming of 5.13—if it had not already arrived, they said, in the form of *The Phoenix* and *Grand Illusion*, two of the hardest rock climbs yet done anywhere in the world. *The Phoenix*, an improbably thin, overhanging Yosemite crack first climbed by Ray Jardine in 1977, was repeated by Hudon and Jones in 1978; *Grand Illusion*, an inconceivably thin, horizontal roof crack near Lake Tahoe, remained unrepeated since Tony Yaniro's first free ascent in 1979. Audaciously, they predicted that the *Salathé Wall* would someday go free, perhaps even the *Nose* of El Capitan—someday, that is, when 5.13 was firmly established and climbers had realized the possibility of 5.14.

All of this 5.13 and 5.14 talk was fantastic. And by fantastic, I mean out of this world. Back then, most of us could lead 5.10 routes competently, which we thought made us pretty good. Those who could lead 5.11, what few there were among our local ranks, were phenomenally good climbers worthy of admiration if not downright worship. And then there were the 5.12 climbers, mythical figures descended from the shining walls of Yosemite Valley, the muted sandstone faces of Eldorado, and the impossibly sharp-edged overhangs of the distant Shawangunks—climbers I had only read about in the pages of *Climbing* or *Mountain*. Climbing 5.12, I imagined, involved clinging to pencil-thin sandstone edges or hanging off fingertips jammed into jagged slits of overhanging granite. Climbing 5.13 would have to involve some form of levitation. Who were these 5.13 climbers Hudon and Jones were talking about?

RAY JARDINE WAS A BIG GUY who parted his shoulder-length hair down the middle and wore thick, black-framed glasses. He looked like a cross between a nerdy football player and a mad scientist. A former high school gymnast who went on to become an aerospace engineer (space-flight mechanic systems analyst, to be precise), Jardine quit his career in 1970 to climb full-time. He ended up in Yosemite, where he pioneered a number of hard free climbs from the mid-1970s into the early 1980s, pushing the ratings to the upper end of the scale. This spurt of productivity was in no small part a result of Jardine's obsessive nature and knack for technical innovation, which led to his development of "Friends," the first commercially available camming protection devices. They revolutionized free climbing.

Jardine was a nice guy, but he wasn't part of the "in crowd." He kept mostly to himself. "I can't remember ever seeing him in Camp 4," Hudon recalls. "He didn't hang out." When Jardine did stay in Camp 4, he was always up early, off with his usual partner, John Lakey, long before anyone else was up. "People didn't know what he was doing," Hudon adds, "but we assumed he was hanging his way up everything."

"Jardine was a kook," says John Long, a Valley regular who made the first ascent of *Astroman* with John Bachar and Ron Kauk in 1975. "He was into his own thing. The way he was climbing was totally at odds with the prevailing style." Although Jardine had climbed only a few routes rated 5.10 when he arrived in Yosemite in 1970, by 1976 he was dispatching 5.12 testpieces. One such route was Ron Kauk's *Separate Reality*, a twenty-foot hand and finger crack splitting a horizontal overhang. Rated 5.12a, the parallel-sided crack was so strenuous that it took considerable strength and stamina just to place chocks to protect the lead, as Kauk had done on the first ascent. Friends, on the other hand, could be placed rapidly, simply plugged into the crack and clipped to the rope, saving strength for the difficult, thin climbing turning the lip of the overhang. Using Friends for protection, Jardine made the second ascent of the route with relative ease, with Lakey photographing him mid-send. Lakey's photo appeared on the cover of *Mountain* 56, where it fueled a strong desire among climbers around the world to acquire Jardine's protection devices, as well as strong resentment from the old guard, who initially considered the use of Friends to be unfair means. Some climbers were so struck by Lakey's image that they forgot Kauk had made the first ascent of the route, let alone that he had done it the hard way.

Jardine climbed several more 5.12 routes in Yosemite during this period, including first ascents of *Crimson Cringe* (5.12a), an arching thin crack; *Hangdog Flyer* (5.12c), a leaning thin crack in a severely overhanging corner; and *The Phoenix*, a steep, thin, overhanging finger and hand crack that he rated 5.12+. It was duly noted in a 1978 article in *Off Belay* magazine, an article that doubled as a convenient advertisement for Friends, that the first ascents of five of the seven 5.12 routes in Yosemite had been protected with Friends.

In May 1979, Jardine and Bill Price pulled off a free ascent of the *West Face* of El Capitan, which the Valley locals had dismissed as "impossible to free climb," according to Hudon. According to Jardine, the 5.9 A4 route established by Royal Robbins and TM Herbert in 1967 went free at a "reasonable 5.11." An article in *Mountain* 69 touted the all-free ascent of this 2,000-foot wall as "a landmark in the history of Yosemite climbing." Some of the Valley locals were not quite as impressed. To them, Jardine was nothing but a hangdogger.

Jardine had climbed his new routes in relative secret, mostly to keep his prototype Friends from being revealed and possibly copied by rival gear designers. There's a story about one of Jardine's climbing partners getting a Friend stuck in a crack. "I couldn't get it out," he was overheard telling Jardine, who handed him a hammer and chisel and said bluntly, "Don't come back without it." But Jardine was also secretive because his tactics went against accepted style, at least the style imposed by the more ethically minded Southern California climbers with their John Muir–cum–Robert Underhill philosophy of ascent. The local ethic dictated that a climber lower off after falling, pull the rope, clean the gear, and start over from the bottom, ostensibly to preserve a sense of adventure and challenge. Jardine didn't subscribe to that overly restrictive ethic. His approach worked for him, and was entirely more practical. Jardine thought it was perfectly fine to hang on the rope and gear to rest, pull himself back onto the rock, and practice the next sequence of moves before lowering off. He likened himself to a gymnast, methodically working out each element of a routine before piecing it all together.

Jardine's technique—referred to as "hangdogging" by his detractors—permitted him to approach a route as a series of short problems that he could work out and practice section by section until he was able to climb the route from bottom to top in one go without weighting the gear. Even though he was not the best free climber (he considered Bachar, Kauk, and Dale Bard, another talented Yosemite climber, to be his betters by far), Jardine was, through sheer persistence, able to climb routes that were harder than any yet done.

This didn't go over well with the Yosemite locals. "He was hangdogging beyond what anybody before him had done," Long recalls. "If he hadn't been so secretive, he would have been ridiculed as a pantywaist.

"It was annoying," Long adds. "Any one of us could boulder him into the ground. It just didn't sit right that he was working routes and climbing harder

stuff than us when we were clearly better climbers. Hats off to him for breaking the rules and pushing the difficulty, though. To his credit, he went against
the grain and did some horrendously hard routes. He took things to the next
level."

Although Jardine was branded as a hangdogger, his style was more akin
to what is now known as "redpointing." He would claim a successful ascent
only after climbing the route from bottom to top and placing all the gear on
lead, without falling or weighting the rope. In this, he was aligned with the old
guard. The only difference was that they insisted on lowering off and pulling
the rope after each fall—an inefficient process in Jardine's scientific view. Jardine figured that if he fell, he may as well "work" the route while he was up
there, practicing moves between rests on gear, then pull his ropes and gear at
the end of the day's efforts and return another day to try anew. "Everybody
had this idea of Jardine as a total hangdogger," Hudon says, "but he followed
rules, and his final ascents were done in good style."

Jardine didn't care what you did while figuring out how to free climb a
route, or how anyone else climbed, but some climbers cared deeply about how
Jardine climbed. To emphasize their opposition to Jardine's hangdogger style,
a gang of Yosemite locals repeated *Crimson Cringe* a few days after Jardine's
first ascent. They climbed it in a single pitch, eliminating Jardine's intermediate hanging belay points and removing some of his bolts, and they did it
without using Friends or hangdogging. As the story goes, Jardine insisted the
route couldn't be done without Friends, which was just the kind of motivation
the Valley hotshots needed to prove him wrong. Bachar won the coin toss and
got the lead, and proceeded to flash the route. Kauk bagged the second ascent
of *Hangdog Flyer*, also without Friends; this time, Jardine offered to let Kauk
use his prototype Friends but Kauk declined, unwilling to use gear that wasn't
available to everybody else because it seemed like cheating. Jardine told Kauk
he wouldn't succeed. Kauk proved him wrong.

For all the controversy it generated, hangdogging wasn't Jardine's worst
transgression. After climbing most of Yosemite's 5.12 routes and making his
successful free ascent of the *West Face* of El Capitan, Jardine had designs on
free climbing the *Nose*. He envisioned a line that would link the lower crack
systems with the upper dihedrals and zeroed in on the *Grape Race* variation
as the shortest and most viable option. This steep slab traverse would be more
conducive to free climbing than higher on the main *Nose* route, where climbers

had to make long pendulum traverses across blank, smooth, dead-vertical granite, and a free variation was unlikely to be found. Jardine thought the traverse would go free at 5.11, but a thirty-five-foot section proved too thin—at least too thin for Jardine to free climb in its natural state.

As Alec Sharp wrote in the preface to his interview with Jardine, published in *Mountain* 69, Jardine was "secure enough in himself that he [could] . . . climb in his own style despite criticism." On his next attempt to free the *Nose*, Jardine brought a new tool: a cold chisel. He was determined to make the traverse go free, critics be damned. It was already common knowledge that Jardine had "improved" holds on *The Phoenix* by placing and removing pitons in the thin crack ("pinning it out") to widen it to allow for fingertip jams. His fabrication of pin scars on *The Phoenix* had stirred some grumbling, but it was nothing compared to the vitriolic fire Jardine drew for openly chiseling holds on the *Nose*. It was unforgivable, and Jardine was vilified.

"Chipping El Cap was bullshit," Long says, clearly still angry about it to this day. "He did it so brazenly. Cold chiseling a blank slab. Oh, man. I mean, I broke every rule of traditional climbing at some point, except chipping. Even I have things I consider sacred. I just can't imagine doing that. It was so disrespectful. It was sacrilege."

Despite having manufactured his "free" traverse, Jardine was unsuccessful in his bid to free climb the *Nose*. He free climbed most of the route, but he wasn't able to get past the Great Roof pitch; the crack was too thin and the climbing too hard. Many wondered why Jardine didn't "pin out" the Great Roof until his fingers fit in well enough that he could "free" it, as he had done on *The Phoenix*. Thankfully, he didn't. After more than forty days of effort on the route over four months, he finally gave up. Tired of being dogged by the locals over his controversial tactics, he left the Valley and all but quit climbing in favor of more solitary pursuits.

IF JARDINE HAD RAISED the free-climbing standards in America, Tony Yaniro blew them through the roof. Yaniro arrived on the scene in the late 1970s like a Tasmanian devil, all energy and enthusiasm and desire to climb hard. By all accounts one of the nicest, most humble people on the scene, Yaniro possessed a work ethic and pain threshold that were the stuff of legend. "He trained and worked out *way* too much for us lazy stoners," remembers one Southern California climber of the day. "That was considered cheating." Inspired by the likes of John Bachar, John Long, and Tobin Sorenson—three of the original Stonemasters, a cultlike group of leading California free climbers of the day—Yaniro trained like mad and progressed rapidly, establishing dozens of hard first ascents by the early 1980s. One of those climbs stands out. In 1979, Yaniro set himself upon an old aid route called *The Fracture*, a thirty-foot thin roof crack at Sugarloaf, a granite cliff just southwest of Lake Tahoe. It proved supremely difficult, requiring many days of effort following months of route-specific training on a simulated crack Yaniro built in his basement. When Yaniro completed his free lead of the roof pitch, he declined to give it a definite rating, but correctly predicted that the route, renamed *Grand Illusion*, would be 5.13—*hard* 5.13. At the time of Yaniro's ascent, and for a long time after, *Grand Illusion* was considered the hardest free climb in the world.

Despite his climbing ability and Southern California heritage, Yaniro was not "in the club." For one thing, he didn't smoke pot like a lot of the in crowd; when he wasn't climbing, he was training, and when he wasn't training, he was designing training systems. And Yaniro didn't follow the rules. He was regarded by the local elite as a "pretty good aid climber" at best, a hold-chipping hang-dogger at worst. *Grand Illusion*, although quite hard, was not a legitimate free climb in the eyes of traditionalists because Yaniro had reportedly fixed pins in the crack on aid to use as free-climbing protection and had hung on the rope to work out moves after falling. Although Yaniro, like Jardine, pulled his rope and gear before making a continuous free lead on his hardest climbs (again, in effect "redpointing" the route—long before redpointing became a thing), *Grand Illusion*, like *The Phoenix*, was dismissed as an aberration, a glorified aid climb unworthy of a purist's attention. And so, the purists ignored it and discounted Yaniro's accomplishments. *Grand Illusion* remained unrepeated until 1982, when German climber Wolfgang Gullich made the second free ascent and confirmed its solid 5.13 rating.

In addition to hangdogging, Yaniro was also known to work a route on toprope before trying to lead it, another "trick" disapproved of by some climbers. To prepare for *Equinox*, Bachar's 5.12c thin crack testpiece at Joshua Tree, Yaniro toproped the route first, then made yo-yo lead attempts with hang-dogging before finally leading it free in a continuous effort. As on *Grand Illusion*, Yaniro claimed a free ascent of *Equinox* only after he had succeeded in climbing it from the ground to the top in one go, placing all gear on lead. But some purists complained: to them, a valid free ascent had to be done from the ground up, on lead, without wiring it first on toprope, and without ever hanging on the rope or pulling on gear. You could fall off, of course, but then you had to lower to the ground and pull your rope and gear—every time. Their measure of success was largely unrealistic; who, besides Bachar or Kauk, if even them, could have lived up to those standards? And who actually did?

To be fair, not all of the Southern California climbers were so strict. Some didn't care if Yaniro toproped, yo-yoed, or hung on the rope, as long as he didn't damage the rock or place unnecessary bolts. Only a small group of climbers seemed to care about hangdogging and other perceived stylistic transgressions. But they were a highly vocal minority, prone to long-winded slander sessions around the evening campfire, verbal abuse of climbers on the cliffs they found engaging in such practices, and furtive acts of petty vandalism meant to deter the hangdoggers from coming around. They liked to complain.

This sort of evangelical preaching and Da Hui–style confrontation some-times resulted in perceived transgressions, such as Yaniro's, becoming magni-fied far out of proportion. Yaniro, like Jardine before him, eventually moved away from the harsh spotlight of the Southern California climbing scene. To avoid controversy, he continued climbing in relative privacy, first in the High Sierra, then later in Idaho and eastern Oregon, where he established a number of hard free climbs in his own style—a style that sometimes included manu-facturing of holds and bolting on rappel, but he could do it without the over-sight of a rules committee constantly barking about his every indiscretion.

HUDON AND JONES WERE PERHAPS the best—or at least the best-known—free-climbing duo of their era, Bachar and Kauk notwithstanding. Although they didn't chip holds or place unnecessary bolts, and Hudon had repeated *The Phoenix* without using Friends (and Jones had followed without any falls), even they had a reputation as cheaters. "We worked routes in a style that wasn't quite up to the local standard," Hudon admits. "We were experi-menting, taking a step. We didn't think we were anything special; we were just determined." The fact that they were validating the legitimacy of such routes was upsetting to some traditional climbers, who wouldn't go near Jardine's "hangdog routes"—especially *The Phoenix*, because it had been pinned out. (John Long, the only old-school Valley climber to try it, made the third ascent. "It was horrendously hard," he recalls.) The promotion of hard free climbing done in bad style was sure to be a bad influence on climbers new to the sport (like me) who were not steeped in the "old" ways.

As for their efforts to free climb the *Salathé Wall*, that route was just too long and too hard to be free climbed, said their detractors. "There were a lot of climbers who could have climbed it," Hudon believes, "but they had a purist attitude: 'It's not going to go,' they said, 'so we won't even try.' We didn't. We were just going to fuck around and see what we could do."

Hudon and Jones's mostly free ascent of the *Salathé Wall*, like their nearly free ascent of the *Regular Northwest Face* of Half Dome, wasn't intended to be free. They climbed in a style they called "as free as can be," which meant freeing what could be freed and aiding the rest—not fooling around too long to try to free a pitch, and not letting a few aid moves stop them from enjoying an otherwise fantastic long free route.

"We thought, 'There's got to be a lot of fun free climbing up there,'" Jones recalls. "We'd done a lot of the short, hard routes in the Valley, and thought some of the aid pitches on El Cap would be really good free climbs. We'd both done the *Salathé* before and realized there were a lot of good cracks up there that would make really good free pitches, so we decided, 'Let's go do that.'"

Hudon and Jones climbed in what was essentially traditional style, swapping leads as they would when free climbing any multipitch route and following the original line without variation unless a convenient detour presented itself. They climbed as much of the route free as they could, as quickly as they could, to enjoy the experience and to see just how far they could push it. They didn't get too hung up on whether they had to resort to aid here and there, which they did, but only where it was too difficult or the leader was too far up a pitch to lower down and start over.

In this manner, they freed all but about 300 feet of the *Salathé Wall*. Much of that was wet at the time of their ascent—impossible to free climb in the moment, but which they felt could "go" under ideal conditions. They believed that all but ninety feet of the route could definitely go free. But they didn't sweat it. They were climbing as free as can be. No need to get crazy about it, even if others did.

5   BACHAR IS GOD

My friend Chris Gentry invited me to take a road trip to Joshua Tree in the spring of 1982. His parents had given him the new guidebook as a Christmas present. It was the biggest, thickest rock climbing guidebook we had ever seen, with more than a thousand routes described and illustrated. We devoured it, poring over it page by page all through the rainy winter, making a list of the dozens of routes we hoped to climb. Our list was pages long and overly ambitious—far more routes than we could climb in a week. Just thinking about all those hard, thin faces, perfect vertical cracks, and rounded golden domes kept me awake at night.

We hit the road at 8 a.m. on a Saturday in late March—Chris, his friend Rich Williams, and I—and drove straight through from Seattle to Joshua Tree in Southern California. We agreed that we would try to make the 1,200-mile drive in under twenty-four hours. The anticipation of arriving in Joshua Tree National Monument and beholding the spectacle of the high desert kept us going through the long day and night.

At 7:45 a.m. the next day, I pulled into a turnout between two high monzonite domes near a sign pointing to Hidden Valley Campground and got out of the car. We had arrived. The air was cold and sharp in the unfiltered morning sunlight, hinting at the promise of heat despite the slight chilling breeze. Everything stood out in sharp relief: boulders, tawny granite domes, Joshua trees poking up across the rocky landscape, arid mountains in the near distance to the south. The thin air of the high desert took an effort to breathe.

"We're here," I said, giving Chris a gentle shove to wake him up. He'd been sleeping in the passenger seat for the past half hour. He sat up and looked out the window, then pulled out his guidebook and began frantically turning pages. He stopped on a page, ran his finger down a list of climbs, and squinted to read.

"There's a four-star 5.7 crack right over there," he said, looking up and pointing toward a rock formation right in front of us.

"Let's do it," I said.

We didn't bother to wake Rich, who was passed out on the backseat. We quietly grabbed a rope and some gear out of the trunk and scurried toward the rock. After nearly a full day on the road with almost no sleep, I was surprisingly energetic, racing wild-haired Chris across the coarse sand, over rough, rounded boulders, and between prickly Joshua trees, yucca plants, and cholla cacti to the base of the dome.

"Who gets to lead?" Chris asked hopefully, catching his breath.

"I do," I said. "I drove practically the whole way here."

"Fair enough," Chris said. "I get the next one."

The route was obvious: a vertical crack splitting a steep, golden wall, about seventy feet from base to top. The rock was delectably cold to the touch. I led up a few moves to the top of a flake, slotted in and clipped a chock, and launched into the crack. It was set in a slightly flaring corner but was straightforward jamming—big, meaty hand jams and foot jams and stems out onto the rough quartzite face. Near the top the flare widened into a semi-chimney and ended on a wide ledge. I rigged a belay with enough slack so I could sit on the edge, legs dangling, and watch Chris climb up after me. He followed quickly and was soon sitting beside me, grinning. We were finally on top of one of the fabled golden domes of Joshua Tree National Monument. We stayed there for the longest time, looking out over the endless domes and boulders and Joshua trees populating the flat desert floor as far as we could see.

Then it got weird.

"Holy shit!" Chris exclaimed.

"What?"

"There!" He pointed to the big dome just across the road, to a group of climbers moving in unison up a left-leaning crack splitting a high, steep wall. One climber after the other, six in all, ascended the crack up the hundred-foot wall, moving methodically just a few feet apart, almost synchronized. We watched them climb the crack to its end, surmount a ledge, and disappear around the back side of the dome.

"They're not roped up," Chris observed, more as a question than a statement.

"No way," I replied, incredulous despite the fact I could see they were not roped up.

This required further investigation. We rappelled off the back side of the dome and walked back to the car. Chris retrieved his guidebook and studied it furiously. "*Left Ski Track*," he said. "5.11." We walked over to look at the crack, to see it, to feel it for ourselves. It was vertical if not slightly overhanging, thin here, wide there, shallow, angling gently to the left up the shaded wall. There were chalk marks here and there in the crack, but otherwise no trace that anyone had passed. The half dozen climbers had climbed it, unroped, in quick succession, and then vanished. For all of this recent activity, the wall was cold, dark, and strangely quiet.

"They just *soloed* this," Chris said, looking at me and then back up at the crack in disbelief. "Who *are* those guys?"

I WOKE UP IN THE AFTERNOON and found our campsite deserted. Chris and Rich had ditched me. I grabbed my rock shoes and chalk bag and headed off looking for them.

I didn't have to go far. I found them flailing on a route right next to the road just a few campsites up, groping their way from bolt to bolt up a 5.10 slab, slipping, falling, grabbing carabiners, hanging on the rope, and ripping their fingertips to shreds on razor-sharp edges and crystals. I left them to their foolishness and went looking for my own. I found it straightaway: big, rounded boulders everywhere around the campground, coarsely sandpapered and bedazzled with crystals like broken glass. After an hour of bouldering, I knew I had better quit before I split my fingers open, but I couldn't stop.

Suddenly, seemingly out of nowhere, a group of climbers appeared, all ratty looking and generally unwashed—hair unkempt, hands and knees dirty, scabby, and swollen, wearing shorts or sweats, torn-up T-shirts, and shredded EBs. They swarmed over seemingly every face of every boulder, one after the other, all at once, then disappeared through a gap between two big blocks, leaving a slight haze of chalk dust and a stale, earthy smell in their wake.

After the swarm had diffused, I tried one of the problems they had done, a little overhanging face on the back side of a rounded boulder. I grasped the initial holds, a couple of sharp crystals, and grimaced. Just pulling off the ground was painful; letting go to make the next move seemed impossibly so.

"You're doing it wrong," someone said from behind me. I turned around to see a young man about my age, a little taller, with a chin-curtain beard and an earnest look. He reminded me of a high school history teacher I had once had, fresh from the university, all serious about Greek and Roman history. He seemed friendly, unlike any of the recent swarm who had completely ignored my presence other than to imply I didn't belong there.

"Show me how it's done," I said, stepping back and gesturing to him to demonstrate.

"Right on," he said. He approached the boulder, chalked up, grasped the opening holds, pulled up, and worked through the moves, clinging to edges and crystals I had not seen or thought to try. He narrated as he climbed. "You grab this crystal," he said, reaching up and pinching a crystal with his left thumb and forefinger, "then lean over to the right and grip this sloping edge, then you drop your left hand to this edge and put your right hand on the crystal and you can pull up, slap the arête, and you're done. You don't want to pull on this with your finger. Hook your thumb over it instead; it makes a huge difference. If you try to pull on it with your finger, you'll be out of balance and will probably tweak a tendon." He made the problem look simple. I tried to repeat his sequence and fell off, but tried again and was able to pull through.

"You're not from around here," he said.

"No."

"I can tell," he said, laughing. "Your pasty white skin gives it away, that and your fingertips. Next time you come you need to work on your base tan. You're going to burn up down here! It's higher elevation than you think. You'll burn faster and won't even realize it because it's not all that warm this time of year. You'll climb all day without a shirt on and the next day you'll be as red as a lobster. Also, you need to work on your calluses. Toughen up your fingers so you don't rip them up. This rock is murder on fingers, and hands. Done any crack climbing yet?"

"Not really."

"Man, you have to go crack climbing!" he gushed. "JT cracks are the best. Four-star routes everywhere. Finger, hand, fist, roof cracks—you name it. We should go climb something."

"Sure," I said. "Why not?"

KERWIN KLEIN WAS, AS FAR as I could tell, a beatnik of sorts from the Pacific Northwest, a transplant from the Midwest who had attended high school in Bellingham, Washington, then relocated to Southern California. Kerwin, a year older than I, attended college nearby and was spending his spring break at Joshua Tree. A gymnast-turned-climber with a bent for hard bouldering, he seemed enthusiastic about everything. He was eager to lead, toprope, boulder, or just hike in the desert. And I was eager to go along. Kerwin led me all over, to obscure cliffs and routes I had not noticed in the guidebook, avoiding the popular four-star routes and the crowds they drew so we could get more climbing in. All the while, he continued to narrate the history and anthropology of the Joshua Tree climbing scene.

"You have your tourons," Kerwin explained, while leading up a steep wall toward an overhang, "like you and your friends, who come in over spring break or in the fall when the weather is good, climb all of the four-star routes but never really get the feel of the place. Then you have people who live close enough that we can come out every weekend. Not really locals, but sort of. And then you have the real locals, who live in Yucca Valley or Joshua Tree and come out every night and every weekend. They really own the place. But also, you have the seasonal climbers, who spend every fall and winter here, months at a time, living out of their cars or tents or whatever, who climb here in the spring until it gets too hot, and then move on to Tahquitz and Yosemite, and come back in the fall for another few months."

Kerwin stopped talking for a minute as he reached the base of the overhang. He jammed his hands in an angling crack, hooked his heel on a ledge high over his head, and levered up until he could reach past the overhang. He pulled over the top easily and set a belay.

"Most of them are Stonemasters, like Bachar, Largo, and Yabo," he yelled down, continuing his soliloquy while belaying me up the pitch. "Basically, if you see a bunch of ratty climbers running around doing boulder problems or soloing shit you can't do, they are probably Stonemasters or their spawn, kids out from Santa Paula, El Segundo, or Simi Valley who are here every weekend or all spring. They spend pretty much their whole lives climbing, moving around from area to area, doing everything together. There's a bunch of them here now."

"I've seen them."

"They're pretty hilarious. Probably the best climbers on the planet, but some of them are retards."

"What do you mean?"

"There's a lot more to life than climbing, dude," Kerwin said. "It's not the most important thing in the world. A lot of them don't realize that. But then," he added, "a lot of the rest of us don't either."

DAVE SORRIC WAS A VERITABLE Joshua Tree local. Even though he lived 200 miles away in Santa Paula, he, like dozens of other suburban kids from the Los Angeles area, spent every spring and fall weekend climbing at the monument, driving out each Friday night and back each Sunday night. He was a scruffy-looking twenty-year-old with sandy brown hair hanging over his eyes, and he wore a red flannel shirt and ripped-up climbing pants that were duct-taped across the knees and ass, the same outfit he would wear every day for the rest of the week. Chris and Rich had met Dave while they were trying that dreadful 5.10 slab I had seen them working on. Dave had wandered by, seen them struggling, offered to belay, and had immediately started giving them shit.

"Hanging on the rope is for pussies," he told Chris derisively after Chris had skidded off yet again. "If you don't get back on the rock I'm going to lower you off."

"Geez, Dave," Chris said. "Why don't you try this?"

"Fuck that. This is a bullshit route. Only tourons climb it."

Chris got back on the rock and tried the moves again, but his feet slipped off and he skidded back down the slab until the rope came tight and held him.

"These shoes just don't stick on this rock," Chris complained.

"That's bullshit," Dave said. "I've seen old ladies climb this route in their tennis shoes."

"I give up," Chris said. "Lower me."

Dave lowered him to the ground. Chris's fingertips were raw. He grimaced in pain.

"I can't even untie the rope. Look! I'm getting blood on the rope."

"That's fucked up," Dave said, smirking. "You need to work on your calluses."

FOR SOME REASON, EVEN THOUGH he hadn't succeeded in leading a 5.10 route all week, Chris decided to try *Bearded Cabbage*, a 5.10c located in the campground loop, within sight of God and everybody. The route was short but ostentatiously positioned, starting with a ledge traverse across an overhanging wall to a shallow, flared crack thirty feet above a jumble of boulders and spear-tipped yuccas. I admired Chris for his lack of fear of public humiliation. So what if he was in far over his head? So what if everyone in the campground could watch him flail? So what if he failed comically? He was having fun. That is what he had come for.

"What's the worst that could happen?" Chris asked, grinning, as he tied in.

"You could be impaled on those yuccas down there," I thought out loud.

"Aw, don't listen to him," Dave said, giving me a dirty look. "You're going to fire it!"

Chris traversed out across the ledge, hooking his right heel over the edge while shuffling his hands across, his left leg more or less dangling. He clipped the bolt at the end of the flake, then reached across to the shallow crack, set a jam with his heavily taped left hand, swung his feet over into the crack, struggled to find his balance, then let go of the flake, intending to jam his right hand in the crack. He promptly swung leftward and lost contact. He dangled there ridiculously in midair in front of the gathering crowd, unable to pull himself back up onto the flake, and had to be lowered off. He tried again, and again, and fell at the same place each time.

"I think this tape is too thick," Chris said. He ripped off some of the tape and gave it another try. He didn't barn-door off this time; he managed to establish his position in the crack and make a tentative move higher, jamming his hand into a slot and pulling up, at which point he let out a yowl and let go, falling a few feet. "That's enough for me," he said, examining the blood oozing from a new gouge in the back of his hand. "Lower me."

A couple of grungy-looking climbers materialized from behind the boulders below us, making me wonder if there wasn't a secret portal from another universe down there. They had seen our rope, and sensed an opportunity.

"Hey," one of them called up, "mind if I give it a try?"

"Sure," Chris said. "Show us how it's done."

"Right on!"

The dude ran up the talus, his curly, long reddish-blond hair bouncing behind him, and started to tie himself into the rope with his grubby, callused hands.

"Do you want a harness?" Chris asked.

"No, man, this bowline-on-a-coil should work. Now how does it go? The rabbit comes out of the hole, then runs around the tree, then . . ." He tied a perfect bowline-on-a-coil, with a single loop of rope around his waist. "Man, I'm not sure I tied this right. Guess I'd better not fall. Watch me."

"I've got you," Dave said.

He started traversing out the flake, no chalk, no EBs, no gear, just slapping along with his hands, his tattered-Nike-clad feet dangling. At the end of the ledge, he swung his right heel up and hooked it over the ledge, smeared his left toe on a tiny hold, and reached up, sinking a hand jam in the flared, shallow crack, then another, and another. Soon, he was standing up on the flake, then jamming his trainers in the crack. He climbed a few moves up the crack, to where it angled back above the steepest section.

"Oh, shit!" he yelled, just as his feet slipped out the crack and were sketching around on the rock in desperation. "Oh, fuck!" His left hand popped out of the crack and was flailing as he hung suspended off of one hand jammed in a shallow, flaring crack. "Watch me! Watch me!"

We were all gaping below, sure this guy was about to pitch off and take a twenty-foot fall on a bowline-on-a-coil. And then he started cackling like a coyote.

"Ha! I had you, didn't I? Suckers."

He reestablished his feet and hands in the crack and calmly climbed down, as easily and methodically as he had climbed up, all the way back to the flake.

"Lower me, dude," he said.

"I've got you, Fish," Dave said, suppressing a smirk.

This Fish character let go of the rock and flipped himself upside down, wrapped his feet around the rope, and adopted a Superman pose pointing straight downward until he reached the talus below.

"Thanks, fellas," Fish said, untying from the rope. "That was fun." He and his companion bounded off, laughing all the way.

"Who were those guys?" Chris asked, wincing as he tore the rest of the tape off his hands.

"A couple of assholes," Dave said. "We should try an easy route. How about that one?" he said, pointing vaguely rightward toward an overhanging wall.

"What? *That*?" I asked, pointing up at an overhanging thin corner crack in that general direction.

"Hell no," Dave said. "Not *that* one; that one's 5.12. The slab on the right. It's only 5.9. Think you ladies can manage it?"

DAVE AND I WERE WAITING our turn to climb when we heard a sound on the sandy ledge behind us. We turned to see a lone climber, tan as the desert stone and just as blond, standing quietly at the base of *Spider Line*. He had shaggy hair, shoulder length in back with a slight curl, and was wearing gray shorts, a blue T-shirt tied around his waist, a blue chalk bag, and gnarled old EBs. No partner. No rope. He seemed oblivious to our presence, like he wasn't conscious of us being there. He chalked his hands methodically, one after the other, digging deep into his chalk bag and pulling out hands white as ghosts and trailing flecks of chalk dust. He rubbed his hands together meditatively, breathing deeply, while looking up at the crack. And then he started climbing, setting his fingertips in the thin crack, toeing in on barely discernible ripples and undulations in the rock, and pulling himself up, move by move. Dave and I stood mesmerized, watching as he climbed upward perfectly, move after flawless move, quietly, without emotion, without any apparent effort, as if the force of gravity had been momentarily suspended to allow his passage there. Within what seemed like a minute at most, he pulled perfunctorily onto the ledge at the end of the crack and vanished over the top.

"Do you know who that was?" Dave asked quietly, almost reverently, after the climber had disappeared.

"That was *John Bachar*. That was God."

6 BACHAR'S CHALLENGE

John Bachar was born in 1957 in Los Angeles, California. He grew up in Westchester, just north of LAX. His parents divorced when he was seven. When he was fourteen, he got his first taste of climbing at Stoney Point, a bouldering hot spot thirty miles to the north at the edge of the San Fernando Valley; he soon became a regular, riding his motorcycle out there after he got his license. Bachar visited Joshua Tree for the first time in 1973 and led his first route, a 5.6. Within a year he was leading 5.11 routes, and he was soon climbing with the likes of Mike Graham, Tobin Sorenson, and Dean Fidelman, "serious" climbers who hung out at Joshua Tree in the spring and climbed in Yosemite all summer. It wasn't long before Bachar was climbing in Yosemite all summer, too. He attended UCLA briefly, but despite good grades, he dropped out in 1976 to climb full-time, much to the disappointment of his father, a math professor at the university.

One day in the mid-1970s, John Long enticed Bachar to free solo *Double Cross*, the 5.7 crack route on the Old Woman formation Chris Gentry and I had climbed the morning we arrived at Joshua Tree. Long was another young Southern California climber who belonged to the loosely affiliated Stonemasters. "If you climbed this route one hundred times with a rope, how many times would you fall?" he asked Bachar.

"Never," Bachar replied. He accepted the challenge and, as the legend goes, completed his first free-solo climb.

Soloing was nothing new—in Joshua Tree, Yosemite, or elsewhere. But it was new to Bachar, and it soon became an addiction he could not quit. He pushed the limits of what was deemed sane with his increasingly difficult unroped ascents, especially in Yosemite, where he shocked pretty much everyone when he soloed *New Dimensions* (5.11a) in 1976. But he wasn't only soloing; he was also establishing hard free routes, including *Hotline*, one of Yosemite's first 5.12 routes, with Ron Kauk, and the classic *Astroman*, a 5.11+ free version of Warren Harding's route up the east face of Washington Column, with Long and Kauk. Bachar was barely out of high school and already he was one of the best rock climbers in the world.

Bachar's climbing ability was in large part the result of his mathematical approach to training and performing. When he first arrived at Stoney Point, he was a scrawny kid, barely able to do two pull-ups; two years later, he was cranking off sets of twenty-seven pull-ups, and a year after that, he was establishing new 5.11 routes. By his midtwenties, he was devoting several hours each day to working out, which included doing weighted one-arm pull-ups off of two fingers and other feats of strength. He developed training apparatuses, such as wooden holds bolted to a beam across a carport entrance where he did fingertip pull-ups and hanging finger traverses, and his best-known invention, the "Bachar ladder," a rope ladder with PVC-pipe rungs. He also trained mentally, using relaxation and visualization exercises to learn how to stay focused on the problem at hand—"the small circle of rock around me," as he later described it in *Alpinist 26*—and remain in control, able to downclimb from anywhere on a route. He was always calculating, breaking down a route and analyzing its features, often rehearsing its moves mentally if not also physically before climbing. For example, before Bachar was mentally prepared to free solo *New Dimensions*, he climbed it numerous times, especially the final 5.11 thin corner pitch, which he toproped successively until he had it wired.

Bachar was strongly influenced by John Gill, the so-called Father of American Bouldering, a mathematician and gymnastic training fanatic who pursued bouldering—defined by Gill as "one-pitch climbing of great difficulty, usually done close to the ground and unroped"—as an end unto itself. Gill, who introduced the use of gymnastics chalk in rock climbing, had done boulder problems in the 1950s and 1960s that were the equivalent of hard 5.13 on the modern scale (a technical difficulty unmatched until the late 1970s) and free-solo ascents of short climbs up to 5.12. He is especially revered for his 1961 ascent of an overhanging face of the Thimble, a thirty-foot-high pinnacle in the Needles of South Dakota, done unroped and unrehearsed, involving 5.12 moves above a guardrail. Gill's ethic was to strive for a "perfect" ascent as often as possible: he would toprope a problem if necessary for safety, but ideally he would do it as an on-sight free solo. It was an ethic Bachar adopted almost wholeheartedly.

Over the next several years, Bachar continued to establish or repeat hard lines and boulder problems. In 1978, he made the second ascent of Ron Kauk's iconic Yosemite boulder problem *Midnight Lightning*, as well as the first ascent on toprope of the quintessential Joshua Tree thin crack *Equinox* (5.12c); in 1979, he soloed the Nabisco Wall, linking pitches up to 5.11c; and in 1981, he did the first ascents of the infamous *Bachar-Yerian* (5.11c X) in Tuolumne Meadows and *Chasin' the Trane* (5.12d) in Germany.

Bachar visited the Frankenjura area of Germany during an extended climbing trip to Europe in early 1981. He and fellow Southern California climber Mike Lechlinski took part in a loosely organized "international free-climbing meet" held there, where Bachar observed that the leading German free climbers not only toproped routes before leading them but also put in protection bolts on rappel as a matter of course. In France, Bachar noted rappel-placed bolts "every five or ten feet" up a given rock wall, not to mention chiseled holds on many of the hardest routes. And in Germany, particularly the Frankenjura where most of the country's hardest free climbs were concentrated, routes featured sturdy protection bolts cemented into the rock every couple of meters. These tactics offended Bachar, a staunch traditionalist, but he remained somewhat ambivalent. This was not his climbing area, so it was not his problem.

Still, Bachar and Lechlinski attempted to make a statement against the "Euro-style" approach by repeating many of the hardest routes in better style, often on-sight. As reported in *Mountain* magazine in the fall of 1981, Bachar made the second ascent of the hardest new route in the Frankenjura, Kurt Albert's toprope route *Sautanz* (IX on the German rating scale, roughly 5.12c); Bachar repeated the thin, technical face climb, also on toprope. He then nabbed the first ascent of an open project, a fingery, technical line up a bulging wall that he called *Chasin' the Trane*. German phenom Wolfgang Gullich soon repeated the route and gave it an X rating on the German scale, confirming Bachar's proposed 5.13a rating. Although the route was later downgraded to IX+ (5.12d), it was still at least as hard if not harder than anything yet free climbed in Europe (with a couple of Ron Fawcett routes in Britain in close contention). Bachar was an instant sensation among the German climbers.

The route's name, from a John Coltrane album title, was "a not-so-subtle dig at the European climbing scene," according to one commentator. By climbing the route on lead from the ground up, Bachar purposely went against the prevailing local style to demonstrate to the Europeans that hard routes could be established without resorting to preplaced bolts and other shenanigans. Although Bachar protected the route with bolts, he placed them on lead, sparingly, and where it was impossible to let go to drill a bolt, he drilled while hanging from hooks set in pockets. Bachar acknowledged that this was a form of aid climbing, but in his view, it preserved the spirit of adventure of a traditional on-sight, ground-up ascent.

Bachar's "redpoint" of *Chasin' the Trane* helped spread the gospel of climbing in a purer, ground-up style, first to the German climbers, and then, through the write-up in *Mountain*, throughout Europe and eventually the entire rock climbing world. Impressed, some of the German climbers gave Bachar's style a try, but they soon went back to their old ways, which they found to be easier, safer, and more productive. In their view, a route created from the top down, with rehearsal of moves and rappel-placed bolts, could be just as high in quality as one led ground-up. They weren't placing their bolts too close together. They were leaving thought-provoking runouts, preserving a sense of adventure, risk, commitment—the same things Bachar was promoting, but which they could accomplish more efficiently. Bachar's style was valid, everyone agreed; it was just impractical.

Bachar had opened minds to an alternative method of establishing hard new free climbs. But in the end, all he did was convince the majority of European climbers that their approach to new route development was, in fact, superior to that of traditionalist American climbers.

After returning to the States, as if in reaction to what he had observed in Europe, Bachar embarked on a series of unprecedentedly bold free solos and first ascents, including the *Bachar-Yerian* and *Body and Soul* in Tuolumne Meadows. The *Bachar-Yerian*, one of Bachar's best-known first ascents, climbs the steepest face of Medlicott Dome, ascending a rash of pimple-like feldspar crystals and knobs through a dark water streak up a 500-foot-high vertical wall. Bachar, with Dave Yerian following, led each pitch, establishing the route from the ground up. He protected the continuously thin, hard 5.11 face moves with slings tied around the larger knobs and crystals and a handful of bolts placed on lead, including several placed with the aid of hooks. A fall on this route would have been long and frightening—not fatal if the bolts and slings held, but there was no assurance of that.

Bachar had explored the route alone, rope-soloing up the initial knob-studded slabs to where the wall steepened, "where Medlicott Dome swelled into this gigantic, ominous thing, a vertical wall hundreds of feet high," as he later described in his 2009 *Alpinist* magazine article. What he saw above his rope-solo high point was a sheet of rock studded with feldspar crystals, some the size of doorknobs, some as big as ice cubes, others as small as dice—bits of rock that might be solid or might snap off with little provocation. It could be a death route, but Bachar was concerned that if he didn't do it in traditional style, the growing contingent of "top-down" climbers would rap-bolt the line, believing, like the German climbers, that it was the only means of establishing the route, or at least the better approach for the sake of safety. Bachar bristled at the notion; it went against his ideal of the pioneers of climbing, "who had always ventured, ground up, into whatever unpredictable mysteries the rock presented them, pushing into more and more difficult terrain with each generation." So, Bachar committed himself to the task of leading the terrifying, knob-studded face of Medlicott Dome from the ground up, on lead, if for no other reason than to show those fools who thought the only possible way to establish this route was by placing bolts on rappel.

To this end, Bachar had accepted a compromise of his traditional ethic: that if bolts could not be placed from no-hands stances, they could be placed from a point of aid, and the resulting climb could still be called a free ascent. Bachar had heard that Dresden climbers, stalwarts of ground-up, traditional climbing, had placed bolts on ground-up leads while hanging from knotted slings wedged in cracks or pockets or from drill bits hand-drilled into the soft sandstone. He decided he could legitimately employ this style on Medlicott Dome, as he had done in the Frankenjura on *Chasin' the Trane*, because it respected the traditional ground-up ethic and would result in placement of only "necessary" bolts, spaced far apart, to protect the leader from a death fall. "It was a compromise," Bachar acknowledged, "but one that would allow me [to] leave the rock as unmarked as I could and still make the first ascent ground up." Bachar further attempted to justify the concept: "The farther apart the bolts were, the more of an artistic statement I could make about the value of skill over technology."

Bachar's sentiments about the route somewhat mirrored Hudon and Jones's "as free as can be" style. "Some people might criticize my use of aid," Bachar explained in the article, "but I'd never intended to call it a free route—just to keep it as free as I could."

The route's reputation for boldness and difficulty kept the "riffraff" off, and still does. But even with its X rating (the "X" indicating protection was so poor that a fall would probably result in serious injury or death), the route caught the attention of hardmen around the globe, who soon began to hurl themselves against it. Gullich visited Yosemite in 1982 and attempted a second ascent. After a thirty-five-foot fall, arrested by a tied-off knob that prevented a death fall onto the slabs below, he gave it up. To this day, even though elite climbers don't view 5.11 as being particularly difficult, the route retains a flavor of difficulty and risk that attracts the young and ambitious.

Despite the boldness of the *Bachar-Yerian*, some climbers were critical of Bachar's seemingly hypocritical use of aid to place bolts to protect free climbing. They argued that placing bolts from hooks was just as much aid climbing as fixing a piton, and if you were going to resort to using aid to place bolts on a free climb, you may as well put in good bolts on rappel instead of leaving a shoddy death route for others. In a move seemingly designed to silence his critics, Bachar went on a binge of hard, scantily protected climbing, establishing several routes that could have been protected with bolts placed from hooks, but where he opted to climb through without any protection instead.

Perhaps the most egregious of Bachar's "statement routes" was *You Asked for It*, a three-pitch line following knobs up another water streak farther right on Medlicott Dome. Bachar led the route placing almost no protection; he could no doubt have placed bolts, from hooks if not from free stances, to make the climbing less dangerous for those who might try to repeat the route, but he didn't. The resulting deadly runouts on sustained 5.10 climbing seemed to be a message aimed directly at his detractors: If they didn't like him placing bolts from hooks, fuck them. He wouldn't place bolts at all.

ONE OF THE MOST WELL-KNOWN STORIES about John Bachar involves "the note." In the fall of 1981, Bachar pinned a handwritten note to the bulletin board in Tuolumne Meadows Campground. It offered $10,000 to anyone who could follow him for a day of climbing. No one accepted his challenge.

The note had its desired effect. It solidified Bachar's status as the undisputed greatest rock climber of his generation. The challenge was symbolic; Bachar knew no one would take him up on it. To accept, it was tacitly understood, would mean following Bachar up difficult routes that were barely protected or not at all—if he even bothered to rope up, in which case one would have to commit to free soloing 5.11 and 5.12 routes. All day. It would be tantamount to suicide.

The note put an exclamation point on Bachar's statement to his critics. Criticize my style all you want, it seemed to shout, but if you can't walk the walk, then shut the fuck up. But the challenge had a different, perhaps unintended consequence. Bachar's note and his other acts of hubris—the bold leads, the death runouts, and the increasingly more difficult free-solo climbs—did not inspire others to adopt his strict traditional stance; instead, they seemed to undermine it.

A reformation had been under way for years, with the seeds of change taking root despite Bachar's efforts to weed them out. Bachar's note highlighted what everybody already knew: you couldn't play the game following Bachar's rules and win. You could climb hard, unprotected routes, sure, but eventually you would die. If the rising generation wanted to make a mark on the landscape of American rock climbing, they would have to play a different game with different rules. So they did.

Within a few short years, rock climbing as Bachar knew it would be irrevocably changed. His challenge marked a pivotal moment in the decline of the traditional climbing ethic. Bachar had made a declaration of war. There was no turning back.

PART TWO

IF NOT NOW, WHEN?

Sitting on those ledges for hours at a time, we finally figured out the three-pronged meaning of our sport. And it is this: To effortlessly crank your hardest projects, to have you fail miserably on ours, and to become the unabashed object of sexual desire to your girlfriends.

—Todd Skinner

OPPOSITE: John Bachar free soloing *Spider Line* (5.11d), Joshua Tree, 1982

7 SHOES OF MAGIC RUBBER

"We're going to Yosemite next week. Do you want to come?" It was Mike Mirande, calling on a Tuesday afternoon in the summer of 1982. "It's just for a week," he said excitedly. "We're leaving Friday morning."

"I don't think I can," I told him. "I have to work."

"Work? *Fuck* work!" Mike said. "Ask for time off. Quit. I said we're going to *Yosemite!*"

Yosemite!

Not with a car payment due, I wanted to tell him. I had to work; I needed the money. I couldn't just quit my job. Then again, Mike had a point. I still had not been to Yosemite.

Being a conscientious employee, I asked for the week off. My boss, Dick, was a former marine who had once told me that if I called in sick I had better be puking or dead. He gave my request due consideration.

"Well," Dick said matter-of-factly, barely looking up from his desk, "the way I see it is, you have to do what you have to do. If you want this job, you show up for work. Get my drift?"

I got his drift alright. That Friday afternoon, I was drifting down I-5 in the back of Mike's yellow-and-white VW van, halfway to Yosemite.

I AWOKE WITH A START just before dawn, at first unsure where I was. I opened my eyes and found myself in my sleeping bag, wedged in a slot between two boulders. Now I remembered. Camp 4 was full, so Mike had dropped me and Greg Olsen off in the parking lot, then had driven off with his girlfriend, Shirley Kollman, to find a campsite elsewhere. Greg and I had sneaked up into the boulders above Camp 4 to find a place to sleep.

It was freezing cold, and the frigid air combined with the paranoia of being busted by the rangers was a rude awakening. I quickly dragged my sleeping bag into Camp 4 under cover of semidarkness and laid it out in a vacant corner of the first campsite I stumbled into. I crawled back inside. I awoke a short time later to the sound of a camp stove being lit, climbing gear being racked, and an awkward silence. I rolled over and squinted up to see several rugged, biker-looking types staring at me as if I had passed out in bed with somebody's girlfriend. I sat up, looked around, and realized I was in the rescue site. Jesus! I wriggled out of my sleeping bag, walked in the other direction, and promptly tripped over a climber sleeping in the next site.

"What the hell?" he groaned, rolling over and shooting me that same look I had just gotten in the rescue site. I was ready to run for it.

"Jeff?"

"Rich?" It was Rich Williams. Thank God! "What are you doing here?"

"Climbing, man! I've been here for a week."

"Right on. Can I crash here for a while?"

"Sure, go for it."

I tossed my sleeping bag in the dirt next to Rich and crawled in. I had moved a total of perhaps four feet, but I was no longer invading the rescue climbers' space. I slept fitfully for another hour or so, lying in the dirt in semiconsciousness, listening to the sounds of camp and the voices coming from the rescue site. They were really talking now, very animated and laughing hysterically. I couldn't make sense of everything they were saying, but I didn't really care. They no longer seemed to want to kill me. For now, someone else seemed to be higher on their shit list.

WHAT I GATHERED FROM EAVESDROPPING on the rescue site residents was that a couple of outsiders were climbing a new route on El Capitan, somebody was dropping bags of shit on them, and they all thought this was freaking hilarious.

The climbers in question, Mark Smith and Richard Jensen, were not Yosemite regulars; they hadn't even climbed El Cap before coming to the Valley in the summer of 1982 with the audacious plan of climbing a new route up the Big Stone. To nearly everyone's surprise, especially the local climbers who harassed them pretty much the whole time they were on the wall, they succeeded, completing a route in thirty-nine straight days of climbing—a new record for the longest continuous ascent of El Cap, breaking Warren Harding and Dean Caldwell's record from their 1970 ascent of the *Dawn Wall*.

Smith and Jensen's ascent was not without its challenges. For one, the first 900 feet of the route was up a steep, nearly featureless slab, long ignored because surely it would require excessive bolting the likes of which had not been seen since the *Dawn Wall*. Smith and Jensen didn't bolt the shit out of the slab as everyone had expected, though. They placed a lot of bolts and rivets, sure, and drilled holes for bat hooks and "dimples" on some flakes here and there, but they climbed large sections of the slab using skyhooks seated on tiny flakes and edges, which required tenuous, delicate, slow climbing to link up discontinuous seams and crack systems. They took repeated long, grating falls down the slabs when their hook placements failed. They suffered injuries. They stuck it out through storms and a near-biblical drenching in a waterfall that formed on the route. These are the kind of difficulties that cause a lot of El Cap climbers to bail off. But the most difficult challenge the pair encountered was the wrath of the Valley locals.

According to various published accounts, one of which includes a confession by one of the so-called El Cap Shitters (who achieved a level of infamy akin to the alleged "second shooter" on the grassy knoll in Dallas on November 22, 1963), the locals threatened Smith and Jensen with violence and even death, harangued them constantly as they climbed, pulled down their ropes and defecated on them when they descended for a night, and chopped their anchors. One pair of climbers reportedly made a leisurely ascent of a route on the wall above Smith and Jensen's line just so they could bombard them with bags of feces every day. Still, despite this despicable display, Smith and Jensen persevered, enduring the daily shitstorm and eventually finishing the climb.

That they completed their ascent under such uniquely trying circumstances was a testament to their spirit of determination. Their route, which they named *Wings of Steel*, stood as the only unrepeated route on El Capitan for almost thirty years. Its detractors called it *Wall of Shit* (*WOS* for short, which worked either way). Not only was the route shunned, it was actively denounced for decades, largely because of the belief—primarily espoused by a vocal minority of Yosemite climbers, rightly or wrongly—that Smith and Jensen were a couple of "hacks" who had climbed the route in the worst possible style, chiseling the rock everywhere to seat skyhooks, drilling holes every few feet for bat hooks, and placing ladders of rivets to get up the blank slabs, then removing them as they cleaned to hide the evidence of their cheating. Smith and Jensen admitted to conservative bat hooking, riveting, and tapping out "dimples" in some flakes to seat skyhooks instead of drilling a deeper hole for a bat hook or rivet. But, they argued, even if they had done all of the things they were being accused of, hadn't those and similar practices long been accepted on El Cap—whacking thin flakes with a hammer to break off an edge where a skyhook could be set, chiseling out seams so that malleable "bashies" could be bashed in, widening too-thin cracks to allow fingers to fit, and the like? In fact, Smith and Jensen wondered, hadn't more than one of their detractors been guilty of those same infringements of the "rules"? Weren't these people being just a little hypocritical?

The problem, in Smith and Jensen's view, was not that they might have chipped off some micro-flakes, used some bat hooks, or placed some rivets—things any other climber might have done during a first ascent of a big wall route—but that they were not Valley locals. Had any of the locals done the same things while establishing a new route, they believed, it would not have whipped up a literal shitstorm of controversy.

This sort of controversy had erupted before, in 1970, when Warren Harding spent twenty-seven consecutive days on El Cap with Dean Caldwell, climbing the *Dawn Wall*, where they drilled more than three hundred holes in the rock during the climb, much to the ire of the anti-bolting crowd. Unswayed, Harding kept going, tirelessly drilling his way up the wall. But then, nobody was dropping bags of shit on Warren Harding.

WOS was finally repeated in 2011. The second-ascent party's report vindicated Smith and Jensen in a way, although it confirmed they did drill a lot of holes. At best, more people may now believe Smith and Jensen's story, but some people don't and never will. The controversy over *WOS* lives on, perpetuated on the climbing message boards. I am sure that by writing about it here, I will be castigated by those who still want to dump on Smith and Jensen, and on anyone who suggests that maybe they were unfairly targeted for abuse. I've heard it all before.

LATE ON OUR THIRD DAY in the Valley, at a time when most climbers were heading back to Camp 4, Mike insisted we drive to Reed's Pinnacle to do *Lunatic Fringe*, one of those classic Yosemite 5.10 thin cracks that just had to be climbed. "We're going to Tuolumne Meadows tomorrow," Mike said. "If we don't do it now, we probably won't get another chance."

When we arrived at Reed's Pinnacle, there was already a party on *Lunatic Fringe*, so we settled for *Stone Groove*, a little corner crack that led up to an open face, with solid finger jams and good footholds on nubbins and knobs the whole way. Rated 5.10b in the guidebook, it seemed easy. A "Yosemite 5.10b," Greg said, meaning it was soft. By the time the four of us climbed the route, the party on *Lunatic Fringe* had gone. So had the sun.

"We may as well climb it since we're here," Mike said, looking up at the route as he uncoiled his rope and started tying in.

While Mike and Shirley climbed the route, Greg put on a strange pair of climbing shoes. They looked like—and in fact were—plain old athletic socks that had been dipped in some kind of rubber, over which Greg laced up a leather sheath to hold the sock in place.

"Rock Socks," Greg said, anticipating my question. "These are proto-types. I'm testing them to see if they will work for thin crack climbing." He pulled the laces tight. "The way they're supposed to work is that you can jam your toes in thinner cracks than you can if you're wearing rock shoes, like climbing barefoot except the rubber will provide cohesion and protect your feet."

Greg Olsen was the smartest person I knew, probably because he rarely said anything, and so said fewer stupid things than most of my other climbing friends. He was a science major at the University of Washington who would go on to get a PhD in physical chemistry. He and another UW Rock rat, Dick "Duck" Novikoff, wanted to be able to jam thinner cracks than the current rock shoes allowed. After discussing the concept at some length, they eventually made some prototypes. Duck's first pair had inner-tube rubber folded over the toes to form a sort of fin, with the foot covered by a true leather "sock"; he tried valiantly to use them, but they didn't really work. Greg came up with a prototype of his own, socks with painted-on rubber applied to the toe area and inner-tube soles. Greg had brought these prototypes to Yosemite to give them a test run on an actual thin crack pitch.

Rock Socks seemed like a brilliant idea, and Greg led *Lunatic Fringe* in them with no trouble, jamming his toes in places where mere mortals like me had to edge or smear. But afterward he tossed them aside. "The rubber is hard and slippery," he complained, "and the socks are stretching out." He pulled on the toe of one of the socks, which had stretched out and was drooping off the end of his foot.

"These could revolutionize crack climbing," Greg added. "Getting the rubber just right is going to be the key."

LITTLE DID WE KNOW THAT a new rock shoe was being introduced to Yosemite climbers at that very moment—a shoe that would, as Greg had predicted, revolutionize the sport. In the mid-1970s, Jesus Garcia Lopez started the footwear company Calzados Boreal SL in Villena, Spain, to make hiking and mountaineering boots. He soon expanded into the rock shoe market at the suggestion of a local climber, Miguel Angel Garcia Gallego. With Gallego's assistance, Lopez produced the company's first prototype rock shoes in 1975 and 1976, which led to the company's first rock shoe, the "El Capitan." Like the favorite rock shoes on the market at the time, EBs, the El Capitan model had flat rubber soles, but these soles were different: the rubber was softer and seemed to stick better to the rock. Still not satisfied, the Boreal team continued to experiment with the rubber, aiming to create a "sticky" sole that was also durable and resistant to abrasion.

Gallego, who was infatuated with El Capitan, made trips to Yosemite in 1978 and 1979 with his brothers, José, Carlos, and Javier, to climb the *Nose* and the *Salathé Wall*, where they tested the newest prototypes. The 1979 prototype worked well on the *Salathé*, and the following year, after fine-tuning the design, Lopez produced a model he called the "Firé," after a rock spire, the Mallo Firé, in Riglos, Spain.

In 1982, the Gallego brothers returned to Yosemite and climbed El Capitan once again, this time establishing *Mediterraneo*, which crossed the *Salathé Wall* and ended between the *Muir Wall* and *Nose* routes—the first all-foreign first ascent on El Cap. They were wearing Firés. After their ascent, they showed off their shoes to climbers in Camp 4, including John Bachar, who tried them out on *Midnight Lightning*. Not surprisingly, Bachar wanted a pair. Gallego gave him one, and not just out of kindness: he was looking for a US distributor. The next year, Bachar and Mike Graham signed on as the American distributors of Firé rock shoes. Their initial shipment of 265 pairs sold out within two hours.

"Sticky rubber made a huge difference," John Long recalls. "Before, routes were scary. The old shoes didn't friction for shit. When the sticky rubber came out, they were way easier. Stuff we were sliding off of before, we were romping up on our first try."

We knew nothing about all of this when Greg climbed *Lunatic Fringe* in his prototype Rock Socks. I followed the pitch in my EBs and didn't have any difficulty either, other than they hurt like hell to wear. And as for sticky rubber, who needed that? Good footwork gets you up routes, and EBs worked just fine.

8 A LITTLE TIME OFF

I returned to Joshua Tree in the spring of 1983. This time, I had arranged to take my winter finals a week early and start spring classes a week late so I could spend three whole weeks climbing. I had barely gotten a taste of JT the year before; just as I had started to settle into a groove, it was time to drive back north and rush to school the next morning, where I nodded off in class pining for the feel of sun-warmed monzonite. This year would be different. I had worked hard all winter to make money for the trip, and I went to the gym before school and worked out at night on my garage wall. I stayed late at the practice rock every night it didn't rain, honing my friction and crack technique. I was determined to step it up, to really do some climbing this time and not just wander aimlessly about the high desert with a bunch of stoners, wasting precious time.

My first morning there, I came upon a trio of climbers with a toprope set up on an overhanging face route in Echo Cove, a semi-box canyon a short walk north of Hidden Valley Campground. A dark-haired young man, shorter, stronger, and a few years older than I, was climbing when I showed up. He climbed a lap, moving rapidly up and down the vertical-to-overhanging wall, lunging precisely past the longest reaches and muscling through the rest of the moves. His belayer, an enthusiastic young man with wild blond hair, was seated cross-legged on the cove floor, shouting up a constant stream of encouragement.

"That's it! You've got it! Brilliant move, Paul!"

A long-legged young woman in blue shorts went next. She stuck the dynamic move and walked up the remainder of the route.

"That's it, Lisa!" the blond guy effused. "That's the crux. You made it look easy!"

By now I had sidled up behind them, hoping they might let me take a turn on the route. With some climbers, especially the locals, you didn't even bother asking, but this group seemed friendly enough. The belayer and his sidekick saw me and quickly looked me over. Breaking into an easy smile, the belayer stood up and walked toward me, still belaying, letting out slack as he came up to me. He held the rope tight in his left hand while extending his right hand earnestly to shake mine.

"Howdy, stranger," he said. "I'm Todd Skinner."

IN THE EARLY 1930S, CLEMENT C. SKINNER moved from Wisconsin to Wyoming with his wife, Viola. Clem, known as the "Old Man of the Mountains," first worked as a government trapper, mostly of wolves and grizzly bears; he later started a successful hunting guide business. Clem and Vi had six children, all boys—Bud, Monte, Bob, Courtney, Quentin, and Ole—all of whom attended the University of Wyoming. Bob and Monte later took over Clem's guiding business, renaming it Skinner Brothers Wilderness Camps. In addition to packing hunters into the Wyoming high country, they started a wilderness school to teach young boys (and later girls) outdoor skills like hunting, fishing, tracking, camping, hiking, horsemanship, and preparing wild meat. The students built log rafts by hand that they floated down the Green River. They camped in tipis supported by lodgepole pines.

In 1956, Bob married his sweetheart, Doris, and in 1958, they had a son; they named him Todd. The Skinner family, which included their first-born son, Orion, and youngest daughter, Holly, spent the summer and autumn months in Pinedale running the wilderness school and packing business. They wintered at local ski resorts.

Tradition ran strong in the family. Todd's uncle Quentin climbed Gannett Peak at age fourteen, and his uncle Ole's son, Ndi, did it at age twelve; Todd beat the record, making the ascent at age eleven. Todd also continued the family tradition of attending the University of Wyoming, where he earned a degree in finance despite taking up climbing, which lured many a less hardy soul to drop out and head to Yosemite.

Todd's father had taught survival skills in the US Air Force and was an experienced rock climber who had established many first ascents. He took Todd and his siblings rock climbing, and climbing was part of the Skinner Brothers Wilderness Camps curriculum. Despite this, Todd did not take a real interest in rock climbing until his college years. He worked for the family business during the summer, packing in gear for hunters, hikers, and climbers, and spent his winters skiing.

The University of Wyoming campus, at Laramie, wasn't far from one of Wyoming's best-known climbing areas, Vedauwoo, and it wasn't long before Todd had found his new favorite place—and his new best friend. One sunny day in 1979, Paul Piana had gone out to Vedauwoo to try a new route. Just as he succeeded in making the first ascent of the 5.11 climb, which he called *Spider God*, a younger climber approached. Paul had met this kid before while buildering on the walls of the university cafeteria; he considered him to be an obviously unskilled and inexperienced climber, but also a determined and irrepressibly enthusiastic one. Here at Vedauwoo, the kid, Todd Skinner, confirmed his naïveté by showing up wearing a Whillans harness and Royal Robbins boots two sizes too big and sporting a rack of gear that included Moac chocks and soft-iron pitons. Then, as Paul described it in *Rock & Ice*, Todd went "clanking up the rock face," eagerly attempting to follow Paul's lead.

"He was falling his way up a route, but he was having a good time," Paul recalls today. "Afterward, he asked me, 'When are you going out again?' He was so enthusiastic about climbing, so psyched to learn and get better."

Impressed with Todd's persistence, and more importantly sensing Todd would make a reliable belay slave, Paul adopted Todd as a climbing partner. Todd quickly adapted to modern climbing techniques, and it wasn't long before the pair were joining forces to climb a slew of hard new routes at Vedauwoo, several of which were reported in a 1982 issue of *Climbing* magazine, accompanied by photos taken by Lisa Schassberger.

Completely infatuated with climbing by the time he finished college, Todd decided to "take a little time off to climb" instead of going to work at an accounting office. Paul came along. So it was that I met Todd Skinner and Paul Piana at Joshua Tree in the spring of 1983.

"WHERE ARE YOU FROM?" TODD BEGAN, immediately assaulting me with a seemingly endless series of questions. "How long are you here? Are there any routes you want to climb while you're here? Are you going to Yosemite in the summer? Have you ever been to Devils Tower? Are there any last great problems in Washington?" It was like this every time I met up with him, and every time he met any climber from anywhere—a good-natured interrogation, a fact-fishing expedition he referred to as the "Skinner Inquisition." It didn't matter who you were, Todd Skinner genuinely wanted to know about you and was not afraid to ask.

"Do you want to try this?" Todd finally asked me after twenty questions.

"Sure. Thanks. I'll give it a try."

"Alright, then get on it!" Todd said. "This is a great climb for mileage," he continued as I tied in. "You have to do mileage in the winter and spring to train for the hard climbing in the summer and fall. I'm going to do fifty laps on it today. I have to get ready for the Tower. There are a hundred first ascents there just screaming to be done. Perfect 5.12 cracks and corners that will require a razor hone. It is going to be a brilliant season. You should join us."

"Really?" I said, a little taken aback at this sudden invitation to join Todd Skinner and Paul Piana and, who knew, maybe even Lisa Schassberger for a season of climbing. They had just met me and hadn't even seen me climb yet.

"Really!" Todd said enthusiastically. "But," he said in a hushed, almost reverent tone, "only if you can leave your wife, kids, lawn, dog, and job for the season. Can you do it?"

"I'm not sure," I said. "I have to finish spring quarter first, then work to save some money."

"That is the saddest thing I have ever heard," Todd said, shaking his head sorrowfully. "Did you hear that, Paul?"

"It's sad," Paul said, shaking his head sorrowfully.

Notwithstanding the sorrow I had sewn in the hearts of my new companions, I tied in and climbed the route, up and down, without falling. Todd encouraged me the entire way. "Nice move!" he said when I stuck the crux statically. "That's usually done as a dynamic move. Way to pull through!" And as I pulled myself up the headwall moves, he called up, "You have it!" And when I touched the ground with a toe and started back up for a second lap, he said, "That's the way, go for it!" And when, after five laps, I stepped off and untied from the rope with a decent pump, Todd gushed, "Well done. That's a brilliant route." And he so genuinely meant it.

My usual climbing partners would have complained if I had wanted to climb a route twice. "Don't be so selfish," they would have said. "Give somebody else a chance. Jesus!" Not only was Todd content to belay me for half an hour while I climbed the pitch over and over, he was enthusiastic about it.

Even Paul and Lisa seemed enthused about sitting there watching me climb. I felt as if I had stumbled into a cult.

"Your turn," Todd said with a slight grin, handing me the other end of the rope after I had untied. "No one rides for free."

Todd tied in and proceeded to climb ten laps, which must have taken close to an hour. Every so often Lisa or Paul would say, "Nice job" or "Stay focused." I just belayed, watching Todd climb. He moved slowly, methodically, almost as if in a trance at times, pulling himself up the brown patina flakes, sometimes seeming to close his eyes and climb by memory, at other times stopping to chalk up in the middle of the most difficult or strenuous moves, just to make it more difficult.

"We're going out to climb *Wangerbanger* and *Hot Rocks* tomorrow," Todd told me as he untied from the rope, his forearm muscles bulging like shipyard ropes under his skin. "Want to join us?"

"Sure," I said.

"Alright then," he said. "We're in the campground loop, down by the big boulders. I drive a white VW bus with Wyoming plates. You can't miss it. Come and find us in the morning."

FOR THE REMAINDER OF MY THREE WEEKS in Joshua Tree, I tagged along with Todd and Paul and whoever else they invited to join them, which was pretty much everyone they met. It didn't seem to matter if you could climb 5.8 or 5.12; if you were a decent person and expressed a sufficient level of enthusiasm and persistence, you were welcome to come along. They bouldered to hone finger strength and technique; toproped laps on 5.10 and 5.11 routes for mileage; soloed for "mind control"; and talked incessantly about the routes they had done and planned to do, here, there, everywhere. Invariably, at the end of the day, they'd end up in Echo Cove for a lap session on *Big Mo*. I probably climbed *Big Mo* one hundred times or more during my stay, up and down, lap after lap, day after day, and I began to feel that razor hone Todd was so effusive about. Climbing every day made you a better climber. Climbing every day made you stronger. Hard bouldering made you tough as nails. Soloing made you mentally strong. No wonder those California climbers were so damn good. I couldn't climb every day like this back home in the land of slugs, moss, and near-constant rain; here, it was sunny, warm, and there was nothing to do but climb all day, every day. It became what you did. It became your life.

Invariably, Todd would tell a story around the campfire each night. "Get this," Todd would say whenever there was a break in the conversation, then he'd launch into a tale about some hilarious or desperate situation—how he led a party of hunters out of the Wind River Range during an arctic storm, survived a week on only a handful of chocolate-covered peanuts, or persevered in leading a desperate route when all his gear had fallen out and he had committed to the crux. The stories were never heroic. They were mostly self-deprecating, with Todd the unlikely hero who survived because of dumb luck, divine intervention, or a little of both. The sun broke through the clouds at just the right moment to reveal the way to safety. A crucial piece of gear, left behind by the first-ascent party thirty years before, appeared at the end of a rappel as he bailed off a climb to escape a furious storm. The one loose match he found at the bottom of his pack miraculously flared to life after all hope had vanished, barely getting the fire going that provided just enough warmth for him to survive the desperate bivouac in sub-zero temperatures. Stuff like that. At first, you might believe every word he said, but after a while, especially after you'd heard him tell the same story a few times with added embellishments depending on the audience, you weren't sure what to believe.

"Get this," Todd began one night after dinner. "One time, me and Paul were in the Needles, and we decided to play a little prank on the tourists. We'd found these lab coats and a stethoscope in a box in storage at the university, so we took them with us on our trip. One day, there were a bunch of tourists hanging around by the Thimble, so we stopped, climbed up to the top of the Thimble wearing our lab coats, and rappelled off, the two of us at the same time. Paul had the stethoscope out and he would put it up to the rock and pretend to listen very intently. I had a magnifying glass out and was looking at the rock really close up, then wrote down notes on a clipboard. The tourists watched us intently and were taking pictures of us. Then one of them asked, 'What are you doing up there?'

"'We're lichenologists,' we told them. 'There's a very rare growth of lichen up here. This is the only place that it grows in the whole world. It used to grow all over the Needles, but now there's just this one square inch of it left in the whole world.'"

"Tourists would ask us, 'How do you get the rope up there?'" Paul chimed in. "There's a way to make a Perlon rope stiff, and you can sometimes get ten feet of it to stand straight up. So we'd stiffen out a rope and hold it up in the air and tell them that's how we got the ropes up there."

"This was back in the day when George Willig was climbing on *Wide World of Sports*," Todd added, "so we'd tell the tourists Willig came around every year and we paid him to put the ropes up. They were eating it up," Todd added, laughing. "Can you believe it? We told them this stuff and they fell for it. I think if you say anything with a straight face, people will believe you."

The next morning, we were toproping laps on a 5.11 route when a pair of climbers approached. Todd, being Todd, went out to greet them and engaged them in his usual interrogation.

"Where're you from?" Todd asked them. "What are you climbing today?"

"There's supposed to be a good 5.9 crack up here," one of them answered. "How about you? What are you climbing there?"

"This?" Todd said, pointing up at our route. "This is a vicious little crack. It starts out easy then gets really thin at the top."

They seemed interested. "How hard is it?"

"It's 5.12," Todd said, looking at one, then the other, with a completely straight face.

"Wow!" said one of them, totally buying it. "That's hard."

They eventually caught on, I'm sure. All they had to do was look at the guidebook to realize Todd was shining them on.

"LET'S GO TRY *BABY APES*," Todd said as I packed up my gear, preparing to head home. I hesitated. If I went with Todd, I might miss my ride. Todd didn't seem concerned. "Leave a note," he said. "They'll come and get you when it's time to go. And if they don't, you can just stay here and keep climbing."

Todd started into another of his stories as we hiked out toward Peyote Cracks. "Get this," he began. "John Bachar climbed this route on a toprope and then Tony Yaniro comes along and says he's going to lead it. Bachar says, 'Go for it,' but Yaniro says he's going to place a bolt. 'Well, not so fast,' says Bachar, and he goes and solos it just to keep Yaniro from bolting it."

"No way," I said.

"Seriously," Todd assured me. "Well, no self-respecting climber's going to drill a bolt to protect a route that's been soloed, so Yaniro left it alone. Except for Bachar's solo, it hasn't been led yet, or so I hear. I'm going to take a look at leading it."

Todd scrambled to the top of the buttress, set an anchor, and then rappelled down, feeling the holds as he went, scoping out the route for possible protection.

"I don't know," Todd said. "It's pretty thin up here. You could get in some wired nuts in a couple of places, but they'd plug up the best jams. If anything came out, you'd probably deck. I think we should stick to toproping."

And so we did. We tried for an hour or so to toprope the 5.12 route, with marginal success. It was a sequential problem, with a roof traverse to a lunge to a pocket on an overhanging wall, then tenuous, strenuous fingertip jamming up shallow slots and flares in the crack, short but fierce, no walk in the park. Establishing on the headwall was not a problem, but it took me several tries to figure out one particularly thin sequence, which ate up my remaining time. Todd had so far fared only slightly better, but we were making progress, inch by inch.

"We are lucky men," Todd said as he untied from the rope after a failed attempt.

"How so?" I asked.

"We're not accountants," he said. "You're sure you can't stay?"

"I have to get back," I said. "I've already missed a week of school."

"I know how it is," Todd said, shaking his head wistfully. "But you know what?" he continued, looking me straight in the eye. "When it comes right down to it, all of that isn't important. I mean, what are you going to school for?"

"I don't know," I admitted. "To go to school, I guess. What should I be doing?"

"Well now," Todd began in a fatherly tone, "I went to college, got a degree, and thought I would go into accounting. But then I woke up one morning and thought, 'You know what, Todd, that's the stupidest idea you've ever had.' Imagine! Sitting behind a desk every day for the next thirty years! So you know what? I said to hell with it. I decided first I needed to take some time off to do a little climbing, and so here I am, out on the road. I don't know when I'll go back. Or maybe I won't go back."

"I don't think I can do that," I said. "Not now."

"If not now, when?" Todd asked, seriously, a fire lit in his eyes. "Now is the only time we can afford to spend the rest of our lives doing what we want to do."

"What if you don't know what you want to spend the rest of your life doing?" I asked.

"Well, you've got me there," Todd said, a slightly perplexed look on his face. Then his face brightened. "You may as well just go climbing then. You don't want to be lying on your deathbed sixty years from now thinking, 'Jesus! If only I had climbed that godforsaken rock.'"

9   MUD TUGGING

In the summer of 1983, I took the long way home from a jaunt to Sun Valley, circling west into Oregon to check out Smith Rock, a climbing area I had read about in an old issue of *Off Belay* magazine. A couple friends had ventured there for a weekend the year before, because it was raining everywhere else, and reported back that it had a few good climbs, although they also mentioned snakes, spiders, and friable rock on routes with names like *Pop Goes the Nubbin*. So I had developed the impression that Smith Rock was not worthy of a six-hour drive from Seattle, even to escape the rain. But, seeing as how I was already in Oregon with a couple of days to kill, and had my EBs and chalk bag in the trunk, I figured why not stop and check it out, shitty rock and all?

As I drove toward Terrebonne, the closest town to Smith Rock State Park, I glimpsed the tan-red tips of several rock spires rising tantalizingly above the horse and cow pastures stretching across the plain. Illuminated by the fiery rays of the late afternoon sun, these hulking walls, buttresses, and pinnacles of gnarled rock thrust upward from the bowels of the earth like flames that flickered higher and higher as I drew nearer.

Despite its desolate beauty, Smith Rock did not seem at first sight to be much of a climbing area. There was plenty of rock, sure—big walls of yellow-and-orange-colored welded tuff several hundred feet high, some of it more or less solid looking, the rest appearing to be frighteningly loose, as if you could pull off great heaps of it with your bare hands. Looking out at the desert rockscape from the overlook, it seemed more like a setting for a western film than a rock climbing area. The Crooked River meandered slowly through the serpentine canyon. Turkey vultures circled lazily overhead against a darkening blue sky flecked with downy white clouds. A falcon's call echoed out across the cliffs.

I hiked down the rocky trail in the diminishing daylight, across a narrow footbridge, and along the Crooked River, one way and then the other, marveling at the steep rock towering everywhere overhead, trying to make out climbing routes. Some of the cracks and corners had evidence of climbing: tattered, faded rappel slings swaying slightly in the breeze, an old bolt here, a fixed pin there, but nothing else. It seemed to be just an ordinary, obscure climbing area in the middle of nowhere, with some crumbly old volcanic rocks that might dissolve in a heavy downpour—the kind of rock that typified everything I had heard about climbing in Oregon.

Bouldering along the base of the walls did nothing to dispel this notion, each flake and nubbin a time bomb ready to explode under body weight. There was no way I was going to climb very high off the ground without a belay. I was completely alone, and it was starting to get dark. If I fell off and hurt myself, it might be days before anybody wandered by. By then, probably weeks later, they would find only a carcass picked clean by the coyotes no doubt lurking nearby.

I hiked back to the rim and stopped at a little store just up from the park to ask where it might be okay to sack out for the night. Juniper Junction was like a miniature version of a tavern or general store from an old western film, with weathered brown siding and a wagon wheel and horseshoes tacked onto the fascia, a bench off to one side, and a sign out front advertising huckleberry ice cream. The proprietor, who later introduced himself as Colin, was a tall, gaunt fellow with long, stringy hair and a scarlet scarf around his neck. He hurried in from the patio behind the store, eager to offer assistance to what could very well have been his only customer of the day.

"Would you like some ice cream?" he asked. "It's very good." I had some and it was very good. "What brings you here?" he asked.

"Climbing," I said.

"Oh, I just love climbers," he said. "There are not very many of them this time of year. But then, there aren't many of them any other time of year either. A few regulars," he lamented, "that's all."

As Colin shared the history of his store, revealing that it had been part of a set for a John Wayne film, I looked out a window at the grassy fields and juniper and pine rolling away toward those jagged rocks, now lit up even more brightly by the setting sun.

"You can camp wherever," Colin told me. "Just throw your sleeping bag out on the grass. There are park rangers, but they won't bother you. You'll be the only one here, I'm sure."

A TRIO OF MAGPIES FIGHTING over food scraps they'd dragged out of a garbage can in front of the toilets gave me a rude awakening. I got up, ate, and washed up in the men's room, then wondered what I might do for the rest of the day. I doubted I would go back into the park; there just wasn't any good climbing there, at least not for a lone climber, and maybe not even for a roped climber. Maybe I would go for a hike around the park, or drive up to the mountains, or just head home.

As I sat in my car deliberating, a white Toyota pickup truck pulled up next to me. A rugged-looking guy with a red bandanna tied around his head of curly hair got out and strode toward me.

"Are you a climber?" he demanded.

"Yes."

"Do you want to go climbing?"

"Sure."

Mike Barbitta had come down to Bend on business the day before and was about to head home to Portland, but he had stopped at the park to see if there was anyone climbing. He was enthused to find me there, so enthused in fact that he dragged me along on an all-day tour of the area, taking me from formation to formation and route to route, rattling off names and ratings and important details such as who had climbed them, which routes to avoid, and which routes had been climbed once and never again—of which there were many. He showed me Picnic Lunch Wall, 600 feet high with only obscure aid routes; Red Wall with its long, moderate crack lines; Monkey Face, 400 feet high like a simian head stuck obscenely on a stake; Christian Brothers with its overhanging, bulbous walls on all sides; the crisp, angular Dihedrals; the sweeping curve of Morning Glory Wall; the crumbling death routes on Shiprock. Mike had a rope, rack, and an extra harness, and we climbed routes as we hiked along—*Pop Goes the Nubbin, Spiderman, Dancer, Child's Play, Hesitation Blues.* These consisted primarily of brittle cracks and flakes and faces with pebbles that threatened to pop out at the slightest tug. With the exception of Red Wall, which had an iron-hard patina in places that made it feel somewhat more solid than the surrounding tuff, the rock seemed little more than sunbaked mud, just solid enough to climb on but not so solid that you didn't expect to pull off a handful of the stuff or have an old bolt or chock placement rip out if you fell.

"This is the core of an old volcano," Mike explained. "The rest has eroded away."

"It doesn't seem like it's going to take very long for the rest of this to erode away, either," I said. As if to emphasize my point, a clatter of spontaneous rockfall echoed across the canyon.

"There's some good rock here," Mike assured me, "but a lot of bad rock, too. Once you get used to it, it's okay. There are a couple of pretty good routes here. Solid rock, good protection." He nodded as he spoke, as if trying to convince himself that what he had just told me was true.

Mike and I put in a satisfying day on the rocks, climbing a dozen routes in all. As we were hiking out past the Dihedrals formation, Mike pointed out some more routes. There was one that stood out, a steep, angular, golden dihedral with a perfectly flat, vertical wall on one side and an inset thin crack that had traces of chalk all the way up to slings a rope length above the ground. "That's *Sunshine Dihedral*," Mike said. "It's 5.12. It used to be the hardest route in the area."

"What's the hardest route now?"

"It's just over here," he said, striding ahead. We walked around a corner and he pointed up at a steep, square buttress pockmarked with holes and little pebbles and edges. "There it is."

I had walked right under this buttress the day before and hadn't noticed the bolts. I had to squint to see that it was a route; there was no crack, no chalk, only a line of innocuous, well-spaced bolts leading up the broad, flat buttress face, difficult to make out in the afternoon shade. "It's 5.12-plus they say, probably the hardest route in Oregon."

Mike told me the history of the route, which I didn't hear because I was still squinting up at it, trying to see the bolts and figure out where one might hang on. It had just been climbed, he said, by a local guy I had never heard of, Alan something.

"It's a controversial route," Mike continued. "It was put up with bolts drilled on rappel, and he cleaned off some loose holds. Some of the old guard are upset about this. They don't want to see a bunch of new routes being put in every ten feet. They like this place the way it is." Mike shrugged, apparently not bothered about it.

"There's room for both kinds of routes here, I think," Mike went on, making a sweeping gesture with his hand as if to demonstrate just how much rock there was still unclimbed, as if this one little route wasn't going to change Smith Rock one bit. Considering the quality of the rock, most of which seemed absolute crap, I could not disagree.

10 NEVER SAY NEVER

Seattle winters are bleak—days and weeks on end with nothing but gray, cold skies spitting incessant rain. There was no such thing as a climbing gym in 1982, at least not in the United States, so there was no possibility of climbing anything unless you were a complete masochist and enjoyed aid climbing in your raingear at the Index Town Walls, the area closest to Seattle. Otherwise, you had to hole up in your basement and do pull-ups, lift weights in a gym, or train on whatever other indoor apparatus you might contrive to maintain some semblance of conditioning.

Thankfully, many local climbers kept up an annual slide show ritual to stave off the winter doldrums. Ostensibly, these slide shows were an opportunity to share photos of our climbing exploits from the previous season, so we could stay psyched about climbing even though it was raining sea otters and geoducks outside and wouldn't let up until March. But in reality, slide shows were a thinly disguised excuse to get together, drink beer, and slander anyone who was unfortunate enough not to be in attendance.

That winter, Dan Lepeska's slide show was the highlight of the season. Unlike the rest of us, Dan had actually gone somewhere that year: he'd traveled to England as part of an international exchange meet. One of the more active Washington rock climbers at the time, Dan had done 5.12 free climbs and big walls in Yosemite—excellent résumé material for his application to the exchange team. He flew off to England in September 1982 to join the group, which included Americans Alex Lowe, Randy Vogel, and Maria Cranor. Such British notables as Jerry Moffatt and Jonny Woodward were among their hosts.

Dan returned with tales of rainy weather, pub games, warm pints, the horrific effects of a constant diet of fish-and-chips, and the climbing exploits of the amazing Brits. His slide show recounted the whole adventure, including a sequence of Woodward making the third ascent of *Strawberries*, the current British testpiece, a route that looked to be insanely overhanging, barely protected, and spectacularly difficult. Dan told us it was rated E7 6b.

"Like 5.12-plus," Dan explained, "with thirty-foot runouts above RPs."

Rough translation: impossible for any of us to climb, and if you somehow could climb it, you'd be shitting your pants the whole way up. The photos, paired with Dan's animated description, had us on the edge of our seats. Thin cracks and face moves up an angular gray wall of overhanging rock. Woodward leading out from RPs, painful, thin jams, thin crack fading, unprotected face moves, ten, twenty, thirty feet out from the last protection. Woodward pumping out, unable to do the last moves, whining like a dog, knowing he was about to pitch. Woodward taking a big whipper, forty feet of airtime at least. Woodward coming straight back after a rest and finishing it off, running it out the whole way to the top, fighting a pump of biblical proportions.

In 1980, Ron Fawcett was the reigning "best rock climber in Britain" (Pete Livesey notwithstanding). He made the first ascent of *Strawberries* that year, preplacing protection on rappel and reclipping his ropes each day to the previous day's high point—"dodgy" tactics at best. But Fawcett had a batch of hot youngsters nipping at his heels, including Jerry Moffatt; he had to do something!

Moffatt snatched away Fawcett's title only two years later; he repeated *Strawberries* in yo-yo style over two days, placing protection on lead but leaving it and the rope in place at each successive high point. Woodward's ascent—the third free ascent overall—was considered to be done in better style than that employed by Fawcett or Moffatt, because he lowered off and pulled his ropes down after each fall. Dan supposed out loud that if Woodward had adopted Fawcett's tactic of preplacing protection on rappel, he would have flashed *Strawberries*.

Moffatt and Woodward were the epitome of the young, brash English rock climbers of the early 1980s, following the long-standing British tradition of making bold, difficult, and dangerous climbs. Clearly influenced by their balls-out approach to climbing (especially Woodward's), Lepeska returned stoked to climb something hard and unprotected. He homed in on a blank, overhanging face on the north side of Jell-O Tower at Castle Rock in Leavenworth, Washington. Most climbers would have seen such a line and thought it needed a few bolts. Not Dan, who was now suffering from that particularly

British delusion: that climbing ground-up with marginal protection was the only sporting way. He led it, running it out between dubious RP placements and a Friend only half-stuck behind a wafer flake, knowing that if his gear failed, he'd probably hit the deck. Dan fell several times, the gear held, and eventually he pulled it off in 1983. *No Such Thing as a Free Lunge* wasn't the hardest route around, "only" 5.11+, but it was certainly the scariest ground-up lead of that difficulty that anyone knew of in the area. The toprope tigers had their way with it, but it was a long time before the route saw its second ground-up lead ascent.

Lepeska also had designs on an overhanging crack on Givler's Dome in nearby Icicle Creek Canyon. Although only forty feet long, the irregular crack split a severely overhanging, angular wall. It was technically challenging from the start, sure to be a real testpiece. A few of the Leavenworth locals had tried it, and even Peter Croft had given it a go, or so we had heard. All contenders had so far failed to get more than a few moves off the ground. It reminded Dan of *Strawberries* in that it was similarly overhanging, but to him it seemed more difficult. He predicted it would be the hardest free climb in Washington one day, perhaps the state's first 5.13. It was clearly too hard to do in good style, though, as Dan would have insisted. It was a route to be done by someone else—someone more foolish or more ambitious, or some combination of the two. The route had Todd Skinner written all over it.

TODD AND I CORRESPONDED REGULARLY after our meeting in Joshua Tree in the spring of 1983. He sent postcards and letters written on the back of whatever piece of paper he had at his disposal, such as a flyer for his "Second Stone from the Sun" slide show tour, a "multi-projector presentation on the wild and varied rock climbing areas of America, Europe, and North Africa," featuring a grainy photocopied image of two climbers simultaneously rappelling off opposite sides of one of the Needles in South Dakota. I guessed that Todd had taken to giving slide shows for money to fund his climbing trips, as Mark Hudon and Max Jones had done before him. The flyer included an endorsement from Beth Wald, who was billed as a member of an American expedition to Dhaulagiri; she gushed that Todd's slide show "presents the brilliant beauty and intensity of our sport and shows it being played on the frontiers of the world and the mind." I was pretty sure Todd had written that.

Todd wrote to me regularly from Laramie, Boulder, Moab, and Yosemite. He kept me updated on the new climbs he had done or planned to do, the various foreign and domestic hardmen he had seen or met along the road, where he would be the following spring, where I should meet him, what routes I should be training for, and where I should mail a box of Pop-Tarts, which he needed immediately to save his life from some imminent imagined peril. One of the routes he brought up was the overhanging crack on Givler's Dome, which I'd told him about in Joshua Tree that spring.

"I've heard tell of that crack," Todd had said when I first mentioned it to him. He feigned only slight interest, but added, "Tell me more."

So I did: It was an oft-tried testpiece, a severely overhanging finger-to-fist crack as steep as the underside of a staircase, pinkie-thin in places, wider than a girl's fist in others, as coarse as gravel, tough as nails, sharp as broken glass. Todd wasn't sure it was worthy. He was on a quest to climb the hardest cracks in America, so only the hardest cracks would do.

"I don't know," Todd said doubtfully, shaking his head. "It may not be hard enough to drive all the way up to the northern swamps."

"It will be the hardest route in Washington," I assured him. "Washington's first 5.13."

"Hmm," he said, pinching his chin harder, "I don't know."

"Peter Croft tried it and couldn't do it," I told him.

"Peter Croft couldn't do it?" Todd asked, raising an eyebrow.

ASIDE FROM *SUPERCRACK*, A 5.12C route on Midnight Rock outside Leavenworth that local hardman Pat Timson led in 1979 (not to be confused with *Supercrack* in the Gunks or *Supercrack of the Desert* at Indian Creek, Utah), there was only a smattering of 5.12 rock routes in Washington as of 1983. Peter Croft had established most of them. A climber from British Columbia who had a reputation for casually climbing routes that were harder than anybody else could do, Croft had done difficult climbs in the Bugaboos and on the granite cliffs of Squamish, including the first free ascents of the *University Wall*, a 5.12 big wall, and *Zombie Roof*, a 5.12+ roof crack. He had also found fertile ground for hard, free leads on Washington's neglected cliffs and crags. For years I never saw Croft climbing in Washington, but season after season I heard reports of his exploits—that he'd freed *Iron Horse* at Index or had done a new 5.12 at Castle Rock. Croft seemed superhuman. If it was true that he had tried and failed to climb that crack on Givler's Dome, it had to be pretty damn hard.

Still, Todd seemed doubtful that the route would be hard enough to be worthy of his attention. In his letters, he referred to it as one of the "last great projects" in Washington and continually urged me to get on it. That was a joke. As if I could ever climb it free. What Todd really wanted was not for me to climb it but to clean it, work on it, then report back to him with information about the route. He wanted to know it was at least possible, so he wouldn't be wasting his time if he decided to drive 700 miles up to Washington to climb it. It would take some persuading, but I knew that once you got Todd hooked on a route, he was determined and crazy enough to eventually do it. He didn't know when to give up. So I lied to him. I promised him, without a doubt, the route would go—and would be 5.13.

I WAS DRIVING UP ICICLE CANYON on the east side of the Cascade Range one day that summer, climbing my way from crag to crag per my usual weekend routine, when I saw a familiar white VW bus parked below Givler's Dome. The Wyoming plates gave it away. I rushed up the trail with my partner, Doug Weaver, and found Todd and his current sidekick, Robin Jones— Todd called him "Royal"—lounging on a boulder in the sun at the base of the crack.

"By God, Smoot," Todd said, grinning, extending his white-chalked hand, "what took you so long?"

"Nice of you to tell me you were coming," I said, shaking Todd's hand firmly as he patted me on the shoulder with his other hand, leaving a big white handprint and a cloud of chalk dust.

"I didn't want you to beat me to it," he said. "I'm not sure I can trust you to keep a secret."

Before I could interject, Todd continued, "Well, this crack is something. It is steeper than I imagined it would be. We've been here two days already and have only managed to get halfway up. But, you were right. It will go."

As Todd explained, on the first day he had aided the crack, scrubbed off some lichen, dirt, and loose rock that might hinder his free-climbing efforts, marked all of the best jams and footholds with chalk, and sorted out a rack for a free lead. On the second day, he had set up a toprope to start working out the moves, and on his first try had fallen off low on the route and swung wildly away from the rock, nearly knocking Robin off his boulder seat and then crashing into the opposite slab. To prevent a recurrence of that sort of pratfall, Todd had rigged a back rope to eliminate the nasty backswing, but this had made it much more difficult for Robin to belay, as he now had to take in the toprope and let out the back rope simultaneously as Todd worked through the continuously difficult, overhanging jams. Having made little progress, Todd was delighted that reinforcements had arrived. Now, the back rope was manageable. With three belay slaves—one to handle the toprope, another to manage the back rope, and a third to provide "beta" (helpful information about the route)—Todd could climb without having to worry about braining himself on the back wall every time he came off.

The back rope proved only marginally helpful, though. The crack overhung so steeply that, even with a back rope, Todd would swing far enough away from the rock after each fall that he could not pull himself back onto the route. After each attempt, he had to lower to the ground and begin anew. There wouldn't be any hangdogging. Gravity had won the day.

"CAN YOU BELIEVE THAT JERRY MOFFATT?" Todd asked, resting on a boulder in the shade of a big pine tree between attempts, shaking his head dolefully. Moffatt's article "What We Did on Our Holidays" had just been published in *Mountain*, describing how Moffatt had jetted over to America in late 1982 after a drinking binge and had his way with every testpiece across the country. He made a casual flash of *Supercrack* in the Gunks (5.12c), which he climbed because he "got bored"; he bagged the second free ascents of *Psycho Roof* (5.12c) and *Genesis* (5.12c) in Eldorado Canyon, both with minimal tries; and he flashed *Equinox* (5.12c) in Joshua Tree.

These were some of the hardest free climbs in America at the time, and Moffatt had made them seem trivial. Even worse, he was being a complete twit about it, not so subtly bragging that he and his climbing partner, Chris Gore, were so vastly superior to American climbers it was shameful. One positive side effect of his insulting swagger was that it inspired climbers across the country to diet and train like madmen so they could climb those routes, too, to prove Moffatt wrong and win their reputations back from those nasty Brits.

"Moffatt's a good climber," I conceded. "It's amazing that he flashed *Equinox*. Imagine walking up to this climb," I said, gesturing toward the crack *du jour*, "and flashing it."

"This is harder than *Equinox*," Todd said flatly. "No one will ever flash this route, by God. No one human, at least."

"So it's going to be 5.13 then?" I asked.

"We'll see," Todd said.

I must confess that after spending a day watching Todd working the crack on toprope, I was less than thrilled at the prospect of spending another day sitting around belaying. Robin was not excited either; this would be his fourth day of hiking up that dirty, sweaty, steep-ass hill to Givler's Dome to do nothing but sit there holding a rope so Todd might figure out how to climb another three-foot sequence. Such was the life of a belay slave, especially one in the thrall of Todd Skinner.

Despite our misgivings, we drove back up Icicle Road the next day, parked behind Todd's van, and trudged back up to Givler's Dome to try to be of service. Having lured him up here, I felt I owed him at least one more day of belaying and encouragement. But by late morning, Doug and I, like Robin, were over it. Fortunately, we were free to leave. Robin was stuck. We promised to return later in the day to see how things were progressing, and we did, but Todd's van was nowhere to be seen. We checked the campgrounds and even drove through Leavenworth, but he was long gone.

It turned out Todd had given up and was on his way back to Wyoming. Not that he had wanted to quit. Robin, it seems, had become "a bit" disgruntled with his role on the "team." Todd had worked on the crack all that morning and into the early afternoon, until the sun had turned the wall into an oven, forcing them to hike down for lunch, water, and a rest. When they drove back up the canyon later in the afternoon to give it one more go in the evening shade, Robin had mutinied, refusing to hike back up to the route that day, or any other day. He was done.

It was not a fun drive back to Wyoming, Todd later confessed, but even he admitted to misgivings about returning to the project. "That accursed crack," Todd wrote to me shortly after. "I don't know why I even bothered. It's not hard enough, and it's painful. My scars will never heal. As God is my witness," he proclaimed, "my hands will never go back in that crack again."

That was not the last time I would hear Todd make such a vow.

TODD WAS BACK IN SEPTEMBER for another go at it. I drove out to meet him and behold the spectacle. He was stronger and more focused this time. He'd been training just for this route. He dispensed with the toprope and went straight to leading, which was, at first, not a pretty thing. As before, because of the angle of the overhang, falling off would leave him dangling away from the rock, too far out to pull himself back in. Efforts to yo-yo failed because the ropes would either get stuck in the crack or block key jams, and falling off down low meant a long, dangerous backswing. You just couldn't hangdog on this route. Todd was forced to lower off and pull his ropes after each fall; consequently, it took much longer to climb than it might have otherwise. Despite this setback, Todd persisted, and in just over a week of effort he had almost finished the climb. He narrowly missed it on an attempt late one day, long after the sun had set; it was too dark for another go.

The next morning, we hiked back up the trail and Todd climbed the crack on his first try. He made it look easy, moving almost sloth-like up the sequential jams, belying the fact that it had taken him thirteen days of effort to be able to piece the moves together. It was all very anticlimactic.

"Well," I said afterward. "That's got to be 5.13."

"I don't know," Todd said. "I'd have to call it 5.12d. I just don't think it's hard enough to call it 5.13."

Todd was sandbagging, of course. The route, which he named *Never-Never*, went unrepeated for twenty-three years. It still has not been flashed. Not even close.

11 LOVE THE PAIN!

By the beginning of 1985, I was taking some time off from college, working at one of Seattle's top four law firms, and living alone in a cheap apartment a block off Stone Way in the Wallingford neighborhood. I paid $200 a month for the shithole, and it was perfect. At twenty-two, I was making more money than I had ever made before. I saved scrupulously, a thousand bucks a month, knowing that as soon as the opportunity arose I would quit my job and hit the road to go climbing for as long as the money held out. I was young and adventure beckoned. What did I need a job for when I had enough money to go climbing? I could always get a job and make more money later.

I suppose I appeared to be an upwardly mobile young man aspiring toward white-collar stability. I seemed to be fooling most of the lawyers and staff into believing I was buying into their law career bullshit. Little did they know I was always a heartbeat away from not showing up for work one Monday morning because I was a thousand miles away on some windswept granite wall or desert spire. I was a climbing bum at heart, one who worked only enough to support his habit.

I had a vague plan that I would go climbing for two or three weeks in the spring, to use up my vacation and sick time, then embark on a long road trip once I'd saved a little more money. Then a letter arrived on the first Saturday in February, postmarked a few days before from Tucson, Arizona. The 20¢ stamp featured a stylized LO♥E repeated five times. Handwritten in light blue ink after each LO♥E was "the pain!" I flipped the envelope over to find more writing: "If we fail, we fail while daring greatly . . . if it is not worth dying for, it is worth risking dying for." It was, without a doubt, a letter from Todd Skinner. I tore it open eagerly.

Hey Pilgrim!

Glad to finally get some news out of the western swamp. Thanks for the slides and the guide book. It looks like a brilliant effort. How is it being taken in Seattle? I'm sure you'll get some guff as well as praise but to hell with the critics! Glad to hear poor Dick took some swings on "Never, Never". How did the photos turn out that day we were all there? All of the shots I took were ruined when I accidentally exposed the entire roll! I will return to Washington to do "City Park" ("One Step Beyond") and maybe the huge roof by the houses down Icicle Creek with you whenever you decide to begin the "great projects"! Allow me to sway you with this plan of a trip down the road of fame, glory and the pursuit of the American dollar: I have just taken a few steps toward the goal at the end of that road and will extend to you now an invitation to come along on the tour of the season. I just bought $975 worth of slide show gear (projectors, dissolve, etc.) to use for promo and $$ on the road. Here is the schedule: Nov 20–Jan 31, Tucson (hard training, bouldering, climbing), superb weather for these months; Feb, Hueco, Texas (best bouldering and strength climbing in America, many supreme new routes, great weather, final razor hone); March 1–April 31, J.T. (cracks, soloing and miles for smoothness and mind honing); May 1–June 30, Valley, Oregon and Washington rads (also "Grand Illusion"!!); July 1–Aug 30, Devil's Tower, Colorado (many specific goals); Sept–Oct, Gunks (long delayed tour). I think that you are going to dissolve if you have to spend another winter in Washington and so why don't you join me on all or at least part of the tour? No money? Absurd! No time? This is the only time of our lives when we dare spend all *of our time. I'm going to do an "On the Road" slide show now for money and expenses and then a "Stay Hungry" show with all of America's 5.13s and many, many 5.12s that should sell here and in Europe and Japan. What I'm trying to say is I need a partner for this rash tour and I want to know if you can leave your wife, children, dog, home, lawn and job for this short period on a quest for glory? It's so hard to find a damn partner for anything over 5.11 but I've done all of the new routes this year without anyone to follow. The summer at the Tower was* really *successful. . . . There are at least 25 more 200 to 600 foot routes to be done there. At the end of that camp I pulled the tipi and had the choice to either do "Circus, Circus" or the "Sphinx Crack". I chose the latter and failed in a four day effort, and*

then started as an elk guide on the fifth of September. I'm on my way to Tucson in 2 weeks and hope to hear from you before then on your plans. Keep dreamin', stay hungry and remember that there is no finish line!
    T.S.

I WROTE BACK TO TODD to tell him I would meet him in Joshua Tree in March. I gave my notice at work and to my landlord. I broke the news to my girlfriend. I told my mom goodbye. I had over $5,000 saved, enough to last through the summer. If Todd's "Stay Hungry" show sold well, or I figured out how to make a few more dollars along the way, I could stay on the road all summer and fall.

Despite his enthusiasm, I really had no idea why Todd wanted me to come on the road with him. I wasn't a bad climber; I was solid on 5.11 and had managed a couple of 5.12s, but he was clearly better than I was, or at least more ambitious. If I was going to climb 5.12s and 5.13s all over the country with Todd on this "rash tour," I would have to get busy. Todd was at Hueco Tanks that winter, working on his razor hone, whereas I had spent much of the winter hunched over a typewriter at my desk job.

Fearing I wouldn't measure up, I spent the next month training harder than I ever had before. I doubled my workouts at the practice rock, working the most difficult crack and face problems and climbing as many laps as possible during each visit. I started cycling to the practice rock in the morning to tick off a thousand feet of crack climbing before work. I did sets of pull-ups off my doorjamb when I walked out each morning and returned each evening, off the bus stop shelter while I waited for the bus, off the stairs behind my office building. Instead of riding the elevator, I contrived a way to climb the staircase railings to the law office, thirty-nine floors up without touching the stairs. If Todd needed a partner to climb the "great projects," I was going to try my hardest to be that partner.

12 HOLD ON AND ENJOY THE RIDE

Dave Sorric and Chris Gentry were two of a kind. After meeting in Joshua Tree on our first trip there, they went to Yosemite that fall and climbed Washington Column and the *Salathé Wall* together. Chris called Dave the "Cretin from Sparta," a name I am sure Dave approved of, if he had in fact not made it up for himself.

In December 1983, I had been the one to call Dave to give him the news that Chris had died in an ice climbing accident. We had hardly spoken before or since, but when I decided I would head down to California to meet up with Todd Skinner in March 1985, I wrote to Dave to let him know I would be taking the train from Seattle and then catching a bus out to Joshua Tree. I invited him to join us for a week or two so we could catch up. He did me one better: he offered me a ride.

We lit out for Joshua Tree at an ungodly hour one morning in Dave's piece-of-crap Mercury. The seats were threadbare, with steel springs sticking up through duct tape; the gas, brake, and clutch pedals showed bare metal; and the muffler was rusted out. But it was mechanically sound, and Dave drove it like a race car eastward from Santa Paula up to Santa Clarita, and out across Antelope Pass into the high desert, taking turns too fast in the dark and scaring me to death. Dave did everything full-on, even driving. The key to hanging out with him was to hold on and enjoy the ride.

We made record time, Dave doing ninety almost the whole way. It was still midmorning when we hit Yucca Valley. We stopped at Vons to get food, filled up our water jugs at a gas station, and then continued down the highway, turning right at the Joshua Tree Tavern and following Quail Springs Road into JT. It was still just a national monument, so there was no formal entry station, no ranger to collect a fee, just a metal gate that was wide open. Dave blew through the gate at a respectful fifty-five miles per hour and kept that speed all the way to Hidden Valley. As we passed the familiar rock formations, I rolled down the window and let the cool, dry air blow back my hair. Joshua Tree again, at last.

We arrived at Intersection Rock, pulled into Hidden Valley Campground, and circled the loop looking for Todd's van. We found it at the farthest point of the loop. You could not miss that white VW van with the Wyoming plates. Todd had snagged a choice campsite nestled among a scattering of big boulders and juniper trees below the steep back wall of The Blob, probably the best campsite in the loop considering the bouldering opportunities and shade. There was a pull-up bar lashed between two of the trees, and a Bachar ladder hung from a third. No one was there, but someone had stuck a note under a wiper blade on the windshield of Todd's van.

"Smoot, we are at Echo Cove getting in some mileage. Get out here quick! T.S."

"WELL, BY GOD! YOU MADE IT," Todd said, grinning. "Give me some slack, will ya, Bill?" The belayer let out some slack, and Todd sauntered over to give me a hearty handshake and pat on the back that left a cloud of chalk and a big white palm print, his usual greeting. "It's great to see you, Pilgrim. How the hell are you? Who's your friend here?" Todd didn't wait for an answer. He smiled and stuck out a friendly paw to Dave. "Howdy. I'm Todd Skinner."

After putting Dave through the Skinner Inquisition, Todd made introductions. "This is Bill Hatcher, and this is Beth Wald. They are both brilliant climbers and photographers. Bill spent the winter climbing with me at Hueco Tanks and is along for the whole tour. Beth was with us at Devils Tower last fall and just met up with us at Hueco."

I hadn't heard of Bill Hatcher before. He was a rugged-looking guy, maybe about my age or a couple of years older, with sandy hair and the grizzled look of a climber who had been on the road for a while. I'd heard of Beth Wald, though, if only barely. She had slack pigtails, sparkling blue eyes, and perfect white teeth. She was wearing a clean long-sleeved blue shirt, a matching star-spangled bandanna on her head, and a color-coordinated chalk bag and rock shoes—a slightly hippie-looking climbing chick with a sense of fashion, such as it was.

Introductions out of the way, Todd climbed a dozen consecutive laps on *Big Mo*, moving slowly and methodically up and down the 5.11 pitch, chalking up in the middle of crux moves, sometimes closing his eyes, milking the route for every bit of training potential. Nothing about Todd had changed in the past two years, except his entourage, which was really not all that different.

"This is a brilliant route," Todd enthused. "It is perfect for laps. I could climb it all day."

"Me, too," I said, and I meant it.

Dave did an obligatory ascent and lowered off and was done with it. He didn't want to climb laps. He wanted to climb *routes*. He thought toproping the same route all afternoon was a waste of time and wasn't afraid to say so.

"Why would you spend all day climbing one route?" he wondered out loud as we left Todd, Bill, and Beth to their session. "There are so many routes to climb."

"For mileage," I told him. "For the razor hone."

"Razor hone, my ass," Dave said. "Let's go climb something."

DAVE AND I CLIMBED LIKE MANIACS the whole week he was there. Each morning we got up before Todd and Beth and Bill, who slept on soft mattress pads in Todd's van or, in Bill's case, the back of his station wagon, insulated from the sounds of other campers stirring, lighting stoves, slamming toilet doors. Dave and I led a more spartan existence. We slept in Dave's tent on gravel with no pads. We were unwashed and filthy. A chilly wind rattled the tent each night, and climbers crunched by on the gravel road in the morning, waking us far too early. No matter. We were off climbing before the others had even stirred.

We climbed whatever we came across, regardless of the number of stars in the guidebook. We didn't care if it was 5.6 or 5.11; if it was a decent line and nobody was on it we roped up and climbed it and then climbed the next good line. We consulted Dave's guidebook every so often, but for the most part we just picked lines based on where we were and how they looked. And in such a fashion we visited nearly every area in Joshua Tree and climbed a tremendous number of routes in a very short time. This was the way to climb.

At the end of each day when we rolled back into camp, Todd would stop whatever he was doing to welcome us. "Well, boys, what'd you climb today?" he would ask, and we would list the routes we had done. Todd would listen intently and nod approvingly when we mentioned a route he had heard of or wanted to climb. Invariably he would ask, "Did you see any hard-looking cracks? Any new desperate problems?" He was ever on the lookout for an unclimbed gem, hoping we would spot a sixty-foot overhanging fingertip crack in a shaded corridor on the back side of a dome that John Bachar, Mike Lechlinski, and all of the other Desert Rats over the past three decades had somehow missed.

One day when we returned to camp, we found Todd hanging in a rectangular wooden frame constructed of two-by-fours with little pieces of wood screwed on. "I call it the Skinner Box," Todd said as he showed it off proudly. "The idea is, you hang on these holds and see how long you can go before you just can't hold on any longer. It's like climbing a super thin roof." To demonstrate, Todd crawled inside, flipped onto his back, then reached up and grabbed the little holds with his fingers. "Some of these are crimpers," he explained, latching his fingertips onto one of the holds that was long and thin, "and some are pinches." He pinched a hold between his thumb and fingers. "Others are like finger pockets," he continued, wedging two fingertips into a curved hold. "So," he went on, "you grab these holds and then pull yourself up and hang off of them as long as possible." He pulled himself up on two thin edges, his heels hooked over a board at the other end of the box, and hung there, his body suspended several inches off the sand. "The thinner the holds, the harder it is to hang on. It's brilliant for honing finger strength." After a minute, Todd lowered himself to the ground. "Or, you can move from hold to hold." He pulled himself back up, and then every thirty seconds or so he would move one hand to a different hold, then the other, and so on. "Here, you try."

I wriggled into the box and pulled up on the biggest holds. "You can do pull-ups, too," Todd mentioned. "Or hang on with one hand." I did a couple of pull-ups off the holds, and then did a sequence of hand switches like Todd had demonstrated. Some of the holds were rounded, others were sharp edged and painful to hold onto. When I tried to move to the finger pocket holds, I couldn't keep myself on. "Ow! That's brutal." I crawled out of the box shaking my fingers. "It is a torture device. I don't like it."

Dave got in and gave it a try. "My fingers hurt," he said afterward. "Fuck that."

"I try to spend thirty minutes or so in the box every day," Todd said, and he maintained the routine religiously, like his laps on *Big Mo*, throughout our time in Joshua Tree. Dave and I religiously avoided it.

If Todd wasn't in the box, he would be pulling laps on his Bachar ladder or doing sets of pull-ups and one-arms on the bar he'd set up between two trees, always working on that razor hone. "If you can do thirty pull-ups in a row, you are strong enough to do a one-arm," Todd professed. Dave and I looked at each other quizzically.

"I can't do thirty pull-ups. Can you?"

"No. I can do about ten."

"Dave doesn't need to do pull-ups," I said. "He eats spinach."

"I have muscles in my shit," Dave added with a grin, flexing.

"Well, alright then," Todd said, feigning mild perplexity, then pumped out another set of one-arm pull-ups.

If Todd hadn't climbed anything hard enough to get a pump that day, he would strap on his weighted vest—a gray-green fisherman's vest with heavy sacks in the pockets—before doing his workout. The thing weighed a ton. Todd made me try it on once before doing a set of pull-ups, and I couldn't do half as many as I should have been able to do. My shoulders and back were sore for two days afterward. Todd would strap the weight vest on and do a set of reps in the Skinner Box, then a set on the Bachar ladder, then a ladder workout on the pull-up bar until his freckled arms were bulging. He would flex and grin at his big biceps.

"We're making progress, boys," he would say with childlike enthusiasm. "We're making progress."

I had thought my winter workouts had been serious, but Todd was a workout maniac. "If I'm going to do the climbs of the future," he would say, with a completely straight face, "I have to be stronger than I ever imagined I could be."

DAVE LEFT JOSHUA TREE LATE on Sunday afternoon. With Dave gone, I joined the entourage full-time, going off with Todd and the gang each day. This was a completely different experience. Rather than go out and visit different areas of the monument and climb whatever looked good, Todd had an agenda: pick one of the hardest routes at Joshua Tree, especially any route that was the subject of current media attention, and work on it all day, every day, until he succeeded, or at least got some good photos for his slide show. Even if the route was too hard, Todd got on it; if it showed any promise, he kept trying. All day. Or at least until the sun hit the route and made it too hot to climb, in which case he'd take a break and come back later to work on it some more in the shade.

Climbing had become something of an industry for Todd. He was CEO and Chief Promoter of Todd Skinner Enterprises, and I quickly discovered I wasn't along on the tour as an equal partner. I was a peon—one of Todd's marketing assistants, staff writers, and photographers brought along to document Todd's quest on film and in the magazines more than to actually climb hard routes with him. As Todd had written in his letter to me back in February, his plan was to get on the hardest routes in America and try to climb them, but most of all to photograph them for his slide show that would make enough money to keep him and his traveling circus on the road indefinitely.

"We must be very careful to cultivate the correct image," he had written in another letter. "Imagery will be more important than reality in the new high-fashion climbing game." If Todd happened to get up a hard route and one of us took a decent photo, we could write it up for one of the magazines for publicity, which would help fuel interest in the slide show, make more money, and extend the tour. Even if Todd didn't actually climb the route, as long as we had a decent picture, that would do just as well. In fact, it might be a little easier.

"COME WITH ME IF YOU want to live," Todd said one morning in a deep, German-accented voice.

"Huh?" I asked.

"We're going out to try *Acid Crack*," he said, grinning. "You're coming, right?"

Acid Crack was one of Bachar's new routes, a "5.12+" overhanging thin crack freshly reported in the magazines. Of course Todd had to get on it, for pictures if nothing else, so off we went, Todd in the lead, me, Bill, and Beth following behind. The three of them spent most of the approach hike repeating the best lines from *The Terminator*. They'd seen the film over the winter and quoted it incessantly.

"Give me your clothes," Todd said.

"Fuck you, asshole," Beth answered.

Whenever the subject of John Bachar chopping bolts came up, one of them would say, "That's what he does! That's *all* he does! You can't stop him! He can't be bargained with. He can't be reasoned with. He doesn't feel pity, or remorse, or fear. And he absolutely will not stop . . . ever, until you are dead!"

We hiked out past Howser Buttress, cracking ourselves up mimicking Arnold Schwarzenegger, telling stories, looking for *Acid Crack*. It took us a while to find it. From the write-up in *Climbing* magazine, I had expected a superb, stunning finger crack to rival *Equinox*. I didn't see anything like that; it all looked like a big talus pile.

"There it is," Todd said, squinting, pointing at the rubble. He started up the talus toward a low, flat wall. "That has to be it."

A left-angling crack split a slightly overhanging forty-foot-high wall. It was a difficult-looking route, but much less impressive than had been hyped in the magazine. Still, it was absolutely something Todd wanted to climb.

Todd went first, as always. He did a few moves, placed a micro-cam, did a few more moves, and placed another cam. "Take me," he said. He hung on the rope to rest, then jammed his fingers back in the crack and started climbing again. He did a move, stuck his fingers in the crack one way, then took again. After a brief rest, he tried the move again, sticking his fingers in the crack a different way. After several more tries, experimenting with one sequence then another, Todd was able to advance three feet up the crack, far enough to justify placing another cam. He hung to rest again, tried the next moves, took a short, controlled fall, then asked to be lowered off.

With a toprope to Todd's highest piece, which was maybe halfway up the crack, Bill, Beth, and I took our obligatory turns trying the route while Todd rested, tearing sufficient skin off our fingers and hands to confirm the jams were thin, the edges sharp, the climbing strenuous. Todd watched us climb, hoping to glean some insight into how best to approach a particular sequence. Bill managed to get up to Todd's high point; Beth tried valiantly but struggled; and I gave it one half-assed effort before giving up, realizing quickly that this sort of climbing by committee was not for me.

Todd got back on the route and eventually managed to do all of the moves, albeit with a lot of hanging on the rope. "That was a good start," he said at the end of the day, while he arranged his rack. "It's hard but I should be able to do it next time. Maybe after a rest day."

We scrambled down the talus to the desert floor. "I'll be back!" Todd said as we hiked away, doing his best Schwarzenegger impression. It wasn't very good.

A REST DAY IN CAMP SKINNER consisted of sleeping in as late as you could amid all the campground noise and dust kicked up by the Winnebagos; eating a big, lazy breakfast that used up all of the remaining perishables; then waddling around the campground or the surrounding rocks to chat up all the other climbers, find out who they were, where they were from, what they had climbed yesterday or were going to climb today, and if they knew of any last great problems that might be worthy of Todd's attention. Then we would head into town to shower and fill up our water jugs at the RV park; stop at the post office to check general delivery, mail out postcards, and send rolls of Kodachrome to the lab in Palo Alto; restock on food, postcards, and film at Vons; and finally splurge on a meal at the cheapest restaurant in town before returning to camp.

This rest day, we met up with Jimmie Dunn at Arturo's, a Mexican cafe by the highway. Dunn was a Colorado climber with East Coast roots, well known enough that I recognized him from a photo in *Climbing* magazine. He had made a lot of first ascents, including the first 5.12 in New Hampshire and the first solo first ascent of El Capitan. We learned from Dunn that he had dropped out of climbing, made a bunch of money building a couple of restaurants, and was now bumming around the desert Southwest in a big Chevy cargo van, living off his earnings, returning to his roots in climbing but also just exploring. He joined us at the campfire later that night and regaled us with stories of his many first ascents of big walls and desert spires, and his recent explorations of previously undiscovered Anasazi ruins. He and Todd, having both climbed Spider Rock, spent half the time talking about their ascents. The other half was spent talking about "Spider Dan" Goodwin and the new Joshua Tree route he had just climbed, *Apollo*. If his 5.13a rating was accurate, Goodwin had established the hardest free climb at Joshua Tree. No one believed it: Goodwin claimed to have established a 5.14 route called *Maniac* in Rhode Island the previous summer that everybody had called bullshit on. (Alex Honnold later climbed it and rated it 5.13c.) From the talk around camp, *Apollo* was just as controversial.

Dan Goodwin was a talented rock climber, but he, like George Willig before him, was better known for climbing buildings. He had climbed the World Trade Center, Sears Tower, and Toronto's CN Tower—on TV, for publicity and for money, which hadn't much endeared him to the climbing community. His ascent of *Apollo* hadn't either, especially to the Joshua Tree locals. Goodwin had sieged the route over several days, and had placed a bolt and fixed pin on rappel to protect the difficult face moves linking the climb's two cracks. These tactics went against the local ethic, violating a staunch ground-up tradition that included bold runouts and desperate lead-placed bolts. Todd predicted the imminent demise of the route. "I have to get on it before they chop it," he said that night.

Abandoning his plans to go back to *Acid Crack*, Todd went out bright and early the next morning to give *Apollo* a try. He wasn't gone long. "Bachar chopped the bolt and pulled the pin last night," he said when he returned, shaking his head, a grim look on his face. "It can't be led without them. Not safely, at least."

It wasn't clear whether it was Bachar or another of the JT locals who had done the deed, but the result was the same: the bolt and pin were gone. *Apollo* was no longer the hardest free climb in Joshua Tree; it was just another 5.12+ toprope. Goodwin's route had been erased.

"Also," Todd added, "the locals have renamed it. Do you know what they are calling it now? Get this. They're calling it *A Pollo*."

13 YOU'RE ALL WANKERS

Kerwin Klein was back in Joshua Tree and giving us a tour of campground boulder problems one afternoon when a group of climbers doing a bouldering circuit swarmed into our camp. This group was more mature than the degenerates we were accustomed to—quieter, better dressed, the kind of climbers who might have driven out from Santa Monica on Friday night, stayed at the Joshua Tree Inn, and had dinner and drinks at Arturo's after each day's climbing. They quickly dispatched all the problems we had just struggled to climb, gliding up holds we had barely managed to hang on to, some wearing only running shoes, which only added to the insult. They even climbed the face of the huge boulder behind camp, a twenty-foot-high nearly blank line that looked to be at least 5.12. We had eyed that problem for weeks and had never dared try it. They scampered up it without any apparent hesitation.

Most of the group had finished their circuit and moved on, except two climbers who were bringing up the rear. They were both tall, brawny hulks, built more like NFL linebackers than climbers, with nearly identical heads of short, curly hair. Showing off their overdeveloped physiques in tank tops and too-short running shorts, they seemed too large, too muscle-bound, to have finessed their way up these problems.

"Who are those guys?" I asked Kerwin.

"That's Largo," Kerwin said, "and the other one's Gaines."

John Long, better known as "Largo," and his current sidekick, Bob Gaines, had invaded our campsite. Long, the quintessential Stonemaster, he of the first one-day ascent of the *Nose*, the first free ascent of *Astroman*, and author of some of the most outrageous climbing stories ever published, was as mythical a character as John Bachar or John Gill. He had probably climbed every route at Joshua Tree a hundred times, most of them solo and blindfolded with one hand tied behind his back, or so one might have believed from reading his stories. Long had a reputation as a spinner of fantastic yarns, prone to hyperbole. There was certainly a grain of truth in all of Long's stories, you could tell, but you could not be sure where the grain ended and the chaff began. Truth be damned, his stories were gripping and usually hilarious. As for Gaines, he was, I was told, also a former college football player turned climber, hence the linebacker build.

Todd subjected Largo to the Skinner Inquisition, grilling him for information about particular routes all over the place: JT, Yosemite, Granite Mountain, Tahquitz Rock. The object of Todd's most grueling interrogation was *Hades*, a route Largo had just climbed on the south face of Suicide Rock, a couple hours' drive south from Joshua Tree. He'd rated it 5.12+, like so many of the newest hard routes. No one dared suggest a grade of 5.13, afraid Jerry Moffatt would come over, flash it, and downgrade it to 5.12c, much to our utter humiliation.

Largo described his ascent of *Hades* like a high school quarterback on homecoming night recounting his game-winning pass. We hung on everything he said. On the first pitch he made desperately thin 5.12 face moves up a nearly featureless wall to reach anchors halfway up the south face. Above the anchors there was an expanding flake that was so precariously perched it threatened to peel off under body weight. Long had to stand on it, all 220 pounds of him, risking death with each move—not only his death, but the death of his belayer hanging helplessly twenty feet below him. From there, the route went up a slab that was even more featureless than the first pitch; he pinched salt-grain-size quartzite crystals and stood on faint ripples in the rough, weathered granite, then executed a crux move involving a desperate lunge from razor-sharp side pulls the width of credit cards. Long had prevailed against overwhelming odds in completing his first free ascent, but the route had taken its toll.

"My fingers were a bloody mess by the time I finished that pitch," Long said. "The nerves are permanently damaged. It could have ended my climbing career."

BY THE END OF APRIL, even though the spring break crowds had abated, climbers were still pouring into Joshua Tree from everywhere. Germans, Brits, Aussies, French, Japanese, and Americans, among them a regular cast of characters you might read about in the magazines: Wolfgang Gullich, Jerry Moffatt, Patrick Edlinger, Hidetaka Suzuki, Jean-Baptiste Tribout, Stefan Glowacz, Kim Carrigan, Jonny Woodward, Russ Clune, Michael Freeman—not just kids on vacation but serious climbers living out of vans and rental cars with plans to travel for months at a time. They would hit all the hot spots to test themselves against the hardest routes America had to offer.

One day I set out with Clune, an East Coast climber on an extended trip out West, to work on *Gunsmoke*, a classic boulder problem that was a must-do on the Joshua Tree hardman circuit. There were a lot of climbers assembled around it, a veritable international gathering. I recognized two Germans, Stefan and Uli, who were in the next camp up the road from ours. Clune knew the Brit, Jonny Woodward, a gangly, bespectacled climber brimming with energy and enthusiasm. And then there was the Aussie, Geoff Weigand, every brash inch of him, calling everybody a "wanker" and saying generally derogatory things about everyone and everything.

The impromptu international climbers meet reconvened in our campsite that night, hosted by Todd, who within minutes was everyone's new best friend. He showed off the Skinner Box and his workout setup, and peppered everyone with questions about the desperate routes they had done and those they planned to do. The presence of so many foreign climbers was something new and unexpected. I had come across the occasional stray Brit, German, or Japanese climber on previous trips, but now I was engulfed by a whole cast of them, all chatting amicably about their hard climbs back home and how they compared with those in the States. The consensus seemed to be that American climbers were pathetic by comparison, with the Brits and Australians being the most vocal about it, the Swiss and the Germans, more diplomatic. But overall, the general impression was that their climbs back home were harder than anything in the States, and American climbers were lagging behind international standards.

This impression was reinforced by each new issue of *Climbing*, *Mountain*, and *Rock & Ice*, which included reports of yet another foreign climber tearing it up on American rock—an influx the climbing media dubbed "the Invasion of the Route Snatchers." Jerry Moffatt, the self-proclaimed best rock climber in England, had on-sighted *The Phoenix*, Ray Jardine's 5.13a testpiece in Yosemite, as well as *Equinox*, Bachar's 5.12c thin crack in Joshua Tree, and he had easily repeated *Psycho Roof* and *Genesis*, nabbing the coveted second free ascents of two of Eldorado Canyon's hardest routes. He added insult to injury by later toproping the latter in his running shoes. Wolfgang Gullich had repeated *Grand Illusion*, Tony Yaniro's futuristic 5.13b/c roof crack at Sugarloaf in the Lake Tahoe region. He was the top German climber at the moment and probably the best climber in the world, considering his new route *Punks in the Gym* at Mount Arapiles was rated 32 on the Australian scale—the equivalent of 5.14a. Later in 1985, during a visit to Colorado, French climber Patrick Edlinger would on-sight *Genesis*, the 5.12c route Jim Collins had established in 1979 after more than fifty tries over several months, and he would also repeat several other hard routes with minimal falls, including *Rainbow Wall*, a rappel-bolted route in Eldorado Canyon regarded as Colorado's first 5.13, and *Sphinx Crack*, a 5.13c crack in the South Platte region. Also visiting the States in 1985 was Kim Carrigan, the self-proclaimed best rock climber in Australia; in addition to repeating *The Phoenix* and *Grand Illusion*, he would establish several new first ascents that would upend the American climbing scene.

What was it, we wondered, that these foreign hotshots had that American climbers didn't? How did they do it? What made them so good? We decided it was their can-do, no-holds-barred attitude about free climbing. They weren't afraid to work routes on toprope before leading them free. They weren't castigated if they hung on the rope while working out the moves. They weren't vilified if they placed bolts on rappel. Also, the Europeans were batshit about training, climbing at least three hundred days each year. They bouldered for technique, did laps for mileage, and holed up indoors for daily hours-long workouts, which made them strong as hell—endless sets of pull-ups, Bachar ladder repetitions, and sessions on their campus boards (a new training apparatus we had only just heard about). They were fearless when it came to leading, even soloing; they didn't balk at running it out, pushing through the pain. They had the physical and mental tools to succeed, and for the most part, the Americans didn't. John Bachar and a few others did, maybe, but Bachar, unlike the foreign invaders, had a mental block: he was hung up on style and ethics; he had to do things the "right" way, which was, it seemed, the entirely wrong way if you wanted to climb the hardest routes.

Geoff Weigand had a much simpler answer. "It's because you're all wankers," he informed us. "We're just better than you are. Get over it."

14 TROUBLE IN DODGE

It was a rare rest day. Todd, Beth, Bill, and I headed into town early to get a shower and have a civilized dinner before returning to camp. The only rule was that dinner had to be cheap, and Todd, as always, knew just where to go. He pointed us to a bar just up the highway with a happy hour that was ripe for exploitation.

"It's a dollar a beer, with free hors d'oeuvres from four to six," Todd enthused. "Cheap beer and free food, all you can eat for two dollars!"

It was something else—a cowboy bar packed with ranchers and farmers and their gals, young and old, having a beer and some crackers and cheese, wings, ribs, and Swedish meatballs, talking over too-loud country-western music after a hard day's work. We didn't fit in at all with the locals, except Todd, who could put on his aw-shucks hayseed charm and win over anyone. Todd was soon chatting with the natives, telling stories about growing up in Pinedale and hunting in the Wind River Range, completely disarming even the most hostile of the bunch. It didn't hurt that he'd worn his cowboy hat into the bar.

We went back the next week, but this time would be different.

Being naturally gregarious and inclusive, Todd had mentioned our plans to some other climbers around camp, and as we were about to head into the bar, a Toyota van pulled into the parking lot and out stepped Jonny Woodward, Kim Carrigan, and Geoff Weigand. This assemblage was something to behold. Woodward looked halfway normal, a lanky, curly-headed Brit in a T-shirt and tracksuit bottoms. The Aussies were not so demure. Carrigan had a New Wave haircut, a curly, bleached fade, and was wearing a pink sleeveless shirt; Weigand had outdone Carrigan with black-spotted Lycra tights, a white blouse with a frilly collar, and a big dangling earring.

"Oh, boy," Todd said, when he saw Weigand's getup. "There's going to be trouble in Dodge."

We hurried into the bar ahead of the foreigners, sat at an empty table, and ordered our first round of beers. Todd and Beth immediately went to the hors d'oeuvres table and heaped their plates with generous helpings of meatballs, cheese, and carrot sticks slathered with ranch dressing. They sat back down and ate greedily. Carrigan and Woodward came in, turning a few heads. Then Weigand sauntered in like he owned the fucking place. For a moment, time seemed to stand still. Everyone in the bar, all the cowboys and ranch hands and their gals, stopped talking, put down their beers, and stared at him. A country-western song was still blaring, but it was as if the room had gone deadly quiet.

"I don't know what everybody's staring at," Weigand said in our direction, loud enough for all to hear as he strode toward us. "Haven't they seen a real man before?"

"Them's fighting words," Todd said quietly, looking nervously around the bar.

Still feeling uneasy about the situation, I was ready to get the hell out of there, but nobody else in our group seemed to pay heed. They nursed their beers, biding time, waiting for the hors d'oeuvres to be replenished. Every time they were, the pack would swarm the spread and scarf them all down, leaving little but scraps for the regular customers, which didn't help our standing. Pretty soon the waitress was looking at us in a peculiar way, and she stopped coming over to ask if we wanted more beer. It was clearly time to go, but nobody was budging. Todd was almost indignant about it. We were going to stay the full two hours, by God!

"America's a free country, right?" Carrigan asked rhetorically, displaying his unique Aussie charm. "We have every right to be here."

When happy hour was over and they stopped bringing in hors d'oeuvres, the whole group left on cue. There was no confrontation in the parking lot, just a cold shoulder from the waitress and other patrons as we left.

"You Americans are so passive," Weigand said, spoiling for a fight.

"Ah, youth," Carrigan said, shaking his head, smiling wistfully.

IT WAS HARD TO READ Geoff Weigand. He was a pent-up character, but that was just his style. If you were an American, you were automatically suspect, except

Todd, perhaps, because he was Todd. If you didn't climb hard routes, Weigand called you a wanker. He said outrageous things right to your face to see how you would react. If you said nothing, he would say more outrageous things. Eventually, after enduring enough of this, I told him to fuck off, to which he replied, "Now that's something intelligent to say." It seemed to work, though; he sneered, walked off, and for the most part stopped talking to me.

Carrigan, on the other hand, was more mature, less brash. He was certainly outspoken, especially against American politics and foreign policy, but he was older and more accepting of American citizens as human beings separate and apart from their government. Both Carrigan and Weigand seemed to outright despise Americans, but at least Carrigan was not completely anti-American on the individual level.

At age twenty-seven, Carrigan was already the "old man" of Australian rock climbing. At twenty, Weigand probably felt a need to prove that he, not Carrigan, was the best rock climber in Australia. He wasn't. Carrigan was clearly in a class above Weigand, and most of the rest of us as well. Like the other foreign rock stars who were in the States that year, Carrigan had an agenda. He wanted to climb the hardest routes in each area, and like Todd he wanted to put together a slide show to take on the road in Australia and Europe and get some photos for his sponsors to use in advertisements—that is, to make money. He had come to Joshua Tree to climb *Equinox*. That was all. He would be there briefly, long enough to tick off his chosen route and hopefully get some photos, then he would head somewhere else. Weigand, on the other hand, was like gum on our shoes. We had to suffer him a while longer.

15 OUT LIKE FLINT

On our last night in Joshua Tree, Todd roamed the campground, saying adios to friends new and old, finding out who was headed home and who might linger here, venture there, and perhaps end up in Yosemite in a few weeks or come out to Devils Tower later in the season. We were invited to hang out at every campsite where we—that is to say, where Todd—had made friends, which was practically all of them. Along the way we came to one of the campsites next to the slabby side of The Blob, where the German climbers Stefan and Uli and their girls were camped. Their big fire cast a pale, flickering light on the golden rock, sending shadows dancing up the slabs. The fire lured climbers from all over the campground, who came with beer and stronger stuff and sat around telling lies about routes they had climbed or failed on and the amazing feats of Patrick Edlinger, Jerry Moffatt, or Wolfgang Gullich they had witnessed or heard tell of. Eventually it seemed that every climber we knew had congregated there.

Todd was a practiced storyteller from his many years as an elk hunting guide. Each night it seemed he had a new story about an epic hunt, a lost climber, a blizzard to end all blizzards, angry grizzly bears or cunning wolves that had to be kept at bay—stories told more than once around a remote campfire to groups of grizzled, whiskey-soaked clients who sat mesmerized as Todd spun his yarn. I imagine Todd learned how to tell stories from his father and uncles, perhaps even from his grandfather, Clem, the old grizzly trapper who had many epic survival stories of his own to tell and no doubt shared them all with his doting grandchildren. There was the one about the time Clem was out trapping alone and fell through a hole in the snow "up to his armpits," as the story goes. Unable to pull himself out because of his snowshoes, which would not fit back through the hole, he had to hang on with one hand while unbuckling the snowshoes with his other, then pulled himself out of the hole, half frozen, and hurried back to camp to build a fire to thaw himself out. There was no limit to the height of Todd's tall tales, and each new story was as infinitely entertaining as the last, whether you had heard it before, whether or not it was entirely true.

That night amid the circle of assembled climbers, after an ember popped out of the campfire so loudly it startled everyone into momentary silence, Todd filled the pause with such a story. My retelling here is entirely from memory. I wish now that I had run to our camp to get Todd's boom box so I could have recorded it, even part of it, so I could share it exactly as Todd told it. But then I would have missed it.

"Get this," Todd said from the shadows of the campfire. "A couple of years back, me and Tom Cosgriff climbed Spider Rock. I'm lucky to be alive to be able to tell you about it. Tom's lucky to be alive, too, but he hasn't spoken a word about that climb since. Neither have I, until now.

"We were dropped off on the Navajo reservation under cover of darkness on a new moon desert night, me and Tom, far away from the canyon rim so the locals wouldn't see us coming. They were still mad, the Navajo, about the last time we had tried to free climb Spider Rock, hopping mad, and they wanted their revenge. We hoped if we came at night they would not be there, or if they were they would not see us creeping in. If they had spotted us they would have known what we were up to and headed us off. We sneaked across the canyon rim, scurrying from pine to pine, looking out and listening to make sure we weren't seen. We had to walk like ghosts, like hungry coyotes stalking prey. The crack of a single twig underfoot would betray us. Once we heard low voices and the sound of men walking. We froze and stood in place for ten long minutes as still as saguaro cactuses and they walked right past us, not a stone's throw away, as if we had become invisible. When we were sure they were gone, we hurried on through the darkness to the rim.

"When we got there, we scrambled down in the dark and across a slab of loose sandstone that led to a cave just below the rim, where we would rappel down into the canyon at dawn. The traverse was dangerous in the dark—fifth-class climbing on loose rock with three hundred feet of dark, empty air below. We could not disturb a stone, and could not risk roping up, because we might make a sound or kick a rock loose and the natives would be upon us. We made it across without a sound and bivouacked in the cave, me and Tom, keeping as quiet as we could be, waiting for first light."

Todd paused and looked somebody in the eye. We all sat there expectantly, looking across the fire at Todd, waiting for whatever he would say next.

"Sometime after midnight, we woke up to the sound of voices on the canyon rim. Navajo voices. They must have spotted my van in town. I was sure they had trashed it and had come to the rim looking to thrash us. We couldn't make out exactly what they were saying, but it didn't sound good for us. Then one of them called out in a shrill voice that shot through the night sky: 'This is Navajo land. You're not welcome here. If you don't come out, we'll kill you.' One of them let out a whoop and the rest followed suit and we just sat there quietly, hoping it was a bluff to scare us out. We knew better than to climb out. We sat quietly, pretending not to be there, hoping they would go away. Then a few minutes later we heard scuffling off to our right and Tom shined his flashlight over that way and there was one of them, a Navajo kid wearing jeans and cowboy boots and a cowboy hat and packing a sidearm trying to do that traverse over to the cave in the dark. We picked up rocks and threw them at him, hit him a couple of times and scared him back. Another one tried it and we chased him off, too, but it was getting desperate. One of them fired a shot from on top of the canyon rim just above the cave. They yelled and threw rocks down at us and threatened to kill us at dawn.

"They had the drop on us," Todd continued. "We were sitting ducks. We had to do something, fast. We waited in the darkness of that cave for an eternity, until we heard them walk away, then waited a half hour more just to be sure they had really gone. We started rappelling down the cliff in the dark as quietly as possible, lowering our ropes a few inches at a time to avoid making a sound. We knew if they had left a guard posted on top of the cliff and he heard us, he might start throwing rocks down on us, or worse, so we moved slowly and carefully, quiet as cats, silently descending into the dark depths of Canyon de Chelly. Rappelling down that cliff in the dark was as dangerous as anything we had ever done. It was completely dark on that moonless night, and when we reached the ends of the ropes we would have to find a crack to set an anchor in and do it absolutely silently under penalty of death from above. We had a tough decision to make, too. If we left ropes fixed they could rappel down after us. We knew we had to pull our ropes so they couldn't do it, but that meant we would have to find another way out of the canyon, and we weren't sure there was another way. We had to make a choice, and we did. We pulled the ropes.

"We made it to the canyon floor just as it started getting light. Suddenly, there was a yell from above and we looked up to see a head poking over the rim looking down at us, and then another, and another. There were three of them, and once we saw them we grabbed our packs and started bounding down the slope like rabbits into the brush. A good thing, too, because they started throwing rocks and sticks and anything they could get a hold of. Rocks came raining down the cliff and then bounded down the slope, flying all around us like artillery. A rock hit my pack, and another just missed Tom's head. We ran for our lives. There would be no going back that way.

"We hurried on down the canyon until we couldn't see or hear them anymore and then kept going all the way to the base of Spider Rock. We weren't sure if we should climb it because those Navajo assassins might be sitting up at the overlook trying to snipe us. We were pretty sure they weren't following us because we had pulled our ropes and there was no other quick way down to Spider Rock that we knew about. Tom was a crazy climber who wasn't afraid of anything. He looked at me and said, 'Let's do it,' and so we did.

"It was an awful climb, if you want to know. All chimneys and corners, just disgusting climbing, and the last pitch was an *offwidth*. Well, it was an ugly affair as I'm sure you can imagine. It took us half the day to climb it and on top we found the bones. Now legend has it that the Spider Woman lives up there and comes down at night and takes the bad Navajo children from their beds and drags them back up there and eats them and leaves their bones up there on top of Spider Rock to bleach in the sun. I don't think that legend is true, but we found bones up there just the same, bleached bones, and no explanation of why they would be up there unless something carried them up there. We didn't want to wait around to find out what it was. It was a bad sign. We were trespassers in the Spider Woman's lair. If she was going to eat anyone, it was going to be us.

"We rappelled off quickly and started the long hike up the canyon to find a way out, not knowing if there was a way out short of hiking through miles and miles of canyon bottom. Then just as we got down to the river we saw off in the distance three riders on horseback galloping toward us, leaving a trail of dust behind them. We turned back and went the other way, past Spider Rock and up the first slot canyon on the right, scrambling up slabs and gullies and hiding behind a boulder, hoping to give them the slip. At first they rode right past us, slowly, scouting for our trail. We stayed hidden, hoping they would keep going so we could backtrack, but then we heard them coming back and peeked out and saw one of them pointing up our way. They started up the canyon and we had to scramble farther up the sandstone slabs to a ledge where we knew they could not get to us on horseback. We traversed that ledge a fair distance, trying to keep to the back wall so they couldn't see us.

"We could hear them riding along in the canyon bottom. Every once in a while one of them would shout up to us: 'There's no way out. It's a dead end. We're going to get you and nobody's gonna know what happened to you. They'll never find you.' We kept on going along that ledge as far as it went, a mile or more up that canyon. It was starting to get dark out. The ledge ended at a talus fan and we had to cross it to get to another ledge that cut back the other way across a huge sandstone wall. The riders were at the bottom of the talus fan, dismounting and calling up at us, 'You're stuck now. You're done for.'

"We had nowhere to go but up. We ran up the ledge as fast as we could, hoping it would lead all the way across the face to a chimney or gully that we could climb up to reach the rim and escape our desperate fate. But our hopes were dashed. The ledge ended at the edge of a great precipice, five hundred feet below the rim. A featureless slab rose above us, and the wall below was steeper and more featureless. There was no way up, no way down, no way out. Those Navajo were coming up fast. They knew we were trapped, knew we would have to come down eventually to meet our fate. We were going to die there in Navajo country and no one would ever find us. All because we had climbed some godforsaken rock.

"Then, looking up the wall from the very end of the ledge, we noticed a shallow dish in the rock, the size of a man's hand, then another above it, and another, a line of them leading up the sandstone slab. At that particular time of day, on that particular day of the year, with the sun hitting the rock at that particular angle, we could see these little dishes running right up the slab as far as we could see. An hour or a day later and from a different perspective we would never have seen them. It was a line of holds, a staircase, carved out hundreds or even thousands of years before. They were very old and had been eroded by wind and rain and were shallow now. But a long time ago, for some unknown reason, some Anasazi had carved a staircase up this cliff to get to the top. It was fate. It had to be. A guardian spirit had foreseen our plight and carved those steps in the rock to lead us to safety a thousand years or more before we were even born. We put on our rock shoes and started up those ancient steps. We moved slowly, trying not to make noise or be seen. It was scary going, climbing up that ancient sandstone staircase in enveloping darkness. But every step was intact, some barely so, and they gave us just enough purchase to keep climbing upward, one hundred feet, two hundred feet, three hundred feet, four hundred feet, until at last the sandstone turned from red to tan and the angle eased back and the steps vanished and we were able to scramble quickly up to the rim. We made our escape just as the sun's rays faded in the west. We hugged like men and slapped each other's backs. We looked down and let out a whoop and waved at our tormentors and laughed.

"We knew it wasn't a first ascent, of course, but every trail has a name and we had to give it a name. So we named it." Todd paused, grinning. "We called it *Out Like Flint.*"

"SPIDER ROCK IS SACRED to the Navajo, and climbing it would very likely result in trouble of some kind, certainly a fine," wrote Eric Bjornstad in his 1988 climbing guide to the desert Southwest. In his book, Bjornstad noted that Todd Skinner and Tom Cosgriff made the first known free ascent of Spider Rock in 1983 and that, during the approach, some Navajo kids threw rocks at them. That is probably all that really happened, but I like Todd's version better.

16 HIGHWAY TO HELL

The next morning we broke camp and hit the road for Suicide Rock. I rode with Bill in his car, following Todd and Beth in Todd's van down Quail Springs Road to the highway and out past Yucca Valley. Todd was eager to get on *Hades* to try those 5.12+ "credit card" edges John Long had described. We were pretty sure the razor-sharp-edge story was an exaggeration, if not complete bullshit. When it came to Largo's stories, it was impossible to know what was real and what was made up.

Suicide Rock was easy enough to find with Tahquitz Rock as a landmark. We parked at the end of a road and hiked in. That winter, Todd had written to me about wanting to climb *The Pirate*, Tony Yaniro's 5.12c testpiece at Suicide Rock, but now that *Hades* was the hot new route there, that's where we headed. After a warm-up climb, we scrambled to the top of the rocks and hiked along the crest toward the south face. We found *Hades* at the farthest end of the rock. It was a beautiful spot—a rounded granite dome overlooking a forested canyon and rolling pine-covered hills in one direction and across Fern Canyon to Tahquitz Rock in the other, almost too pristine a wilderness to be believed. Raptors soared in the distance. According to a legend that may have been fabricated to boost the local economy, two lovers, one the daughter of a chief of the ancient Cahuilla tribe, committed suicide by jumping off the rock rather than be separated.

Looking down the long, nearly featureless slab, we could see a bolt belay at the base of a thin flake, pretty much as Largo had described it. Todd and Bill rappelled to the anchors, feeling the holds and testing the moves all the way down. After getting roped and racked up, Todd led up from the belay, gently laybacking up the thin flake and gingerly manteling on top of it, which was not nearly as tenuous as Largo had described but still would have caused some sort of injury if the flake had cut loose and fallen on the belayer. From the top of the flake, Todd stretched to clip in to a cheater sling that was tied to the first bolt.

"I'll bet Largo can make the reach all the way to the bolt," he said. "It was nice of him to leave a sling for me."

From there it was hard, thin slab climbing all the way to the top. The slab was rough and edgy—the kind of slab that would shred your fingertips if you hung on for dear life and would grate your skin raw if you fell off and slid down the rock the wrong way. Todd climbed up a few moves, decided he had the sequence wrong, and jumped off to avoid a grating slide. After a couple of tries he was able to work out the moves to get to the next bolt. He lowered back to the flake, and on his next try was able to climb through and clip it. Todd spent an hour working out the moves from bolt to bolt, yo-yoing up the slab until he reached the bolt protecting the crux moves. He hung there for a minute, rubbing his fingertips and chalking up, then reached over, pulled on the "credit card" edges, and let out a shriek.

"Jesus!" Todd said, hanging on the rope, shaking out his hands and then inspecting his fingers. "Side pulls from credit cards is right!"

Todd lowered to the belay, leaving the rope through his high point, and after a long break he was on it again. He cruised up the lower part of the slab and was soon back at the crux. He pulled sideways off one of the thin holds and reached over to the other, pulled tight on both and brought his feet up to crystals on the steep slab, held on there, looked up for a hold to lunge to, and cried out, "Now what?" He let go and swung back to the left, hung for a minute, then tried again. Again he got to the penultimate move and hung on there, unclear on what to do next.

"What am I going for?" Todd asked, studying the slab desperately, wincing in pain. "I don't see it."

He lunged up at what he thought was a hold and it was just a ripple; he skidded off.

"Goddamn it!" he yelled. "Look at my fingers!" He held up his fingertips for me to see; they were already skinned down and red. "I don't have many tries left before they're a bloody mess. I need to stick this on my next try."

I was hanging from the rappel rope, taking pictures, so I swung over and inspected the holds. Putting myself in the leader's position on the crux moves,

I looked to see if there was a hold that Todd might use that would get him through the crux. There were sharp crystals and undulations in the rock, but no good edges, except one little slanting edge that might work. I reached up for it, grabbed it, and pulled on it, taking my weight off the rope momentarily.

"How was that?" Todd asked.

"I don't know," I said, shrugging my shoulders. "Seems tenuous. Try it."

Todd pulled himself back up to the bolt, established himself on the rock, pulled up on the side pulls and got his feet high, then slapped at the edge and stuck it. He held on there for a second, looking to see what was next, and let go, skidding back down the slab.

"I think that might work," he said. "It better, because I don't think my fingers will last more than one more try. Lower me," he called down to Bill, and was soon back at the belay, rubbing his fingers.

After a rest and some work on his fingers, Todd gave it another go. He climbed up the lower slab, complaining all the way. He reached the high bolt and pulled into the crux moves.

"God that hurts!" he yowled as he pulled hard on the side pulls. He brought his feet up, got his balance just right, and made a semi-dynamic reach over to the little edge. He teetered there for a second, as if he was going to swing back, groaned again, tightened his grip, and held it.

"Curse you, John Long!" Todd growled as he yarded on the hold, brought his feet up, and pulled through.

In a few moves Todd was scrambling up the easing slab to the top. He clipped in to the rappel anchor and sat down, bemoaning his fingers' cruel fate while Bill jumared up the slab, cleaning the pitch.

"My fingertips will never be the same," Todd lamented. "Look! I won't be able to do any face climbing for at least a week."

On the hike out, Todd decided he wanted to climb *Insomnia*. "It's going to be dark soon," I protested.

"We have plenty of time," Todd said. "Besides, when are you going to come back here to climb it? Let's do it now."

Todd dropped his pack and started racking up. Bill flaked out a rope. Beth pulled on her harness. I looked up at the crack and thought, damn it, it's a long hike out and it's getting dark.

"I'm hiking out," I said, sighing. "See you at the van."

"Suit yourself," Todd said, tying into the rope. "We'll be there in a flash. This shouldn't take long. It's only 5.11."

I hurried down the trail, racing the impending darkness. By the time I reached the road, the sky was almost black. I laid back with my rucksack for a pillow, looked up at the stars, and fell asleep. Some time later I woke up to the sound of voices and cracking branches. They had missed the trail and were whacking their way through the dark woods, lost. I walked down the road toward the racket, flashlight in hand, and guided them out. One by one they stumbled out of the woods, smiling. They had been lashed and poked by trees and tripped by roots and rocks but had survived.

"You should have stayed and climbed *Insomnia*," said Todd, a huge grin on his face. "It was brilliant."

I knew Todd was right. But I also knew that if I had stayed, the four of us would still have been fighting our way through the dark woods with no one on the other side to guide us out. If I had to miss out on the fun, so be it. I was, I had decided, the smart one of the group, or at least the one with the most common sense, although I also seemed to be the one who was missing out on all of the fun, if you call getting lost in the woods in the dark fun, which I in particular do not.

Despite his ordeal, Todd was satisfied with having made the second ascent of *Hades*, even though he had skipped the initial 5.12a pitch. Todd had only wanted to climb the crux pitch, with its credit card side pulls, because it was the one Largo had hyped. But that's not how it was reported in the magazines. The official story was that Todd had repeated *Hades* "in an easy afternoon" and felt it was 5.12c; there was no mention of rappelling in, skipping the first pitch, and hangdogging.

Todd was probably right about the rating, but even so, the news of Todd's second ascent set off a flurry of letters to the editor. A local climber had been lurking below and had watched the goings on for a while. In a later issue of *Climbing*, he reported that Todd had repeated only the upper pitch, and that he had pretty much hangdogged his way up it, which was true. He didn't feel that there was anything wrong with what Todd had done, only that it had been reported inaccurately and was not really a free ascent by local standards. As he saw it, *Hades* still awaited a legitimate second free ascent.

"I'm impressed that Todd led the second pitch without toproping, which is how others have approached it," Long says, "but he missed something by not doing the first pitch. That first pitch was a Jim Dandy. It was 5.12a climbing where you could get some air if you fell off. You have to try it from the ground first, otherwise you're not doing the route."

This little snippet of controversy was still a long way off, though. By the time it came to light, there were bigger fish flaming in the frying pan.

17 SIN CITY

Todd Skinner's Flying Circus pulled into Las Vegas a few days after *Hades*. Todd led me, Bill, and Beth to a small casino well away from Glitter Gulch. According to Todd, we could eat dinner there for free. The true cost of the meal, however, was that you had to spend an hour in the dingy casino before you could eat food that had been sitting out since the lunch buffet. Its edibility was suspect at best.

"The trick," Todd told us quietly as we walked into the casino, "is to sit at a slot machine and pretend to play. If you're gambling, they'll bring you free drinks. Watch for the cocktail waitress. When you see her coming, put a quarter in and pull. Works every time."

John Long had told Todd that he absolutely had to stop at Red Rocks and climb *Levitation 29* the next time he was in Las Vegas. According to Largo, it was the best route in Nevada, if not the entire world. Long had made the first free ascent of the route in 1981 with his then girlfriend and climbing partner, Lynn Hill, and Joanne Urioste, who had done the first ascent with her husband, Jorge, the month before. *Levitation 29*, Largo assured Todd, was *the* route to do at Red Rocks. As a bonus, it was almost completely bolted.

Prior to the arrival of Joanne and Jorge Urioste on the Red Rocks scene in the 1970s, routes at Red Rocks tended to be wilderness adventures involving labyrinthine approaches, long cracks, scary offwidths and chimneys, bold runouts, loose rock, and difficult descents. The Uriostes did not want to put up scary, dangerous routes; they wanted their routes to be accessible, safe, and—above all—fun. So they placed bolts, lots of them, drilling as often as possible hundreds and sometimes thousands of feet up this wall and that. Their approach opened up miles of untouched desert sandstone to long, new, relatively well-protected routes. It also went against the grain of the prevailing

123

climbing tradition at Red Rocks, which dictated that routes should have a degree of risk to retain a sense of adventure. Word of these long, bolted free climbs eventually leaked out. And so, at Largo's urging, we stayed a couple of extra days in Nevada instead of heading straight to Yosemite.

Todd had a hand-drawn map of the approach to the route. By sheer luck, after only one wrong turn, he found the road that led to the canyon that would give us access to *Levitation 29*. The four of us started hiking, following a dry creek bed that traced a mazelike path through a narrow canyon, the kind of place you would not want to be caught during a heavy downpour. As we rounded a bend, we saw our destination, a red-and-tan-streaked sandstone wall a thousand feet high rising up in profile. We continued up a gravel wash until it looked feasible to start up toward the wall. Without a guidebook, we picked our path by dead reckoning, hoping Todd's scribbled notes would lead us to the route. We started up a brushy gully, then scrambled up interminable sandstone slabs, traversing rightward, until we reached the base of the wall. Our objective rose before us in plain view: a direct line straight up the middle of the face. The mostly bolted route followed what appeared to be a crack and corner system halfway up the angular sandstone wall, deep red in color and hard as steel. There would be no routefinding trouble here.

We had not gotten the earliest of starts, and it was already early afternoon. I quickly calculated that there was no way our group of four was going to climb a 1,000-foot wall, descend, and hike out before dark. The route was nine pitches long. Todd wanted to climb the whole thing. Even with three people, it would be a stretch. With four, it wasn't going to happen. I decided to sit it out, anticipating an epic hike out in the dark, or worse.

"You're not going to climb?" Todd asked, incredulous. "It's a brilliant route."

"Yes," I agreed, "but if I stay down here you three can probably get to the top and down before dark. I'm not hiking down those slabs in the dark. And also," I said, making up a plausible excuse, "I hauled my telephoto lens up here so I'd like to use it."

"Alright then! Get some good shots," Todd said.

Todd, Beth, and Bill roped up and started climbing, one at a time. Todd would lead up, belayed by Beth, and Bill would photograph; then Beth would follow the pitch and photograph Bill coming up behind. Then Bill would lead up and pull the rope and rappel down and photograph Todd leading. In this fashion, they climbed at a snail's pace, three pitches, four pitches, five pitches, thoroughly documenting the climb for future slide shows and magazine articles. I set up with my long lens on a sandstone tabletop feature and shot close-ups of the action for the first few pitches. When the shadows started creeping in across the wall, I decided it was time to get out of there.

"I'm hiking down," I yelled up. "I'll wait for you by that big boulder we passed on the way in."

"Okay," Todd yelled down. "See you there."

I scrambled back down the slabs to the creek bed and hiked down to the boulder, a long rock about fifteen feet high on all sides and flat on top. It was in the sun. I spent the next two hours bouldering, climbing the steep faces and overhangs, traversing, moving dead branches and loose rocks to open up more problems. Although I would have dearly loved to have climbed *Levitation 29*, in a way I was glad I hadn't. The simple pleasure of climbing alone on a stray boulder in a wilderness canyon in the middle of nowhere was far better than being stuck in a clusterfuck on a route with three other climbers, waiting for a turn to climb or rappel, worrying about whether we would get caught on the route after dark without a flashlight among us.

Long shadows soon fell over the canyon. Birds began to twitter and dart through the trees and along the cool wash. As the canyon grew darker, it became ghostly quiet. The birds were still now; there was no wind. I sat on a rock at the edge of the wash below an overhanging wall, growing anxious. It was nearly pitch-black now and there was no sign of Todd and the others. This kind of stuff probably happened all the time when Todd was guiding hunting parties in the Wind River Range, but out here it was unnecessary, and unnerving. I didn't want to be a character in one of Todd's epic campfire stories. I wanted to get the hell out of there.

I was preparing to hike out alone and wait at the cars when I heard voices up the canyon, then the crunching of gravel under feet. Beth, Bill, and Todd came around the corner, all smiles and laughs. They had climbed the entire route, Todd said. I was glad. My sacrifice had made it possible, and it was really no sacrifice at all: to be honest, I had enjoyed my time alone.

PART THREE

THE RENEGADE

Although this climb may not have been done exactly to our taste, and although we might have fretful little criticisms that envy always produces, we can better spend our energy in ways other than ripping and tearing, or denigrating the accomplishments of others.

—Royal Robbins

OPPOSITE: Beth Wald in the Skinner Box with Todd Skinner and Australian climber H.B. looking on, Joshua Tree, 1985 *(Photo by Bill Hatcher)*

18 LET ME GO WILD

The whole trip up to this point, Todd played his Violent Femmes cassette constantly, especially the first track, "Blister in the Sun." The song blared from Todd's boom box in the van, on the picnic table, or at the base of whatever cliff we were climbing. Todd played the song during the opening montage of his slide show and had even named a new route at Vedauwoo *Let Me Go Wild*. He and Beth Wald played that song so often, I was ready to chuck the cassette off a cliff. It wouldn't have mattered. Even if the song wasn't playing, at any given moment Todd or Beth might bust out singing, "Let me go wild . . ." and so on. Except they had it wrong. Those weren't the lyrics.

It was not until we were in Yosemite, sitting in the Camp 4 parking lot listening to the song for the hundred-thousandth time, that I broke the bad news to Todd.

"It's not 'let me go *wild*,'" I told Todd. "It's 'let me go *on*.'" He didn't believe me.

"It's 'let me go *wild*,'" Todd insisted.

"I think it's 'let me go *on*,' Todd."

"Let's listen to it again," Todd said. He rewound the cassette, pushed the play button, leaned forward, cradled his chin on his fingers, furrowed his brow, and stared deeply at the boom box, listening intently to the lyrics as if contemplating some eternal human mystery.

"Again," he said, not satisfied.

But after three or four replays, his expression softened and he was nodding his head earnestly as if he had reached a profound understanding.

"By God, it is 'let me go *on*,'" he said. "Jesus, what a bunch of buffoons we are." Then he shrugged and grinned. "Hey Beth, get this . . ."

And so it was, and on we went, although this revelation did not reduce the frequency with which the song was played or sung aloud. At least now they weren't butchering the lyrics. I don't think they knew what the song was about, though. It wasn't about climbing, that's for sure, although as near as I could tell, the song's subject and rock climbing had a certain commonality.

CAMP 4 WAS ALIVE IN THE SPRING of 1985 with climbers visiting Yosemite from all over—from Spain, South Africa, Germany, Japan, Colorado, New York, England. There were familiar faces: the Germans from Joshua Tree, friends from Seattle, and some of the Valley regulars who strolled by every so often, congregating at the edge of the parking lot, keeping together in small groups like a clique of high school jocks parading through the cafeteria the day of the big game. Given that our campsite was right next to the toilets, we got to know everybody within a short time.

As a rule, people were attracted to Todd Skinner. Everyone liked him. Even if they hated his style of climbing and despised his disrespect of their so-called traditional approach, they all liked Todd as a person, right down to the most hard-core bolt-chopping son of a bitch who ever cursed his name. Even John Bachar. Why was not a mystery: Todd was irrepressibly enthusiastic, unfailingly polite, and genuinely interested in everyone he met. He remembered everyone's name, where they were from, where he had met them, and what they had climbed. He asked about you and listened, really listened, when you answered.

Todd was sitting at the picnic table poring over the new issue of *Climbing* magazine when I strolled into camp one afternoon after a particularly desultory session on the Camp 4 boulders. My article about the Index Town Walls had just come out. When he saw me coming, he put the magazine on the table.

"So tell me more about *City Park*," Todd said.

The article, a survey of the climbing history and routes at my favorite home crag, was pretty much an advertisement for *City Park*, a thin crack I had told Todd about years earlier. There was a full-page photo of my friend Brian Scott aid climbing it, and a head-on shot of a climber on an adjacent route that showed the entire 120-foot crack from top to bottom.

"It would seem that Washington climbers must master 5.12s before they attempt what may become this state's first 5.13," I wrote in the article. It was perhaps unkind to suggest in a national publication that Washington climbers—my friends, climbing companions, and I—were lagging behind the standards, but it was true. For almost a decade, the locals hadn't been trying very hard to raise the standards, and they had a penchant for underrating everything. There was an old joke about Index: "There's one 5.9 and everything else is 5.11d." The 5.12 barrier remained elusive at Index largely because the locals, whether out of stubbornness or just plain spite, had so far refused to call anything 5.12. Even after Peter Croft had free climbed an aid pitch called *Iron Horse* and rated it 5.12, the locals went and downgraded it to 5.11d. A couple of routes had been begrudgingly given a 5.12a rating, though. And as for *City Park*, if anybody free climbed it, it was going to be harder than that.

"Definitely 5.13," I said. "Hard 5.13."

"Will it be 5.14?" Todd asked hopefully.

I shrugged my shoulders. "Maybe," I said. "I mean, if anything's going to be 5.14, it's *City Park*."

Todd nodded approvingly. "I may just have to come and visit the western swamps again."

JERRY MOFFATT ARRIVED IN THE VALLEY a couple of days after we got there. Everyone was still talking in reverent tones about Moffatt's ascents of some of the hardest routes in America, including on-sights of *Supercrack* in the Gunks and *Equinox* and *The Phoenix* , but he'd done a lot more beyond those feats. Moffatt had proclaimed himself to be the best climber in England and was backing it up. He'd outdone both Wolfgang Gullich and Patrick Edlinger on his first US trip, then had made first ascents of *The Face* in Germany's southern Frankenjura in 1983 and *Revelations* at Raven Tor in England in 1984, both French 8a+ (5.13c). *The Face* was the first 8a+ route in the world, and *Revelations* was the hardest route then climbed in England. In addition, Moffatt had led *Master's Wall*, a long-standing problem at Clogwyn Du'r Arddu, in 1983; rated E7 6b (5.12d R/X), the route was as sparsely protected as the *Bachar-Yerian*, if not more so, and a full number grade harder, with ground fall potential on the lower half of the route and a possible 100-foot fall near the top. Although Moffatt inspected *Master's Wall* on rappel prior to leading it, he had removed a protection bolt beforehand, feeling that bolts didn't belong on mountain walls such as Cloggy, only on limestone where they were necessary.

It could be argued that not only was Moffatt the best climber in England at the time of those ascents, he was possibly the best climber in the world (although a couple of German and French climbers might have disagreed).

There was no disputing he was heads above the best American rock climbers of the day.

Flush with pride at the publication of my first feature article, I had an idea. I walked to the nearest pay phone and called *Climbing*'s then editor, Michael Kennedy.

"Jerry Moffatt is here," I told him. "Would you publish an interview with him?"

"Definitely," Kennedy said. "Do it."

I did not know how to get Moffatt to consent to an interview. I didn't feel confident enough to just walk up to him in Camp 4 and ask him. He tended to hang out with Ron Kauk, John Bachar, and some of the other Valley hotshots and, frankly, I didn't want to go near them. I was still very much intimidated by Camp 4 royalty. So I lurked around the campground, hoping Moffatt would walk by alone, or be on a boulder problem when I just "happened" by. Basically, I started stalking Jerry Moffatt.

I finally got my chance to hit him up the next night at the Mountain Room bar. He was there with a small group of climbers I didn't recognize. After a couple of beers to loosen my inhibitions, I walked over and introduced myself, feeling very much like I had back in high school when I had asked a girl to the prom and been turned down. If Moffatt declined, I would be crushed. Every climber in Yosemite would know. I would be the laughingstock of Camp 4.

"Hi, Jerry," I said, getting on with it. "I just got off the phone with Michael Kennedy at *Climbing* magazine, and he wanted to know if you'd do an interview for the magazine."

I was fully expecting a "Fuck off, wanker," but he was cool about it.

"Yeah, sure," he said nonchalantly, sounding very British. "When do you want to do it?"

"How about tomorrow morning?"

"Yeah, sure," he said. "Meet me here at ten?"

Well, that was easy. I was going to interview Jerry Moffatt in the morning. All I had to do was ask.

I had never interviewed anyone before and had no idea what to ask him. I wanted to pose at least a few intelligent questions so I didn't seem like a total dumbass. Having read all of the recent climbing magazines, I knew in general the things he had done, but I needed questions with depth—questions that would reveal the soul of Jerry Moffatt.

"What would you ask him?" I asked Todd at breakfast the next morning.

"Hmm," Todd said, furrowing his brow and biting his lower lip. "Ask him about his training regimen. I want to know."

After brainstorming with Todd and looking at some back issues of *Climbing* and *Mountain* that Todd had stashed in his van, we came up with a list of questions covering pretty much everything we could think of: who had inspired him to climb, how had he flashed all of the hard routes, what did it take to climb at that level, what did he think about American climbers, what did he plan to do next, was he still the best rock climber in England or even in the world, and so on.

Todd loaned me his boom box and a couple of blank cassettes to record the interview.

"I will let you have these if you promise that I can listen to the interview first," Todd said, knowing that without the tapes and his boom box I could not record the interview. I could hardly refuse.

Moffatt was already at the Mountain Room eating breakfast with some other climbers when I arrived. We found an outdoor table off the dining room and sat down. I loaded a tape into Todd's boom box and hit the record button. "Test, test, test," I said, then played it back. "Ready?"

"Yeah, sure," Moffatt said, leaning back in his chair.

I hit the record button again.

"I'll begin with an easy one. How did you start climbing?"

THE INTERVIEW WENT SPLENDIDLY considering I could barely understand what Moffatt said. It wasn't so much the words—I could understand those even through his thick British accent—but the colloquialisms, the slang, I didn't always get straight off. I stopped the interview a couple of times to ask what the heck he had just said.

Moffatt talked about his early inspirations, his hard flash ascents, how he liked to travel to new areas and climb hard routes, and how much he loved climbing in general and pushing the standards and inspiring others to follow his example.

"I like to try and push myself," Moffatt told me, "to do routes people are going to find hard to repeat or ahead of their time."

My sometimes leading questions revealed that despite Moffatt's fondness for the American climbing scene, he thought it lacked the spirit of competitiveness found in Europe. In particular, he called Yosemite climbers "apathetic," though he considered many of them to be his close friends.

"Yosemite climbers have been here for so long, and they don't seem to travel very much," he told me. "It's just stagnated, that's all. Yosemite is the most apathetic climbing scene that I've seen anywhere, but they all seem to have a good time."

Moffatt was outgoing and gregarious during the interview, which seemed more like a conversation than a formal interview. Despite his reputation as a "super brat," Moffatt seemed genuine, down-to-earth. He wasn't some poseur trying to be something he was not; he was a good climber, and he knew it. He was for real.

"HAND THAT TAPE OVER," TODD SAID when I returned to camp. "You made a deal."

I gave him the tape, and he put it right into the boom box and played it. We all crowded around. Todd listened intently, nodding in agreement with much of what Moffatt said about pushing himself and trying to climb things that are ahead of their time.

"That was brilliant," Todd said when it was over. "Hey, Jerry reminded me of something," Todd continued. "You know how he mentioned Livesey and Fawcett?"

Moffatt had talked about Pete Livesey and Ron Fawcett, two of his role models during his early years as a climber. Livesey and Fawcett were the British equivalent of John Bachar and Ron Kauk during the 1970s, competitive with each other but sometimes partners, two of the best free climbers in Europe at the time. They established many of the hardest routes of the decade on both sides of the Channel.

"Get this," Todd began. "Back in the seventies, when Livesey and Fawcett made their first trip to the States, they came to Yosemite to climb *Butterballs*. It was the newest hard route in the Valley, and it was the only route they wanted to climb, so they could see if they were as good as those Yosemite climbers. So they showed up in the Valley and told the locals that they wanted to climb *Butterballs*, and the locals said, 'Yeah, sure, man,' and they took them out to the Cookie Cliff and showed them this thin crack and said, 'Here you go, guys. This is *Butterballs*.'

"Well, of course, Livesey and Fawcett got right to work on it. They're from England, so they didn't know one granite crack from another. But after several tries, they had only made it twenty feet up the crack. 'This is quite difficult,' they said, and the locals assured them it was. 'Yeah, it's *Butterballs*; it's 5.11c, the hardest free climb in Yosemite. Keep trying, you'll get it.' So they kept trying. They couldn't climb it the first day, so they came back for a second day and still couldn't get more than about twenty feet up it without falling off. They shook their heads. 'These Yosemite climbers are quite good, aren't they? This is 5.11? Bloody hell!'

"About then, the locals started busting out laughing and told them it was all a prank. They weren't on *Butterballs* at all. The locals had set them on an old aid crack at the base of the wall, *The Stigma*. What do you think about that?"

"That's funny," I said. "What would have been funnier is if they had pulled it off."

"You're right," Todd said, nodding in agreement. "That would have been even funnier."

Todd added, almost to himself, "I wonder if anybody has ever free climbed *The Stigma*?"

19 A RIPPLE ON THE POND

After a week in Yosemite, we had immersed ourselves in our usual routines, which involved Todd going off to climb the hardest routes he could find, usually with either Bill Hatcher or Beth Wald in tow to belay and take pictures. I went along sometimes, but more often struck out on my own. I'd come on this trip to go climbing, not watch Todd hangdogging. Fortunately, I was able to hook up with climbers I met in Camp 4 or at the Mountain Room or at the base of whatever cliff I happened to show up at that day—climbers from all over the United States and other far-flung places, tackling whatever they were keen to climb, whether it be bouldering, toproping, leading, or soloing.

Some days I'd hike up to Vernal Falls or Half Dome, or just kick back in El Cap Meadows pondering the immensity of the Big Stone and taking peeks through Steve Schneider's telescope as he checked in on his friends' progress on the wall. Sometimes I stayed out late watching a crescent moon rise as the sun set in deep orange and purple hues beyond Cathedral Rock, and then wandered back to camp alone in the dark, because I was in Yosemite and wanted to embrace it, to soak it all in and experience every sublime aspect. I wanted to climb everything I could climb, take in every view I could see, breathe deeply the scent of bay and pine and dust. I reveled in the innate fear of standing at the edge of the void on the summit of Half Dome. I gazed at the full moon from the top of North Dome. In the evening I raced back to the Valley to have drinks with Moffatt, Schneider, Warren Harding, and whoever else was hanging around at the Mountain Room bar. I didn't care what Todd, Bill, and Beth were doing. I was having a marvelous time.

I soon found out that they were going out to the Cookie Cliff and hangdogging on *The Stigma*. After getting his first look at it, Todd had thought, "You know what, maybe those Valley climbers weren't so far off when they tricked Livesey and Fawcett into trying to free climb it. Maybe it was too hard for anybody back then, a good prank to pull on the visiting Brits. But now? Could it be that climb of the future I've been looking for, America's first 5.14, is just sitting here in plain sight in Yosemite Valley, right under everybody's noses?" Todd figured it was worth a try, at least on toprope to see if it was even feasible—if you could get fingers in anywhere, if there were any footholds, if it would take protection. A lot of ifs. "But," thought Todd, "what the hell?" Nobody else was lining up to do it. It was an obscure aid practice crack, too thin to get fingers in and with no good footholds, impossible to free climb, right? Everybody knew that. Everybody but Todd Skinner.

Nobody said anything about it for several days. Todd played it cool, and Bill and Beth were sworn to secrecy. Todd first aided up the crack (apparently a comedic struggle since he was completely inept at aid climbing), rappelled down it to clean his gear and get a feel for the crack, then gave it a few tries on toprope. Even if folks had known about this, no one would have gotten very riled up. After all, toproping was not viewed as an illegitimate style in and of itself. John Bachar toproped routes all the time. The idea of Todd Skinner trying to toprope an old aid crack wasn't anything anybody would get too excited about.

Todd, though, was excited and bursting to tell somebody. After a few days of toproping, he could no longer keep his project a secret. People had seen him on it more than once; clearly, he was working the route. He began to talk about *The Stigma*, not loudly enough that any Valley locals could hear him, but in hushed, almost reverent tones. He had, during his initial efforts, been able to do every move on toprope, albeit with a lot of hangs. Some of the moves were as hard as anything he had ever climbed before, or so he said, but he knew the route would go. That is, if he could somehow manage to piece all of those moves together, and if he could figure out a way to protect the pitch on lead.

"It is so thin," Todd told me and others he trusted with his secret, "that you almost can't let go to place protection. At best, you might have just enough time to clip in before you fell off, but even that would be right at the limit of possibility. But it will go. Mark my words, it will go. And it will be hard."

Todd paused, seemingly for dramatic effect. "I don't want to speculate too much," he continued, lowering his voice and looking around to see who might be lurking in the shadows to overhear, "but it could be harder than anything yet done in Yosemite."

The crux of the pitch was a thirty-foot section of crack splitting a flat, nearly featureless vertical granite wall—a crack so thin in places you could not even get fingertips in. Because of its unrelenting difficulty and his belief that he wouldn't be able to place protection on lead, Todd came to the conclusion that he would have to fix pitons in the crack to protect it. The idea of fixing nuts in the crack occurred to him, but he quickly dismissed it: chocks would plug up the best jams and make it much harder if not impossible to free climb the route. Bolts were out of the question; placing bolts next to a perfectly good crack would be heresy, and he didn't want to be burned at the stake. Pins would work, though. Nobody would object to a few pitons being hammered into an aid crack, would they?

The only problem was that Todd didn't have enough pins for the job. He needed a half dozen Lost Arrow pitons to sew up the thin, parallel-sided crack. As he went around Camp 4 one afternoon begging to borrow Lost Arrow pitons from the big wall climbers, people must have wondered what he was up to. His efforts to free climb *The Stigma* were still a secret, and Todd was not known to be an aid climber; in fact, those who knew him well knew he was a particularly incompetent aid climber.

Whatever lies Todd told about why he needed them, he came back to camp a while later with a self-satisfied look on his face and a bounty of Lost Arrows in his cupped hands. He went out to the Cookie Cliff the next morning and whacked them in, strategically avoiding the widest pin scars so as to not plug up the best jams. And with that, his journey to fame, glory, and the American dollar truly began.

Day after day for the next two weeks, Todd and his crew would ride out to the Cookie Cliff first thing in the morning and not return until evening. Todd would come back to camp with Bill and Beth, and whomever else might have tagged along, and talk about the day's progress—about how he had managed to lead all the way to the second piton without falling off one day, how he had worked out the six-foot section of moves to the third piton over several hours of effort the next, or how in a brilliant effort he had made it to the third piton without falling another day and was assured of leading all the way to the fourth piton the next day. He had made a good attempt on the fifth day, he said, but after that was stymied by increasingly hot weather that made it impossible to work on the route except very early in the morning and very late in the afternoon when the cliff was in the shade. Although discouraged by the lack of progress, Todd was not about to be sensible and give up. *The Stigma* was going to go free, by God. He would spend all day, every day working it, for as long as it took to climb that godforsaken crack.

"SO, MICHAEL," I BEGAN. I was back at the pay phone, ringing up Michael Kennedy at *Climbing* again. "Peter Croft is here. He showed up yesterday and soloed the *Northeast Buttress* of Higher Cathedral Rock, *Braille Book*, and *Central Pillar of Frenzy*, on his first day here, after driving all night from Canada. Do you want me to interview him, too?"

"Sure," Michael said without hesitation. "Do it."

I knew Peter Croft by reputation before he arrived in Yosemite in May 1985. His 1982 free ascents of *University Wall*, an eight-pitch 5.12 route, with Hamish Fraser and Greg Foweraker and *Zombie Roof*, a thirty-foot horizontal roof crack rated "5.12+," both in Squamish, were widely known, at least in the Pacific Northwest. Croft, a Canadian, had done most of the hardest first ascents on Washington rock to date, and was probably the best climber in the state on any day he deigned to visit. I was always hearing about how he had climbed this roof or that crack at Index or Leavenworth, usually a new 5.11 or 5.12 route, an obvious plum that he had breezed in and climbed while we Washington climbers were asleep at the switch. To me he was already a local legend, but to the rest of the climbing world he was just getting started.

The previous year, Croft had become a blip on everybody's radar when he soloed the *Northeast Buttress* and the *Steck-Salathé* in the same day, one of the more notable solo link-ups yet done in the Valley. Royal Robbins had called Henry Barber's 1973 free-solo ascent of the *Steck-Salathé* "an act of vision." The way Croft was climbing, he seemed to have more than vision; he had ESP.

The buzz around Camp 4 the night after he arrived was that Croft had driven all night to Yosemite from Squamish and then immediately gone on a rash of free-solo climbs. Upon rolling in late in the morning, he jumped out of the car and free soloed the *Northeast Buttress* of Higher Cathedral Rock, a 900-foot-high 5.9 route, then *Braille Book*, a 600-foot 5.8 route, and as a finale, he flew up the first five pitches of *Central Pillar of Frenzy*, another 500 feet of 5.9 crack climbing. He did it all during a rainstorm that had driven me and most other climbers off the rock that day. These weren't the hardest routes in Yosemite, but the idea of driving twenty straight hours and then racing up 2,000 vertical feet of 5.8 and 5.9 rock, unroped and in marginal weather, sent a ripple across the Valley. We all heard about it, and we were all impressed.

Back home, Croft regularly soloed miles of 5.10 and 5.11 routes in a day. Literally. One Saturday I had witnessed him soloing Castle Rock in Leavenworth—600 feet up, 600 feet down. He did it ten times, which added up to 12,000 feet of vertical and overhanging rock up to 5.11 in difficulty before lunchtime. Hell, he'd even free soloed *ROTC*, a 5.11c overhanging thin crack at Midnight Rock. It was mind-blowing stuff. I wasn't sure if anybody else in Yosemite knew what Peter was capable of, but by the time I interviewed him, everybody knew. By then, he had linked up the *Northeast Buttress*, the *Steck-Salathé*, and *Snake Dike* on Half Dome in a single day, one of the most impressive Yosemite enchainments yet done. They epitomized Croft's approach: get in as much climbing as possible in a day and on as much terrain as possible, whether 5.2 or 5.10. Climbing solo is far faster than climbing with a partner, so when faced with the choice of working on a 5.13 route all day or linking up a series of long 5.9 routes high in the mountains, Croft always opted for the latter. He climbed hard; he climbed in traditional style; he free soloed like a madman. He did his own thing.

And then, just in case he had not already announced his presence with sufficient authority, Croft free soloed the *North Face* of the Rostrum, an 800-foot 5.11c route, a few days later. The ripple became a shock wave. Who the hell was this guy?

"HEY, PETER," I SAID, jogging over to intercept Croft as he walked through Camp 4 one afternoon.

"Hey, Jeff," he said. "How's it going, eh?"

Croft was an anomaly on the climbing scene. He came across as something of a loner, which wasn't so unusual, but he took it to extremes, as if he seemed to prefer at all times to be alone—even while climbing. Not so many years earlier, he had spent a season at Squamish, climbing every day and sleeping in a cave under a boulder. He was the pillar of the Squamish climbing community, universally liked and known for his sense of humor and entertaining stories. But in Camp 4, he didn't seem to hang around with anybody. Sure, you'd see him talking with Bachar, Ron Kauk, or one or two of the other locals, but rarely with a group of any size. Still, he was not the least bit standoffish or intimidating. He was the equal of any Yosemite hardman, but also approachable. You could talk to him, even go climbing with him, and he didn't treat you like you were nobody—even if you were.

Croft agreed to the interview, and we arranged to meet in El Cap Meadows the next morning. The following day, I hitched a ride out to the meadows and found Peter sitting on a log, gazing up at El Capitan.

"Are you ready?"

"Yeah," he said, "but I need to make it quick. I'm going climbing."

Peter was unpretentious and taciturn. He said he loved to travel, to meet people, and to climb. He was genuinely humble; self-confident, sure, but not at all cocky. He didn't think of himself as the best climber around, even if he probably was. He spoke of his climbs as if they were nothing special, even his hard free-solo climbs; they had been fun, an amazing adventure, but no great accomplishment. To hear him tell it, he thought every climb he ever did was the best climb he had ever done. He had an insatiable appetite for rock. It could be 5.8 or 5.12, he didn't care as long as he could climb. Sitting for a forty-five-minute interview beneath the glowering visage of El Capitan must have been torture for him. He kept looking over his shoulder at the Big Stone.

I had one question in particular I was dying to ask him, a question a group of us climbers had hatched the previous winter while sitting around Dan Lepeska's house drinking beer and staving off another cold, wet Seattle winter. We were speculating about this and that climber's motivations and what they might do next, including Peter Croft and where all of his soloing was headed. I waited until near the end of the interview to spring it on him.

"You've soloed the Rostrum now," I said, setting him up. "Do you think you will solo *Astroman*?"

It was a fair question. If Peter was willing to solo 5.11c thin crack routes like *ROTC* and the *North Face* of the Rostrum, why not *Astroman*? Todd and I had mulled over the possibility in camp, and thought it would be brilliant if he did it. It would be, we agreed, the next great leap forward in Yosemite free climbing, Todd's pending efforts on *The Stigma* notwithstanding.

"No," Peter answered. "It's just too thin in some places."

It was a lie: he would free solo *Astroman* two years later, then free solo both *Astroman* and the Rostrum in a single day, then climb the *Nose* and the *Salathé Wall* in a day, among a bunch of other incredible big wall link-ups and speed records. But for now, with his usual humility, he denied such aspirations. For Peter, it was all about getting into the flow and climbing, climbing, climbing. His message was clear: climb as much as you can for as long as you can and have a hell of a good time doing it.

20 DEAL WITH US

A week after we arrived, Kim Carrigan and Geoff Weigand showed up in Yosemite Valley and invaded our campsite, where Todd welcomed them eagerly. I will admit that they added a certain boisterousness to our daily routine. Being Australian, they were naturally cocky and imposing in a here-we-are-deal-with-us-you-wankers sort of way.

Carrigan had no doubt been a brash, arrogant youth like Weigand, but he had matured. He still carried himself with a certain swagger, but in a more genuine, infinitely more sufferable manner. You could actually have a discussion with Carrigan, if you could ignore his anti-American, Aussie-centric bombast. With Weigand, you had no hope of a give-and-take discussion. At least I didn't.

Todd immediately persuaded the Australians to come out and try *The Stigma*. This was one of Todd's tricks. He hoped one of them would work out or improve on a crucial sequence and reveal the key to a free ascent, then bow out gracefully, leaving it to Todd to reap the glory. There was the risk that one of them would take interest in the climb and beat him to the first free ascent—a risk that was very real with the likes of Carrigan, who was as fit as ever and had his sights on climbing the hardest routes the Valley had to offer, if only to show up all the American climbers. Ticking off the hardest new free route in Yosemite would have fit right in with Carrigan's agenda. But Todd had spent over a week on *The Stigma* already, and he was confident that nobody, not even Carrigan or his sidekick, could come in and cruise something that hard.

I went out to the Cookie Cliff that day for the first time, to see what *The Stigma* was all about. A lot of hangdogging, that's what. This whole business with *The Stigma* was not at all impressive to me, once I saw what was going on. The pitch—a very thin, pin-scarred crack, perhaps seventy feet long—split a flat, vertical wall where the old road met the base of the cliff. Leading about three-quarters of the way up the crack was a line of evenly spaced Lost Arrow pitons, all placed on rappel about four to six feet apart and preclipped with carabiners. They stopped at a slight ledge twenty feet short of a single bolt just above where the crack ended. It was blasphemous, really. Even I was mildly appalled. But then, who was I to have an opinion about it? I wasn't up there trying to climb it, was I? I was against it on principle but had no standing to complain, and so I kept my mouth shut.

When I arrived, Weigand was engaged in an attempt on the route. More accurately, he was hanging from the rope clipped to a piton six feet above him, which must have been Todd's high point that day. Weigand hung there for a while, then started climbing. He did a couple of moves, laybacking awkwardly up the crack, then barn-doored off and hung, rested, then started climbing again. After a couple of moves, he fell again, cursed in Australian, and hung there, shaking out his arms. Eventually he reached the high point, tried a couple of times to climb higher, then asked to be lowered off. Beth and Bill were also there, along with a handful of curious onlookers, whom Todd regaled with his prediction that the route, when completed, would be the hardest free climb in the Valley, possibly America's first 5.14. I looked around for Carrigan; he was long gone.

On the way back to Camp 4, I ran into Charles Cole, one of the Valley locals I had gotten to know from hanging out at the Mountain Room with Jerry Moffatt and Steve Schneider.

"Hey, Charles."

"Hey, what're you up to?"

"Nothing. I was just out at the Cookie Cliff. Todd's trying to free *The Stigma*."

"He's what?"

"He's got fixed pins in it. They're—"

"*What?*" Cole said, his eyes suddenly burning with fierce intensity. "He's got *fixed pins* in it?"

"Yeah," I answered, a little taken aback. "All the way up it."

"That's bullshit!" Cole snorted, then stormed off into the depths of Camp 4 without another word.

I continued walking, wondering why Cole seemed so angry. I feared I might have said too much to the wrong person. Had I just unleashed the Valley hounds on Todd?

"JOHN BACHAR STOPPED BY TODAY," Todd told me, feigning sheepishness, when he returned to camp that evening. "He took me aside and gave me a fatherly lecture."

"Was he mad?"

"No. He just said—" Todd continued in his best father-knows-best tone, "'Son, you shouldn't hangdog, you shouldn't fix pins. We frown on that sort of thing around here.' He tried to talk me out of it, that's all. He gave me a disapproving look. There were some other locals up there, though, hanging back, giving us dirty looks. I worry about those hombres. I fear those pitons might not last the night. If they take them, I don't know what I'll do."

KIM CARRIGAN HADN'T INVESTED much effort in Todd's project. After a cursory try, he had gone off to look at something else, and had within the week established a new route on the Cookie Cliff, a 5.12c crack pitch he called *America's Cup*. The Aussies had won the 1983 America's Cup and were apparently still beating their chests about finally taking international sailing's most prestigious prize. Carrigan had to aid up the first bit to clean off some dirt and lichen, then came down and led the pitch without falling, which was impressive style for an unabashed hangdogger. Soon after, he and Weigand made the first completely free ascent of the *North Face* of the Rostrum, bottom to top, including the 5.12b finish through the *Alien Roof*, a feat that had eluded everyone since Mark Hudon and Max Jones first tried and failed to do the complete route in 1979. Ray Jardine had done the first free ascent of the roof in 1977 by rappelling in from the top, a tactic Bachar had criticized, but nearly ten years later, no one had made a free link-up of the full route from bottom to top including the roof. Carrigan not only did it, he did the climb on-sight, without falls—brilliant style for such a long, hard free climb. In the course of just a few days, he had made two first ascents that were almost as hard as anything that had been established in Yosemite in the past several years, and he had done them in exceptional style. This Carrigan guy was something else.

I didn't bother phoning Michael Kennedy about interviewing Kim Carrigan. I just went ahead and did it. If I hadn't interviewed him, someone else
would have.

By the time he landed in Yosemite in May 1985, Carrigan had already
amassed an impressive list of hard ascents, including repeats of *Equinox* (5.12c)
and *Grand Illusion* (5.13b/c), two of the hardest free climbs in California, with
the latter standing as the undisputed hardest free climb in America at that
moment. He came to Yosemite with a specific agenda: to climb *The Phoenix*
and *Cosmic Debris*, the two hardest free climbs then done in the Valley, both
rated "5.12+" but pretty much agreed to be 5.13; to see if he could do some
high-level first ascents; and to try to shake up the scene. He made no pretense
about this. He was there to show up the Americans, to shock them out of their
lethargy and see what they might do in response. His ascents of *America's Cup*
and the *North Face* of the Rostrum certainly impressed the locals, especially
the latter, which he had done in impeccable style. There wasn't much to dis-
parage about a ground-up, on-sight, no-falls free ascent of a big, hard route
that had defeated all previous attempts.

Carrigan and I seemed to get along well, though perhaps he was only
humoring me. He was opinionated and outspoken and seemed to despise all
things American, and yet on a personal level he was bright and articulate and
quite pleasant. He had a punkish attitude, and he wore shocking Lycra tights
and earrings; his appearance and demeanor had "fuck you" written all over
them. But he was, behind this iconoclastic façade, decent enough. His sense
of humor bordered on sardonic, though without real hostility, and while most
of what he said had more than a hint of irony and contempt, it was measured
and often funny. He had an enormous ego, but unlike many other top climbers
of the day, he was well aware of it and made obscure comedic references about
himself and his ego that only his friends seemed to get. For everyone else, he
was not an easy person to like. Carrigan had once interviewed himself for a
climbing magazine, even going so far as to declare himself the best climber
in Australia. Like Moffatt, he was unapologetic about this; it was true and he
could prove it.

Carrigan and I sat down on a picnic table in Camp 4, I turned on the boom
box tape recorder, and we started talking. Kim enthused about his early climbs
at Arapiles and the notable first ascents he had made, and about his love for
travel, for meeting other climbers and making new friends all over the world.

"I don't have many rivals in Australia," he said at one point. Carrigan spoke his mind; he said what he wanted to say whether anybody liked it or not. And he said some horrible things about Americans. In his guidebook to Mount Arapiles, describing the route *Dead Americans*, Kim had written, "There should be more of these." I had to ask about that.

"Why are you Australians so anti-American?"

"We're very much down on America for its imperialist politics," he said. "The way it criticizes Russia and then acts just like Russia."

His feelings extended to American climbers, especially Yosemite climbers. He was not afraid to rip them out loud even as we sat there in the heart of Camp 4.

"I find American climbers to be very complacent, especially in California," he said. "A big problem is the ethics. Because they won't hangdog, people are afraid to try something that might be over their limit. So that has the effect that they will try nothing. Rather than trying and failing, they try nothing and then go bouldering all day. There are a lot of foreign climbers here this year, and they're actually keen and interested in doing new things.

"Todd Skinner trying to free *The Stigma*, that's pretty controversial," he continued. "For someone relatively unknown to come into the garden of the Valley demigods and give something they all think's impossible a go, I'd say that's very controversial, as will be the style in which he'll eventually do it. It's over his limit, sure. He's hangdogging up it, so what? He fixed some pins in it, big deal. Like nobody's ever pounded in a pin in Yosemite? The thing is, he's pushing himself, he's trying, and when he succeeds he'll be a better climber and will leave something for the next person to aspire to do in better style.

"Hangdogging on routes doesn't detract in any sense from someone else's attempts to do them in good style," he went on. "It gives them something to aspire to. If you don't have that, you just don't have anything. You just live in this little world thinking that the routes of five years ago are the hardest routes in the world. The Valley's a little world, a very little world, with little people."

I glanced nervously around Camp 4 to see if anyone had overheard Carrigan's rant. He hadn't whispered it. Thankfully, no one was around, although Carrigan wouldn't have cared if the whole rescue site gang had been strolling along the path right behind us. No doubt he would have said it louder, to make sure they heard every word. He wasn't afraid to stir things up. He would have fought them all.

"So, what about rappel bolting?" I asked, figuring if we were already in the frying pan, we may as well jump right into the fire. "It's accepted in Australia and in Europe, but not here. What do you think about that?"

"This resistance to rappel bolting is hypocritical and limiting," he answered. "It's why you Americans are falling behind the Australians and the Europeans. What's the difference between drilling on lead and drilling on rappel? As far as ethics go, you're still drilling. The ethic restricts what everywhere else has been the natural growth of the sport. I mean, the hardest route in Yosemite is five years old. Look at what Alan Watts has done at Smith Rock. He's practically established 5.14 in America all by himself!"

21 THIS IS IT

"Well," Todd said one afternoon a few days later, sloughing off his gear after coming back from the Cookie Cliff, "that route won't have me to kick around anymore."

"You did it?"

"Yep. It's done."

"How hard is it?"

"Well," he said, putting his hand to his chin, stroking his imaginary beard, pondering for dramatic effect, "I can't say just yet. It is harder than anything I have ever imagined. I think if I was going to rate it using the current Yosemite Decimal System, I would rate it 5.14. I'm calling it 5.13-plus, but if anything in America is 5.14, this is it."

Through sheer stubbornness and determination, after thirteen days of effort and in defiance of the local ground-up ethic, Todd had free climbed an "impossible" route and possibly established the first 5.14 in America. He was more than a little pleased with himself. Others were not so pleased.

As was later reported in *Climbing*, Todd had not climbed the entire crack to its end, but had stopped at a ledge about twenty feet short of where the crack petered out, a no-hands stance where the hardest climbing ended. He had reckoned this hands-free stance was a logical place to stop climbing, because although the rest of the crack could be climbed at a relatively pedestrian 5.12a, the existing anchor was way off to the right and could not be clipped to complete a free lead of the entire crack. If he had thought about it, he might have fixed a pin at the top of the crack and slung it to the bolt to create an anchor that could be clipped at the end of the crack, and then climbed the final twenty feet to do a proper complete free ascent of the entire first pitch of the route. After all, what would another couple of fixed pins have mattered? I'm sure he thought about it, but he hadn't done it. He had spent nearly two weeks working the pitch, piecing together a desperately hard sequence of painfully thin moves to get to the stance. He had pulled himself up onto the stance and clipped the final fixed pin placed as an anchor there. He wasn't about to risk falling off on the 5.12a finish and blowing the whole thing. What if he wasn't able to repeat the crux section? No, he'd done what he set out to do. He rappelled off, coiled his rope, packed his gear, and hiked away, flush with his success.

As a gesture, half magnanimous, half braggadocio, Todd left his protection pins in place so others could try *The Stigma* as a free climb. Todd wanted other climbers to get on it, to succeed even and validate the route, perhaps confirm it as being 5.14. He left a note at the base, proclaiming that he had free climbed it, had rated it "5.13+," and had renamed it *The Renegade*. He asked that the fixed pins be left in place, so others could try it as a free climb.

As if that was going to happen.

Todd's free ascent of *The Stigma*, such as it was, rattled the Valley locals' cage. He was like a boy taunting a rattlesnake at the zoo by tapping on the glass, trying to provoke a strike. They struck fast. The pins were gone the next day. Then the rumors started, that such-and-such Yosemite climbers had been seen overzealously nailing *The Stigma*, unapologetically bashing in pitons and wailing them out, as if to emphasize that Todd's ascent had been nothing more than a glorified aid climb. It was overheard that these post-free aid ascents were done with the intention of actually pinning out the crack further so the route would be easier, so *The Stigma* would not be—could not be—the first 5.14 in America. If true, this sort of retaliation would have evidenced a huge hypocrisy—the ethical elite purposely damaging the rock just to spite another climber's attempt to raise the standards of difficulty. There was no proof of this; it was just a rumor. There was, though, a lot of grumbling in the Valley over the next week. No heated debates in the parking lot, no fisticuffs, no ropes being pulled down and shat upon, just quiet meetings of two or three locals who would give furtive, dismissive looks our way or refuse to acknowledge us in passing. Pretty much business as usual, although I found that the friendships I had started with some of the Valley locals suddenly evaporated, I assumed because of my association with Todd.

Not everyone shunned us. A few regulars came over to talk about *The Stigma*, some to congratulate Todd on his success, others to let him know that while they respected him as a person and climber they did not respect his climbing style. No hard feelings, just a difference of opinion. But some of them were just overzealous assholes about the whole thing. Me included, as it would turn out.

22 GONE TO TERREBONNE

"I'm going home," I told Todd a few days later. I wanted out of Yosemite. I was sick of hanging around with Todd and the gang, and after just over three months on the road, I also felt a little homesick. As luck would have it, Kim Carrigan was heading up to Smith Rock in a few days to see about some hard new routes that had recently been reported in *Climbing* magazine. From there, I might be able to hitch a ride to Seattle. If not, I would take the bus.

"You can ride along with us," Carrigan said. I knew that by "us" he meant himself, Geoff Weigand, and Jonny Woodward. I didn't like the idea of being stuck in a car with Weigand for half a day, but a ride to Smith Rock would take me more than halfway home.

"What? You're leaving already?" Todd asked.

"I need to get home and type up the interviews and get them off to the magazine," I said. This was true—a thin excuse, but true.

"Alright then," Todd said. He seemed slightly dejected, although not exactly surprised. Bill Hatcher had left Yosemite a few days earlier. "You can rejoin us later on the tour," he offered. "We'll be heading to the Tower, then to the Gunks, then to Mexico. You have to come to Mexico," he gushed. "There are miles of unclimbed routes there. It is going to be brilliant."

"I'll meet you somewhere, I'm sure," I said. This was true as well, but also a lie. At that moment, I had no intention of rejoining the tour. I loved Todd, he was my friend, but I had had enough of being on the road. I was leaving the band, striking off on my own. I would meet Todd somewhere eventually.

"Maybe you could come up to Index and give *City Park* a try?" I suggested. "It's still there, waiting."

"I don't know," he said. "My fingers are still numb from *The Renegade*. That kind of climbing is so painful. I don't think I ever want to put my fingers in another pin scar again."

"That's okay," I said. "Maybe Alan Watts will come up and try it."

"Well, now, don't get hasty," Todd said. "I didn't say I *wasn't* going to try it. You say it's going to be hard?"

"As hard as anything I've ever seen."

"Do you think it will go?"

"I know it will go. When you rappel down and put your fingers in the crack, you know every move will go. Piecing them together will be the key. You've done *The Stigma*. You could do *City Park*."

"I don't know," he said, shaking his head. "Crack climbing is dead. Face climbing is the future." Then he looked at me straight on, an earnest, hard look. "Will it be 5.14?"

"I don't know about that," I said. "But I think it will be at least as hard as anything you've ever climbed."

"As hard as *The Renegade*?"

"Maybe," I said. "Maybe harder. It's the same kind of climb, only longer."

Todd pondered that, and then said, "Under penalty of death, you are not to tell Alan Watts one word about *City Park*. You have to swear."

I laughed. "Okay, Todd. I swear. I will never tell Alan Watts one word about *City Park*."

"Well," Todd said, extending his hand, "adios, Pilgrim. We'll see you along the trail somewhere."

"Definitely," I said. "See you up north, I hope."

"Maybe," he said, "if there's anything up there worth climbing, which I doubt."

WE DROVE OUT OF YOSEMITE in the early afternoon and followed Highway 120 to Stockton, then headed north on I-5 through Sacramento and past Mount Shasta, turning off onto Highway 97 at Weed. We were soon in Oregon. Carrigan drove stoically through the afternoon and into the night, saying almost nothing. I rode shotgun. Weigand and Woodward sat in the back, mostly sleeping, or at least trying to.

We stopped for gas and food around dusk in Klamath Falls and then continued north toward Bend, following long, straight stretches of narrow highway through fir forest. Carrigan drove fast the whole way, making good time.

Somewhere near La Pine Kim uttered an Australian oath, and I looked back to see flashing red lights. The state trooper ticketed Kim for doing 75 in a 55 mile-per-hour zone, although he was probably going closer to 90. Kim was polite but curt. He had no intention of paying the fine or appearing in court, so there was no point in making a scene. "Tosser" was all Kim said, and as the trooper walked back to his car, he unceremoniously crumpled up the ticket and dropped it on the passenger-side floorboard.

We arrived in Terrebonne around midnight, turned right just past Terrebonne Jack's, and drove down dark roads to the park. We were the only ones there, which didn't seem unusual to me, based on my previous visits. There was never anybody at Smith Rock. Nobody had ever heard of it, nobody ever went there. Carrigan parked at the edge of the picnic area and we piled out.

"Are we here?" Weigand asked, looking out into the darkness. "Is this it? Where are the fucking rocks?"

"You'll see them in the morning," Carrigan said.

We threw down our sleeping bags on the sloping grass. I lay awake for a long time, breathing in the luxuriant sage-scented desert air, looking up at the millions of stars shining brightly in the black night sky, and thinking about going home. Unless I could find someone to give me a ride, which seemed doubtful, Carrigan would drive me to the Trailways bus station the next day and I would be on my way.

We were up early, Carrigan first, then me and Woodward, and finally Weigand. We ate whatever we had to eat, washed up, then hiked down into the Crooked River Gorge and across the bridge. Like kids on their first trip to Disneyland, the Brit and younger Aussie gawked at the acres of vertical and overhanging sunlit rock. Even I still looked up with a measure of awe at the immensity of Picnic Lunch Wall, which had a distinctive monolithic presence. It was no El Cap, just a 600-foot-high pile of loose, flaky rock, but it loomed impressively. Carrigan was the most focused of the bunch. He had been to Smith before, he said, and had dismissed it as crap, but the rumors of hard new routes had lured him back.

We hiked along the river, around the toe of Shiprock, and up a traversing side trail that led through grass and tan-colored boulders to the base of Morning Glory Wall and across to the edge of the Dihedrals. There were quite a few more routes bolted now than on my last visit, especially on the east wall of the Dihedrals, above *Karate Crack*. Carrigan pressed for details; I told him what I knew, which in some cases wasn't much other than "Alan Watts says those routes are 5.12" or "That's what it said in *Climbing*."

Carrigan looked at the routes and decided to try *Watts Tots* first. I suggested *Karot Tots* as a warm-up.

"Bring some wired nuts for the traverse," I advised, trying to seem authoritative so Carrigan might think of me as useful. "It has one bolt the whole way across."

Carrigan led up *Karate Crack* and across the 5.11 traverse, and I followed. We rappelled straight down the buttress so Carrigan could get a sense of *Watts Tots*. He rappelled slowly, groping the pockets and edges on the way down. As soon as I hit the ground he was already racked up and ready to lead it. He jetted up the steep face, moving easily from pocket to pocket, and got high on his first try, falling at a spot where the holds thinned out, a slight crack angled up, and there was only one thin, rounded edge and nothing good for the feet. He did the sequence wrong, muttered his usual oath, and pushed off, falling ten feet. He hung for a minute, inspecting the rock, then pulled back on and climbed up to the crux again. He tried it a different way, stuck the move and pulled up, then pushed off again and fell fifteen feet.

"It's like a one-move 5.12 boulder problem at the end of a 5.11 lead," he observed while resting on the ground briefly between attempts. "I think I'll get it this try." And he did, firing right up it on his next go, nailing the sequence at the crux and pulling through.

Meanwhile, Woodward and Weigand had followed us up *Karot Tots* to get a closer look at the headwall routes above *Karate Crack*. I couldn't offer any route details beyond that they were 5.12.

"It's all runouts between bolts," I offered. "You can get Friends in some of the pockets."

Woodward led up to the Peapod, a recess at the top of *Karate Crack*, and set up a semi-hanging belay. Weigand followed and then led up the dead-vertical face, which involved thin climbing interspersed with huge pockets and very few bolts. Weigand climbed methodically, taking forever, working out short cruxes and then milking rests out of the big pockets into which he plugged Friends to supplement the intermittent bolts. He climbed forty feet up the wall, a brilliant display of on-sight leading on hard rock, but then lost his nerve in the face of a long runout and downclimbed back to the Peapod, also an impressive feat. He let Woodward have a turn. Carrigan got impatient watching them. He wanted to climb something.

We went back around the corner to *Sunshine Dihedral*, which was brilliant in the morning sun. "This is 5.12 then?" he asked.

"They say either 11d or 12a."

"Let's find out."

Carrigan led up the corner easily, stemming out on the golden-yellow rock on either side of the crack, jamming, laybacking, and smearing with his hands, flashing the pitch with no hesitation. He lowered off and I seconded, although not as cleanly as Carrigan had led it.

"You have a bus to catch then?" Carrigan asked. Since there was no one else in the entire park, I wouldn't be able to finagle a ride to Seattle. I'd have to take Trailways.

"Yeah, it leaves Bend at 3:30."

"Alright, then we'd better get you there. I want to come back and climb a bit more tonight. Are your things ready?"

"All set to go."

"Alright, boys!" Carrigan yelled up at Weigand and Woodward. "I'm taking this Yank to the bus. I'll be back shortly."

"Good riddance," Weigand yelled down. "Goodbye, wanker!"

I smiled as I gave him the finger. He laughed and gave it right back.

I HAD NOT KNOWN, HAD NOT HAD even an inkling, that this would be looked back upon as one of the seminal moments in the evolution of American sport climbing. Up until that morning, when Kim Carrigan, Geoff Weigand, and Jonny Woodward hiked down into the Crooked River Gorge, grasped handfuls of welded tuff, and pulled skyward, Smith Rock had been a bucolic backwater of a climbing area. After their visit, Smith Rock was on the map. Word spread quickly through the climbing world that Smith had steep rock, hard climbing, and infinite sunshine.

If I had known this, I would have stayed for a week or longer and photographed the hell out of the three of them climbing everything, and probably dispatched an article to *Climbing* or *Rock & Ice* about these wide-eyed strangers in this unlikeliest of climbing paradises. Instead, stupidly, I went home.

Carrigan drove me to Bend and dropped me off at the bus depot.

"Well, Jeffrey," he said. "Thanks for the tour of Smith Rock. Send me those photos of *Cosmic Debris* and *The Phoenix*."

"I will," I said. "Thanks for the ride."

I gathered up my things and dragged them into the depot. Carrigan drove off fast, back to get in another climb or two before the day was gone. I sat down and waited impatiently for my bus to arrive.

PART FOUR

THE GODFORSAKEN ROCK

I have often been asked why I seldom, if ever, write my views on all this ethics business. In thinking about it, I realize I don't give a damn.

—Warren Harding

OPPOSITE: Alan Watts on *The Stigma* (5.13b), Yosemite Valley, 1985

23 THE KID FROM MADRAS

In the late 1950s, a handful of climbers including Vivian and Gil Staender, brothers Jim and Jerry Ramsey, Alan Green, and Jack Watts started rock climbing at Smith Rock. They weren't the first, nor the only, but they were the earliest ones to climb there regularly. Rock climbing "looked like a cool thing to do," Jim Ramsey recalled in an article about the early days of climbing at Smith. Equipped with hemp ropes and soft-iron pitons, wearing hiking boots or tennis shoes, they climbed the easiest routes to the summits of the various pinnacles and spires throughout the area on predominantly rotten rock. Most days, they were the only climbers there. Ramsey described it as a "huge deal" if they happened upon a piton or sling left by a previous party, as if they had discovered some important historical relic.

With reaching the summit being their primary goal, not how they got there, they often improvised. There were no rules to follow. On their first ascent of Gunsight Rock in 1958, the Staenders climbed the main pinnacle with the aid of a ladder. On another climb of an otherwise "impossible" spire, the first-ascent team shot a wire over the summit with a bow and arrow, hauled a rope over, and ascended the rope to the top. Lassoing a pinnacle or flake of rock and prusiking up the rope was another technique taught by the Mazamas and The Mountaineers and used in the mountains whenever the opportunity arose.

Smith Rock became a state park in 1960 because of its "significant geological features" and "to serve as a resource for public recreation." In January of that year, Dave Bohn, Jim Fraser, and Vivian Staender made the coveted first ascent of one of the area's most significant features, a 400-foot-high pinnacle on the northwest side of the park called Monkey Face because of its remarkably simian countenance from the west. One of the last unclimbed summits at

Smith Rock, Monkey Face was considered impossible to ascend because of its consistently overhanging rock and lack of cracks. It was too high for a ladder or bow and arrow to be of any help, but Bohn and Fraser, two enterprising college students, figured out another way: bolts. They'd heard about big wall climbers in Yosemite placing bolts on El Capitan, and, lacking a better option, they set out to try it. On December 31, 1959, the pair started the climb by drilling a rudimentary bolt ladder up the most direct and least overhanging line to the top, from a ledge on the south side of the spire to a cave below the summit overhangs. It was an all-day effort to drill bolts up 100 feet of rock to the cave, where Bohn and Fraser bivouacked. Staender joined the boys on New Year's Day, and the three of them pushed through the intimidating overhangs to the top.

After Monkey Face, the few remaining unclimbed summits in the park were soon surmounted. With no new first ascents left to do, climbers turned their attention to more difficult routes up the various walls and spires. As at other areas in the United States, particularly Yosemite, aid climbing predominated at Smith Rock during the 1960s, with climbers establishing some difficult multipitch aid lines on the overhanging "big" walls of Monkey Face and Picnic Lunch Wall. Aid climbing at Smith Rock could be a serious, sometimes desperate affair because of the poor consistency of the brecciated tuff, which was more like compact mud than solid granite and would flake off or crumble in places with little provocation.

Then in the 1970s, mirroring the evolution of climbing elsewhere in the country, free climbing became the focus at Smith Rock. Tom Rogers, Del Young, Dean Fry, Wayne Arrington, Jeff Thomas, Chris Jones, and other local climbers pushed the standards progressively higher, establishing such routes as *Karate Crack* (5.10a), *As You Like It* (5.10b), *Morning Star* (5.10c), *Minotaur* (5.10d), *Lion's Chair* (5.11a), *Wartley's Revenge* (5.11b), and *Rising Expectations* (5.11d). Of particular note were *Methuselah's Column* (5.10a), a runout face climb on the far left side of the Dihedrals formation done in 1973 by Dean and Paul Fry, which was Smith Rock's first bolt-protected free climb; *Revelations* (5.9), a face climb up a prominent arête on the Testament Slab done in 1975 by Tim Carpenter and John Tyreman, one of the area's first entirely rappel-bolted free climbs; and the bolted face climb *Monkey Space* (5.11b), the first free route to the top of Monkey Face, worked out by Chris Jones and Bill Ramsey in 1979.

The 1970s could well be called the "Thomas Era" of Smith Rock climbing. Between 1976 and 1978, active and influential local climber Jeff Thomas redefined Smith Rock as a free-climbing area. He firmly established the 5.11 grade with ascents of such routes as *Brain Salad Surgery* (5.11a), *Shoes of the Fisherman* (5.11b), *Lion's Chair* (5.11a), *Wartley's Revenge* (5.11b), and *I Almost Died* (5.11a). Thomas was without a doubt the best free climber at Smith Rock up to 1978, and he established the prevailing local ethics of the period. A firm believer in the ground-up approach, Thomas refused to place bolts on rappel and chastised those who did. However, he had no qualms about hanging and working out moves before returning to complete a free ascent. His early approach—later termed "redpoint"—became the prevailing style at Smith Rock. But his anti-rap-bolting stance was not destined to survive. A new wave of climbers were coming up who would think placing bolts on rappel was just fine.

IN 1980, JACK WATTS'S SON, Alan, dropped out of college, moved back in with his parents, and started climbing full-time. From their home base in Madras, Oregon, the Watts family had gone on regular trips to the mountains, and Jack had taken Alan climbing as a boy. Alan climbed the South Sister at age eight, and by the time he was thirteen, the father-and-son team had climbed most of Oregon's highest peaks. Alan was a scrawny kid and not much good at rock climbing when he started, but he fell in love with it anyway—and got better. As soon as he could drive, he began hanging out at Smith Rock with a group of youngsters who climbed there under the tutelage of Jeff Thomas. Thomas impressed the younger Watts and his peers with his hard free climbing and aura of casual nonchalance, a sort of Smith Rock version of Jim Bridwell. Although some of the younger climbers were outperforming Thomas by the end of the decade, for several years during the late 1970s, Thomas was "the Man" at Smith Rock.

By 1980, Smith Rock was considered pretty much climbed out. Thomas and his generation had snagged all of the low-hanging fruit, and unless you were going to start drilling bolt ladders up blank faces, it seemed everything worth climbing had already been done. There were still unclimbed cracks here and there, but they tended to be what one would now describe as "chossy"— filled with brittle, friable flakes and loose rocks. But Alan Watts was eager to establish new routes, so he climbed these lines anyway. Instead of following Thomas's ground-up approach, however, Alan would rappel down a potential climb, clean off the loose rock, and place any necessary bolts in advance of the lead. Leading these routes ground-up would have been dangerous—both for the leader, who risked having holds break the whole way up, and for the belayer, who would be bombarded by rockfall the whole time. In this fashion, Alan was able to create several good-quality, relatively safe routes up to 5.12b in difficulty, although he considered crack climbing increasingly unappealing—a dead end when it came to route development at Smith Rock. For an ambitious young climber, there was nowhere else to go but to the faces.

Alan began exploring face-climbing possibilities, but initially dismissed most of them as foolish or impossible. The faces at Smith Rock tended to be steep, blank, and loose. The welded tuff wasn't as solid as the name implied; it was strafed with thin, friable flakes—little time bombs waiting to snap off under the weight of a climber. And the vesicular pockets were so small in places you could get only one or two fingers in them. One face Alan inspected was the wall to the right of *Tator Tots* on the Dihedrals. When he rappelled down it in 1981 to scope out a possible route, he deemed the holds "far too small." But after a season during which he did several 5.12 first ascents, he revisited the wall and found he could now hang on everywhere; the seemingly impossible crux didn't feel as impossible as he had predicted. It would be hard, sure, but he was confident he could do it. He brought out his bolt kit, rappelled down, drilled six bolts, and got to work. Seven days of effort later, in early 1983, he had established *Watts Tots* (5.12b), the area's first modern sport route.

He didn't stop there. Within a month he had established the hardest free climb at Smith Rock: *Chain Reaction*, a 5.12c line up an overhanging arête on the left side of the Dihedrals. Although *Watts Tots* was the first route of its kind at Smith Rock, it was *Chain Reaction* more than any other route that opened Alan's eyes to the potential of the area. If this improbably overhanging arête could be free climbed, what couldn't? The next year, he pushed the standard even higher with the first ascent of *Split Image* (5.12d), a technical arête on the back side of the Christian Brothers formation, followed closely by the first free ascent of *Double Stain* (5.13a/b), a gripping overhanging crack-and-face line on the front side of the formation—the new hardest route at Smith Rock.

By the time Kim Carrigan and his crew visited Smith Rock in the spring of 1985, Watts had almost singlehandedly brought free-climbing standards at Smith Rock up to the level of the hardest routes in America—nothing quite as hard as *Grand Illusion* (5.13b/c), but as hard as anything in Yosemite or elsewhere in the States. He wasn't finished, though; 1985 would shape up to be quite a year at Smith Rock.

24 MONKEY OFF MY BACK

When I returned to Smith Rock in the summer of 1985 to rendezvous with Alan Watts for a trip to the High Sierra and Yosemite, the Aussies were gone and the place was insufferably hot and back to its usual neglected state. Alan wanted to try a new hard route Hidetaka Suzuki had just climbed at Donner Summit, then swing down to the Valley for a go at *The Stigma*.

I don't remember the first time I met Alan Watts. He had been in Joshua Tree in 1983 when I was there, and probably climbed with me and Todd Skinner then, but I don't remember him. His name didn't ring a bell when Mike Barbitta mentioned him later that year as the author of the new hardest route at Smith Rock. I definitely met Alan in Joshua Tree in the spring of 1985, though. Todd and I had gone out to toprope *Baby Apes* again and found Alan working on *Moonbeam Crack*, a 5.13a thin crack first toproped by John Bachar that Alan was able to climb and we were not. That summer, during one of several visits to Smith Rock, Alan and I did a couple of routes together, and he asked me if I'd accompany him on a trip to Yosemite. Having temporarily dropped out of college and with no job, I agreed to go along.

I arrived in the early afternoon and found the park vacant as usual—not a soul in sight except a tourist family huddled in the shade of a tree in the picnic area, two resident magpies picking food scraps out of a garbage can, and a trio of vultures circling in the thermals. While waiting for Alan, I lurked around Mike Volk's trailer, the locals-only hangout across the street from the park, and leafed through the latest issue of *Climbing*, reading the write-up about *The Stigma* and my Jerry Moffatt interview for the umpteenth time. Alan showed up a while later in his rusty yellow Datsun pickup, complaining about soreness in his fingers but still wanting to climb something.

"What, in this heat?" I asked.

"Sure, why not? Let me take some ibuprofen first." He opened the bottle, shook out four pills, downed them with a gulp of water. "There. Let's go."

We hiked down into the gorge and into the shade of Picnic Lunch Wall, which was pleasant despite the oppressive heat. We contoured the base of the cliffs to the Christian Brothers formation, where Alan dropped his pack at the base of *Golgotha*, a 5.11 face route with no bolts, a rarity at Smith Rock. Alan threw five pieces of gear on his rack and flew up it like it was 5.6. I managed it well enough but took a short fall when a foothold broke off.

"That's the great thing about climbing at Smith Rock," Alan said, smirking down at me from the belay. "You think you're something special and then, *pow*! You're hanging at the end of your rope, wondering what happened."

He pointed to the base of the climb. "A guy fell off right there last week," he continued, shaking his head sympathetically. "Pulled all his gear and hit the ground. It was ugly."

"Why hasn't somebody bolted this?" I asked. "Everything else is bolted."

"What, and ruin all the fun?" Alan said. "Besides, if somebody had bolted it, that guy wouldn't be able to tell his grandkids the story about how he lost his teeth."

The reason the route had not been bolted was that it had first been climbed in traditional style, back before bolting on rappel had caught on. Even in an ethically challenged backwater such as Smith Rock, the Rawl-wielding hang-doggers had so far respected the sanctity of a traditional ground-up, natu-rally protected lead. It wasn't as if rappel bolting had ever been strictly taboo at Smith Rock: *Revelations*, a 5.9 face climb on the Testament Slab, had been bolted on rappel back in 1975, long before *Watts Tots*, which wasn't bolted until 1983. Nobody ran out to chop *Revelations*, a popular climb, but rap-bolting didn't really catch on until the early 1980s. And even then, nobody was rushing to rappel bolt entire blank faces, at least not yet.

The next morning, I rode with Alan to his parents' home in Madras to pick up some things for the trip. We were back at Volk's trailer by early after-noon, pretty much packed and ready to leave but for one bit of unfinished business: Alan wanted to have one more go at the *East Face* of Monkey Face.

In defiance of gravity, Monkey Face overhangs on all sides. There is no easy route to its summit except the original route, which begins from the highest notch and ascends a bolt ladder to a cave. By walking across the floor of the cave, you can avoid the steepest rock and instead reach the summit via a short vertical step, 5.7 in difficulty. Subsequent routes attacked the overhangs head-on, producing some of the hardest rock climbs in Oregon. By the mid-1980s, several of these original aid routes had been free climbed, but the *East Face* so far had not succumbed. Following an incipient crack up a vertical-to-overhanging wall, this A3 line was one of Alan's long-standing projects, his current nemesis, one of those leaps into the future that Todd had always proselytized about. Over the past year of effort, Alan had pieced together the moves section by section, bolted the line sparsely, and worked it to the point that his fingers were inflamed with tendonitis. Free climbing this route was his obsession, and he could not leave for Tahoe without giving it one last try.

"I don't want to come back in two weeks and find out some hotshot Brit has come and climbed it," Alan said. "I am *not* the best climber in the world, as you know." He had watched Australian climber Kim Carrigan flash the first pitch during his visit that spring and had reason to be concerned.

"Kim gave it a good shot," Alan continued. "If he'd worked on it for a solid week, I think he might have pulled it off. What if Jerry Moffatt shows up tomorrow?"

"I don't think you have anything to worry about," I said. "Who would come here? This is still a pile of crap as far as the climbing world is concerned. It's just not on anybody's radar."

"It will be."

"Well, then, we'd better get down there before Moffatt shows up," I said. "Although, as bad as his tendonitis was in Yosemite, I doubt if Moffatt could get ten feet up it right now."

"I'm hoping to get at least that far," Alan said, contorting his swollen fingers into gruesome claws, then popping another handful of ibuprofen.

We hiked down into the gorge, up the switchbacks to the top of Picnic Lunch Wall, then down the other side to the base of Monkey Face. The east wall was in full shade by the time we reached it. We scrambled up to a broad, sloping ledge at the base of the wall. I lay back and looked up at the tan-and-red-streaked face looming ominously overhead, all but blank except for two thin cracks, one on the far left edge of the face and the other to the right. Alan's rope ran halfway up the wall through a carabiner clipped to a bolt and back down, passing through a few other pieces of gear left behind as backup. He had not pulled the rope as was the usual practice; instead he was yo-yoing, lowering to the ground after each fall but leaving the rope through his highest piece of protection. Although the practice of redpointing a route—which required pulling the rope and all protection before the "send"—had been adopted at Smith Rock during the Thomas era, it wasn't yet the compulsory style. In Alan's view, yo-yoing remained good enough, at least on this route. They were still yo-yoing in Yosemite, and Todd had yo-yoed on *The Stigma*. In any case, there weren't any rock police lurking about, waiting to cite Alan for his stylistic infraction. He tightened his shoelaces as tight as he could, wincing in pain as he pulled. The ibuprofen hadn't kicked in. He tied in, chalked his fingers, and went through his pre-climb routine, pantomiming the moves, eyes closed, visualizing each hold and each sequence of hand and finger placements to the anchors 130 feet above, which took almost two minutes. After a couple of deep breaths, he established himself on the opening holds and pulled delicately onto the wall.

The *East Face* of Monkey Face overhangs consistently, gently at first, then more steeply. Alan climbed to his high point smoothly, without any apparent difficulty despite the fact that the moves were thin and sequential—long reaches between fingertip jams, 5.12 move after 5.12 move. From his high point, the wall reared back through a wave of reddish tuff. The old aid crack was too thin to jam, but the many piton ascents over the years had left pin scars into which one could theoretically stuff one or two fingertips, wrench, and pull. Alan had the physique to pull it off. He was small and wiry, with thin, cable-strong fingers that could cling to the tiniest of holds that a larger, heavier climber could not control, at least not as easily. The crux of this route was not only thin and overhanging but technical as well, requiring an exact sequence of desperately hard moves to succeed. Pulling off this 5.13 crux on top of the hard 5.12 climbing required to get there was near Alan's physical limit, and beyond nearly everyone else's.

Alan almost stuck it on his first try, but soon uttered a familiar oath and let go, falling twenty feet before the rope held. He dangled in space for a few minutes, looking at the rock, massaging his fingers. He finally started swinging until he could reach the rope and pull himself in. He reestablished on the rock, then repeated the sequence through the section where he had fallen. He stuck the move he had missed the first time, held his position for a beat, then let go. He fell again, twenty feet, then asked to be lowered off.

"I almost had it," he said. "Next time. Do you want to try it?"

"No thanks," I declined. "I'd embarrass myself. I'm here to belay you."

"That's what I like about you, Smoot," Alan said. "You're all about me."

Alan took a long rest before he got back on it, massaging his fingers again, then stretching them. After fifteen minutes, he was ready to go. He climbed smoothly up to his high point and pulled through the crux. There was some grunting and groaning, and a couple of swear words along the way. It was not pretty, but it was done. Alan gave a whoop as he clipped the anchors, then pulled up the ropes and rappelled off. He had just established the hardest free climb in America. Not in impeccable style, mind you, but the monkey was finally off Alan's back.

"If anything in America is 5.14, this is it," Alan said as he rappelled down, with not just a hint of irony. "Be sure to quote me on that."

He reached the ledge, sat down, and tried to untie his shoes. He gave up and started rubbing his fingers again.

"But really, I think it's only 5.13d. Let's go see what *The Stigma*'s all about."

WE STUFFED OUR GEAR BEHIND THE SEATS of Alan's pickup truck and headed west to Eugene, on the first leg of our journey to Yosemite. Alan had to make a stop at the Metolius climbing shop to pick up some gear. Back then, the shop was run out of a garage behind Doug Phillips's house in Metolius, Oregon. Phillips handed Alan a rack of small cams and some nuts threaded with various lengths of wire. "Secret weapons," Alan told me, handing them over while he started the truck and got back on the road. From there, we traced the Old McKenzie Highway past black lava fields and the Three Sisters volcanoes and down through forested river valleys into Springfield and Eugene. We stopped at McDonald's for dinner.

"So," Alan said, pulling out a quarter, preparing to school me, "I'll bet you that if I flip this quarter ten times, it won't come up heads or tails five times in a row."

"Sure, what's the bet?"

"Tell you what. If it comes up five times heads or five times tails, in a row, in just ten throws, I'll buy your dinner."

"Here?"

"Yeah. A Big Mac."

"Sure. I'll take it."

"If you lose, you buy me dinner at Degnan's when we get to the Valley."

"Deal."

"I just took a statistics class. Do you know what the odds are against this happening?" he asked, smugly, as if I had just made the stupidest bet ever. He flipped the quarter. It came up heads.

"No. What are they?"

"Astronomical."

He flipped the quarter, caught it, and slapped it on his wrist. Heads again.

"If you say so."

Another flip, heads again. Alan frowned.

"Do you want to throw in some fries and a shake?" I asked.

"No way. A Big Mac. That's the deal."

Heads again.

"What kind of grade did you get in that class, Alan?"

He flipped the quarter up and caught it, then turned his hand over onto his other hand and paused. "This isn't supposed to happen."

"Show me the coin."

"It's not heads. Trust me."

"Show me."

He pulled his hand away to reveal George Washington's shiny silver-plated head.

"What the fuck!"

"That's what you learned in college? How much did you pay for that class?"

Alan didn't buy me a Big Mac. He didn't have enough money, or so he claimed. But I did get a place to crash for the night, on the floor of some guy's house in south Eugene, a couple of beers, and an evening of entertaining conversation that consisted mostly of slandering other climbers, so I didn't complain. But I have not forgotten that, against all odds, Alan Watts owes me a Big Mac.

Early the next morning, we drove back over the mountains to Klamath Falls, where Alan had to make yet another stop, for what I don't remember, although I think it involved a woman. From there, we took back roads to Alturas, California, then went south on 395 through Susanville to Reno, a day's drive that led us to a friend's house where we would spend a few days while Alan tried to make a second free ascent of *Star Walls Crack,* Hidetaka Suzuki's new "5.12+" route at Donner Summit. But first we checked out the Biggest Little City in the World.

Reno reminded me of that all-you-can-eat-buffet casino Todd had dragged me, Beth Wald, and Bill Hatcher to in Vegas before they climbed

Levitation 29. At the big casino in Reno, instead of Siegfried and Roy and their white tigers, they had a guy riding a unicycle on a slack rope juggling flaming batons and chainsaws, which to be honest was really a lot more impressive to me and Alan.

We drove up to Donner Summit the next morning and set upon *Star Walls Crack* in the early afternoon, once the sun was off the climb. The crack was thin and shallow, a vertical seam splitting a flat, overhanging gray-and-orange wall. It ended some sixty feet up the wall at the base of a roof capped by a featureless headwall. A red sling and a yellow sling hung from pitons pounded into the last vestiges of the crack, anchors left in place by Suzuki. Alan spent a few hours working on the route while I belayed him, and then I took photos while his Reno friend belayed him. I gave it a couple of half-assed tries between Alan's efforts and managed to climb the first twenty feet, a boulder problem start that Alan assured me was 5.12b, probably to make me feel better. But for the most part I had to content myself with belaying, taking pictures, and hiking up to the top of the buttress to survey the beautiful subalpine landscape of Donner Pass.

Alan had flown up the initial moves to the horizontal break, where the real climbing started. The crack bottomed out a few inches deep in places; it didn't allow for sinker hand jams like you would find in Yosemite. Alan's sequences involved half-jammed hands, finger locks, and laybacks, with toes jammed in the crack where they would fit, otherwise splayed out on vertical and horizontal edges on the flat, nearly featureless wall. He worked the crack in sections, trying out sequences until one worked, placing cams as he climbed higher, fell off, then tried again. The wall was only slightly overhanging, so it didn't prevent hangdogging; it was easy to swing back in after a fall and reestablish on the rock. As Alan climbed higher, he ran it out more and more above his protection, and the length of his falls increased to the point that, as he neared the anchors, he was taking repeated twenty-foot falls. He worked methodically and efficiently, dialing in the sequences of moves section by section until he reached the anchors. He let go, fell again, and repeated the final moves to the anchors once more to be sure, then clipped the anchors and asked to be lowered off. After only a few hours of work, Alan had it wired. He called it a day. We would return tomorrow for the send.

On the way back to Reno, we stopped at a grocery store. There was a line of video poker machines just inside the door. Despite the astronomical odds against winning, of which Alan was no doubt keenly aware, he put a dollar in a machine. Perhaps he was feeling lucky since I had so recently shown him that dumb luck was apt to prevail over statistical probabilities. He won twenty-five bucks.

"This place is great," he enthused. "You don't need a job. Just put a dollar in the machine and it gives you twenty-five bucks. Now I can afford groceries."

"Maybe you can buy me that Big Mac," I suggested.

"Yeah, sure," Alan retorted. "Where's my gas money?"

"SO, WHAT NOW?" I ASKED, as Alan untied from the rope the next morning, having dispatched *Star Walls Crack* on his first try of the day. It was still early.

"Hey, let's try *Crack of the Eighties*," Alan said. "It's right over there."

"Where?"

"That little buttress there, with the light green lichen, just off on the right side of Snowshed Wall, the big wall there. See it?"

"I think so, but I don't see a crack there."

"It's a thin crack. More of a seam really."

"How hard is it?" I asked.

"Nobody knows," Alan said. "It hasn't been climbed. Hudon and Jones used to try it and they couldn't do it. They said it wouldn't be climbed until the nineteen-eighties, so everybody calls it *Crack of the Eighties*. Lots of people have tried it. Almost everybody tries to toprope it. Let's check it out."

We drove down the road and pulled off in a gravel turnout. We hiked along the base of Snowshed Wall to a steep buttress split by a vertical seam. As we walked, Alan recounted the list of climbers who had tried and failed to climb the crack: Mark Hudon, Max Jones, John Bachar, Ron Kauk, and lately Kurt Smith, "the Kid," an upstart trying to establish himself as the rising star of the next generation of Yosemite hardmen. He had climbed the *Bachar-Yerian* the year before, which hadn't hurt his reputation any. And he had supposedly been trying hard to make the first ascent of *Crack of the Eighties*, hoping it would vault him into the next realm.

"It would be funny," Alan thought out loud as we hiked along, "if I could swoop in and bag the first ascent."

"It looks pretty thin and shallow," I observed, after scrambling up to the base of the buttress. "Maybe there's a reason they've been trying to toprope it."

"Maybe," Alan said. "Let's see."

Alan roped up and I put him on belay. He started climbing, traversing across the blocky, weathered granite wall, then pulling up on a flake and jamming past a little roof to where the tiny crack split a slightly overhanging, green-tinted headwall. He plugged in a cam just above the roof, pulled back on an edge of the crack, and reached for a flaring slot higher up. He stuck it, then started fiddling with a nut that was the wrong size. He put it back on the rack and tried another nut that also didn't work. He pushed off, falling only a few feet onto the cam.

"I can do this," Alan said. "I just need to figure out how to hold on to get a nut in. Hold me here."

After hanging on the rope for a minute, Alan climbed back up to the cam and hung there. He pulled a few HB nuts off of his rack and tried to find a spot where one would fit and hold. Finding a placement he trusted, he pulled up onto the rock and tried to place the nut while in a climbing position. He tried a couple of different hold combinations until he found the one that seemed to work best, then he pulled the nut out and clipped it in the front of his rack.

"That should work," he said. "Lower me."

After a short rest, Alan was back on it. He cruised up to his high point, placed the nut as he had practiced, clipped it, then pulled on the crack edge. He reached up for the slot, stuck it, pulled up, and stuck a higher fingertip jam. He placed a shallow cam and cranked upward, laybacking the thin edge of the seam, placing a nut here and a cam there as he climbed. In a few minutes, he was pulling onto a big ledge. He set a belay and peered down with a big grin on his face.

"Somebody's going to be pissed," Alan called down. "You want to follow?"

"No thanks. I know my limits."

"Okay, suit yourself," Alan said. "I was going to rename it *Watts-Smoot* if you followed it. You would have been famous."

Alan rappelled down to retrieve his gear, then scrambled back up to the top and dropped his rope. By the time he got back down, I had the rope coiled and was ready to depart.

"So, how hard is it?" I asked.

"I don't know. Not as hard as *Star Walls Crack*." Alan had decided that *Star Walls Crack* was 5.12d, so *Crack of the Eighties*, seeming easier, must be 5.12c. "I mean, I practically walked up it," he said. "How hard could it be?"

We hiked back to the truck, wondering why, given the amount of effort over the past decade, nobody had been able to climb *Crack of the Eighties* before, even on a toprope. Plenty of solid 5.12 climbers had tried it. Why hadn't they been able to climb this "miserable, busted-up seam," as Alan was referring to it? Alan had a theory, which he explained to me on the drive back to Reno.

"They're good enough," Alan explained, "but they don't hangdog, so they get stuck on a crux move or section and keep falling off at the same spot and get tired and give up before they work it out. Or they get a mental block, so the route becomes bigger and harder in their minds. It psyches them out, and they fail.

"A hard route is like a gymnastic routine," Alan continued, "a sequence of difficult elements linked together in a routine. Imagine if a gymnast didn't wire each element before putting it all together, but had to start over every time they screwed up? It would take them ten times as long to do it. Same thing with the Valley climbers. Their ethics are holding them back. I know why they're doing it, and I think it's admirable, but it's counterproductive. They sit around complaining. 'He's a hangdogger. It's not a legitimate ascent.' Meanwhile, everybody else is climbing all these hard routes. The sport is changing. They need to get with the program or get left behind. I mean, this route, they've been trying to toprope it for ten years, and I come in and lead it on my second try?"

"I think you could have done it without hanging," I suggested.

"Maybe," Alan conceded. "It wasn't as hard as I thought it was going to be. I guess if I had known it was that easy I would have approached it differently. But for all I knew, it was going to be really hard and I was going to be falling off a lot. I needed to be sure I had at least one good piece of protection. Having that one good nut made all the difference. And I placed it on lead, and did the whole route in one go without falling or hanging, so it's a legitimate ascent.

"They'll complain about it anyway," Alan continued. "I'm a bolt-drilling hangdogger. Everything I do is suspect."

We drove back to Reno in the late afternoon shadows, delving deeper into the psyche of Yosemite climbers along the way. In the morning, we would be on the road to the Valley so Alan could give *The Stigma* a try. If he could bag the second free ascent of *The Stigma*, it would be a coup de grâce, a fatal dagger in the heart of the last bastion of traditional ethics, or so I imagined it. With all the controversy Todd Skinner had stirred up with his ascent that spring, I was not sure I was looking forward to Alan potentially repeating the route. But Alan didn't want to make a statement. He just wanted to take the measure of this new, hard route that might, just might, be 5.14.

THE 5.14 BARRIER HAD ALREADY BEEN BROKEN, only not in the States. At least there was not a verified, consensus 5.14 route in America as of August 1985. Wolfgang Gullich's route *Punks in the Gym*, established that April at Australia's Mount Arapiles, was rated 32 on the Australian scale, which translated to 5.14a, a notch harder than Stefan Glowacz's *Lord of the Rings*, also at Arapiles, rated 31 or 5.13d. (John Sherman would immortalize *Lord of the Rings* by posing for a photo while clipped to a hidden bolt, pretending to free solo the route in his sandals while drinking a beer.) The fact that two German climbers had established the hardest free climbs in Australia more than hinted at the efficacy of the European approach to hard free climbing. American climbers who were open to adopting the so-called Euro tactics were determined to establish a 5.14 in the United States before some hotshot foreigner did the deed.

So far, foreign visitors to the States had been content to repeat established hard climbs in better style, hence all of the flashing of 5.12 and 5.13 routes across the country. Alan had come close to 5.14 on the *East Face* of Monkey Face, and Todd had apparently come close on *The Stigma*, but nobody had cracked the barrier, not yet. But it wouldn't be long. Alan had projects at Smith Rock that would be 5.14 when he finished them. He was sure of that.

25 MY FANS ADORE ME

The pitons were long gone, having been whacked out by incensed Yosemite locals the day after Todd climbed *The Stigma*. We already knew this. We'd also heard rumors that, in their zeal, the locals had deliberately widened some of the pin scars to make the route easier, so it couldn't be 5.14. It was a big enough sore spot with the Valley locals already; if it turned out to be 5.14, every piece of hangdogging Eurotrash would be on it, rubbing salt in the wound.

Alan and I were the only ones there, which was fortunate. I did not want to get caught up in a confrontation with any of the Valley locals. I was leery of anyone finding out what we were up to. To Alan, it was just part of the fun.

"Hey, where is everybody?" Alan wondered aloud as we walked up to the Cookie Cliff. "I thought they'd be here with pitchforks throwing rotten eggs and tomatoes."

"They'll be here tomorrow, I'm sure," I said. "As soon as word gets out, they'll be here."

Alan turned his pack upside down and shook out his rack, which clanked like steel as it hit the ground. Among the tangled mess of slings, chocks, and carabiners were a dozen Lost Arrow pitons.

"You know," I said thoughtfully, picking up the rack and giving the pins a pointed look, "you might want to see if you can lead it on gear. They might not be so pissed off if you don't fix gear. They really hated that Todd had placed pins on rappel to protect it."

"Now why would I want to do that?" Alan asked.

"Just to see if it can be done," I replied. "I don't know if Todd even bothered to see if it could be protected with gear. When I told Charles Cole that Todd had preplaced pins, he was livid. They all thought that was bullshit, and I guess it *was* bullshit if it could have been done from the ground up.

You should at least see if you can do it in better style, even just a little better. They might even accept it, or at least not hate you as much, because you tried."

"Hmm," Alan said, seeming to be giving it some thought. "Smoot, when did you get to be such a pain in the ass?"

"Just now, I guess."

"I doubt that."

Alan did his recon ascent, freeing the initial 5.12 section easily, then aiding up to the stance where Todd had finished his free ascent. He climbed slowly and meticulously, studying the crack to see where a nut or cam might fit without plugging up a pin scar or slot where he would have to stuff his fingers or toes. This was why Todd had opted to preplace pins: He was able to whack them into the thinnest parts of the crack, into places where his fingers would not fit, leaving the best jams wide open. Plus, he could space them at convenient intervals where he could clip them more easily, resulting in shorter falls. What Todd did was anathema to traditional crack climbing. Climbing a crack on lead-placed gear meant taking what the rock gave you and making the best of it. Preplacing fixed pins every six feet up the crack was, in some ways, no better than bolting it, other than that you weren't drilling a hole every six feet, which made it only slightly less offensive.

Alan continued aiding past Todd's no-hands stance to the bolt anchor at the end of the crack, another twenty feet higher, whacking in a couple of pitons because the crack was too shallow and flared at the end to take any-thing else. When he reached the anchor bolt, I had him haul up my old rope and fix it so I could shoot photos of him leading, if we could find someone at Camp 4 willing to come along to belay, which seemed unlikely. More likely, I thought, we would ask someone to belay, and they would sneak out during the night and pull my rope and shit on it instead.

Alan rappelled slowly, hanging here and there as he slid down the rope, pulling on the edges of the crack, poking his fingers into pin scars this way and that, feeling the rock like a blind man reading a Braille book. He inspected nubbins and crystals as potential footholds and fiddled with cams and nuts to determine where protection would best fit. By the time he reached the ground he had a rack of a dozen pieces that included no pitons.

"Go ahead," I said. "Tell me I was right."

"Shut up, Smoot."

The preliminaries completed, Alan was ready to start working the route on toprope—the usual method employed by hangdoggers to practice the moves on a route before committing to the lead. He had left his rope hanging for just this purpose.

"No way," I said. "You should try to lead it from the ground up. If you do a full-on hangdog ascent, you'll just piss off the locals. At least try it from the ground up."

"Jesus, Smoot!" Alan said. "What are you, some kind of ethics coach?"

"Nope," I said. "Just your belayer."

"Good God," he said, shaking his head. "Why did I bring you along on this trip? I should go get John Bachar to belay me."

"Hey, if it doesn't work out, I'll jug up the fixed rope and reset your toprope for you," I offered. "Just give it a try. What's the worst that could happen?"

"I could fall off and pull all my gear and land face-first on this boulder."

"Just think of the story you could tell your grandkids."

ALAN GAVE IT A TRY ON LEAD, and by the time it was getting dark he had led about halfway to the stance, again cruising the initial 5.12 section and then working out a few moves before falling and hanging. After practicing a move or sequence a couple of times, he would have me lower him off and he would start over from the ground, pull through the moves where he had fallen previously, set another nut or cam, clip it, then fall off the next move and repeat the process: a garden-variety hangdog ascent that somewhat respected the local ground-up effort. If Bachar could toprope a route before leading it, or lead it placing bolts from hooks, there didn't seem to be much wrong with Alan aiding the route first and then leading it, placing all gear on lead. No bolts. No fixed pins. No preplaced chocks. The monkeying around while hanging on the rope after taking honest falls didn't bother me. I could never quite figure out why it bothered the Yosemite locals so much.

After Alan's final effort of the day, I swung the fixed rope over to where he could grab it and he rappelled off, removing all of the gear he had placed. We hiked off into the twilight, leaving behind only my old rope, which I was sure I would never see again, at least intact and undefiled.

In the morning, Alan decided to take a rest day. His fingers were sore from all of the thin jamming. He'd made good progress and was confident he could finish the job with a little rest. I was worried about my fixed rope being stolen or vandalized, though, so Alan drove me down to the Cookie Cliff and dropped me off.

"I'll be back later," Alan said. "If you aren't here when I come back, I'll assume you've been thrown off the cliff."

I sat there all day, guarding my rope from the Valley locals who I imagined were lurking nearby. I didn't care much about the rope itself. The sheath had been cut or worn through in places, and it was faded and dirty. But I wanted to use it to take photos of Alan on the route—photos I hoped to sell to a magazine. If the rope got cut down, I would not be able to get it back up there. So I sat on a boulder at the base of the cliff the whole day, reading a book and keeping a wary eye on my investment.

The only Valley local I saw that day was John Bachar, who came by in the early afternoon. He paused briefly at the base of the route and looked up inquisitively. I imagined he was looking for signs of foul play, for fixed pitons or rappel bolts or such. Maybe he knew Alan was in the Valley and assumed Alan was out here. I don't think he did, though, or other Valley climbers would have come around. After a minute, Bachar continued walking up the road right past me without so much as a nod or sideways glance. That was fine with me. I did not want to get into a debate with Bachar.

He swaggered back down the road a half hour later, having soloed something farther up the cliff. He looked up at the crack again as he passed, then departed without a word. The gig was up. Even though I hadn't spoken a word, everyone would now know that someone was in the Valley working on *The Stigma*. Alan would no doubt be spotted in Camp 4, and some genius would put two and two together and convene an angry mob.

Alan came back to get me later in the afternoon. I did not want to leave my rope, certain it would be gone in the morning. But I was hungry and tired of sitting there and aware that I could not stay all night.

"Did you have fun, Jeffrey?" Alan asked sarcastically.

"I did," I said. "John Bachar came by. He says you are the devil incarnate."

"That's so nice of him to say."

"He said something about your mom, too. I forget what."

"Well, he and my mom go way back."

THE VALLEY WAS FAIRLY VACANT for mid-August, occupied mostly by foreigners it seemed. Alan had not run into anyone he knew who might belay him on *The*

Stigma so I could take pictures. Then again, Alan had also not run into any-one who might come out, pull down my rope, and shit on it. Still, if we could not find a belayer, I'd be stuck taking unpublishable butt shots, which nobody would want to see.

We went to Yosemite Village and bought food for dinner and the next day. As luck would have it, two Japanese climbers were in front of us in the check-out line. They became very animated, talking excitedly and pointing at Alan as we waited behind them.

"Alan Watts?" one whispered.

"Alan Watts!" the other exclaimed.

"You are Alan Watts?" one of them finally got up the nerve to ask Alan.

"Why, yes," Alan said, quite magnanimously. "Yes I am."

"Ah. Very pleased meet you, Alan Watts."

They bowed deeply and shook Alan's hand and smiled and laughed like a couple of schoolgirls backstage at a Van Halen concert. They were thrilled to meet the very famous Alan Watts, who was apparently a celebrity in Japanese climbing circles. Alan played the object of adoration with only the faintest hint of mockery.

"Alan," I whispered, "get them to come with us tomorrow morning. We need a belayer so I can take some pictures."

Alan arched an eyebrow and nodded.

"So, where are you guys climbing tomorrow?" he asked slyly. "Do you want to come to the Cookie Cliff? I'm going to climb *The Stigma*."

"Oh. *The Stigma*. Todd Skinner. *The Renegade*. Yes! Yes! We come, okay?"

"Yes, okay. Meet us there at ten o'clock."

"Okay, yes. Ten o'clock. We see you there right on the time, okay?"

They bought their groceries and we bought ours and they followed us out to the parking lot, talking excitedly and bowing. Alan had to extricate himself from this socially awkward situation, and did so as politely as possible. They were still standing there, waving, as we drove away.

"Good grief," I said.

"What can I say?" Alan said. "My fans adore me."

KURT SMITH WAS STANDING by the kiosk at the end of the Camp 4 parking lot, talking with a group of climbers. I hesitated and started to walk the other way. Alan started toward them.

"Don't do it," I said.

"What?" Alan asked, feigning innocence. "I'm just going to say hi."

"Don't."

"Hey, Kurt," Alan said casually as he approached Smith, as if he had nothing much to say.

"Hey, Alan," Smith said, almost sneering. "You're working on *The Stigma*, huh? That route is such bullshit. Skinner didn't even climb it. He aided it."

"It's still pretty hard," Alan said. "I'm going to try it ground-up, no pins."

"No hangdogging?"

"I'll work out the moves," Alan said. "I already worked on it some yesterday. It isn't that hard. Have you tried it?"

"No. I wouldn't try it," Smith said, now definitely sneering. "It's a hangdog route."

"Hey," Alan said, changing the subject, "I was just up at Donner Summit."

"Yeah?"

"Yeah. I did *Star Walls Crack*. It was 5.12d, pretty hard."

"Yeah?" Kurt said, standoffishly.

"Yeah," Alan said. "And I climbed *Crack of the Eighties*."

Kurt's eyes narrowed. He stared at Alan.

"You climbed *Crack of the Eighties*?"

"Just a couple of days ago," Alan admitted. "It's not really that hard. Maybe 5.12c."

"Did you toprope it?"

"No. I led it."

"Did you hang?"

"Just once to figure out where an RP would fit in. I did it on my second try."

"That's bullshit," Smith said, his face turning red. "My grandmother could have climbed the route that way."

"I'm sure your grandmother could have climbed the route," Alan replied, trying hard to suppress a smirk. "It wasn't very hard."

Smith's hands curled up into fists. I thought he might punch Alan, but instead he launched into an apoplectic rage, cursing Alan and the horse he rode in on for desecrating his sacred project. I knew how he felt. Kurt loved that route; his sense of self depended on the mythology of him making the first ascent in perfect style. He had worked on it for years, following the rules, making love to it instead of seducing it, only to have it stolen away from him by this punk, this hangdogging route rapist Alan Watts.

"That's fucking bullshit!" Kurt said. "Bullshit," he repeated as he strode off angrily.

"Thanks, Alan," I said as we walked away. "Now we're in for it."

"I wouldn't worry about it," Alan said. "What's the worst they could do."

"I don't know. Burn your truck? Smear the crack with shit?"

"Wouldn't that be something," Alan said thoughtfully.

AFTER ALAN'S ALTERCATION WITH Kurt Smith, I braced myself for a torch-wielding mob at the Cookie Cliff the next day, but we arrived to an empty parking lot. We hiked to the base of the cliff and there was my rope, still hanging from the bolt, apparently untouched. I tugged hard on it to be sure someone hadn't loosened the knot to sabotage me. I sniffed it. Nobody had defiled it as far as I could tell.

"See?" Alan said. "Nothing to worry about."

It wasn't long, though, before a strange chorus of owl-like hooting and screeching started up. "Hangdogger! Haaaaang-dogger!" someone yelled.

The hoots continued for a while, seeming to come from a half dozen lurkers camouflaged among the trees and boulders on a ridge a hundred or so yards away, spying from afar but unwilling to reveal themselves.

"Must be some of the locals come to welcome you," I said to Alan.

"It is awfully nice of them to do that," he said. "I'm touched."

Our Japanese friends showed up shortly, and after they assured Alan that they knew how to belay and could understand simple English commands such as "take," "slack," and "falling," I jugged up the fixed rope with my cameras and film and got into position to shoot a couple of rolls of Alan working on the route. Alan put on his rock shoes—a La Sportiva Mariacher on his left foot and a Boreal Firé on the right, to maximize his ability to edge, smear, and jam as needed on the limited footholds. He clipped his minimal rack to his harness loops, checked his knot, made sure his Japanese belayer really, really knew what he was doing, and started climbing.

Alan got past his previous day's high point on his first try before finally falling off. He hung for a minute, pulled himself back onto the rock, rehearsed a sequence, then let go and lowered off to a renewed round of hooting from the woodsy knoll. The Japanese climbers looked off at the hooters and then at each other, puzzled. After a brief rest, Alan tried again, climbing a few feet higher. From his high point, he placed a brass nut specially made by Doug Phillips. It was a standard-issue RP nut, but with a longer cable so it could be placed out of reach of a standard RP—a secret weapon that extended Alan's reach by six inches and avoided the use of a fixed pin at that particular spot. He clipped the rope in and continued climbing, placing another nut five feet higher. At a point where his feet were just above the nut and he was engaged in a complex sequence of outward side pulls and pinkie jams, he realized he was going to fall off. "Take!" he yelled, then let go, expecting to take a short, controlled fall of perhaps ten feet. Instead, he fell and kept on falling, and didn't stop until thirty feet later when the rope finally came tight with Alan dangling upside down ten feet off the deck.

"What the fuck?" Alan said, looking down at the belayer. "I said *take!*"

"Slack?" the belayer asked, preparing to give Alan some more slack.

"Take! Take!"

"Oh. Take. Sorry."

"Okay," Alan said, shaking his head then looking up at me, dumbfounded. "Lower me."

Alan was fuming but said nothing further. I rappelled down, knowing I was done taking photos for the day. We told our Japanese friends that Alan was going to take a long rest and that I had all the photos I needed, so they didn't have to hang around all afternoon. They waited for a while, hoping to see Alan climb the route, but we outlasted them. Eventually they nodded and bowed and said goodbye, finally getting that we were giving them the bum's rush.

THE LONG REST DID ALAN GOOD. He sent the pitch, repeating Todd's route up to the ledge on his next try. The crux involved cranking up several small, well-spaced pin scars, including a straight pull on one finger twisted in a slot and one of the most improbable Gaston moves I have ever seen accomplished, applying counterforce to opposite sides of the crack where it was too thin to jam while smearing on minute ripples and edges. He ran out the last fifteen feet to the ledge, placed a cam, then jammed his fingers into the crack above it and levered himself up to a standing position.

"Flip that rope over to me, would you?" Alan asked.

"No way," I told him. "You should finish it. It isn't free until it is all free."

"Damn it, Smoot," Alan insisted. "Flip me the rope."

"Hold on there," I insisted back. "You've repeated Todd's climb, but there's still twenty feet of crack that's what, 12a?"

"So?"

"If this was at Smith Rock, would you stop there?"

"No," Alan admitted.

"There you go."

Todd had been criticized for stopping short of the end of the crack. Since Todd had fixed pins in the lower half of the crack, he could easily have fixed one more pin in the last twenty feet of the crack and finished the climb. He did not, I suspect, because the hard climbing was over at the stance, and he didn't want to blow it on the 5.12 moves to the top and have to start over from the bottom. Once he had managed to climb the 5.13 section, he wanted it to be over. I explained all of this to Alan as I held him hostage on belay. Under my implied threat not to lower him off unless he kept climbing, Alan agreed to give it a try.

There was the matter of protection. Alan didn't have any more gear on his rack. He had carried a pared-down rack with only the gear he needed to get to the stance. The upper crack needed a piton. He needed a hammer. He hadn't expected to succeed so quickly and wasn't prepared even to place piton anchors to rappel off. He had planned to rappel off using my fixed rope. The cam he had placed above the stance was protection enough for the moment.

"Okay, smart guy. Now what?"

"I'll tie some pitons and a hammer to my rope. You can pull them up, then place a pin and go for it. You can place pins on the lead and then climb up to the end of the crack and clip in to the anchor."

"Easy for you to say."

"You can do it."

It went pretty much as I had suggested. Alan hauled up the hammer and pitons with one hand, pulling an arm's length of rope up and holding it in his teeth, then pulling up another arm's length of rope, and so on, until he could untie the gear and clip it to his harness. Alan whacked in a piton at the ledge, then free climbed a couple of moves above the ledge, whacked in another pin while hanging off a finger jam, clipped it, did a move, fell, hung, tried the move again, then lowered to the stance, shook out both hands, and climbed through to the end of the crack like it was nothing—a yo-yo ascent on the last bit, sure, and some shenanigans pulling up gear, no doubt, but still a complete free ascent of the entire crack. Unfortunately, the anchor was well out of reach from the end of the crack. There was an intermediate bolt between the crack and the anchor, but it could not be clipped from the crack. Lacking a better plan, Alan lunged past it for the anchor sling but missed and fell. He lowered back to the stance, then climbed up and tried again, with the same result.

"If the anchors were a foot lower and to the left, it would be perfect," he said.

"How about tying a sling to that bolt so you can clip in without lunging?" I suggested. "Just use that bolt as the anchor for the end of the pitch?"

Alan gave it a gander. "That might work."

I tied a long sling to the fixed rope and Alan pulled it up, pulled himself up the fixed rope to the anchor, tied the sling to the bolt, then lowered himself back onto the lead rope. I lowered him to the no-hands stance, and after a short rest he climbed through from the stance to the top of the crack, reached up easily to clip a carabiner to the sling, then pulled up a bight of rope and clipped it, and that was that. Alan swung over to the anchor and clipped in, untied my fixed rope and dropped it, and rappelled off using his rope. He pulled his gear but left the two pins he'd fixed in the upper crack, even though he knew they would be gone by morning.

ALAN'S REPEAT ASCENT OF *THE STIGMA* had, we hoped, given it an air of legitimacy. It was not a perfect ascent, but it wasn't bad considering the shenanigans that had preceded. A decade later, no one would have thought twice about lowering the anchors to the top of the crack and calling that the end of the route. In fact, within only a few years, the anchors had been lowered and two bolts had been added to the pitch, a sign that sport climbing had gained a measure of acceptance—even in the Valley. Not only were climbers rappel bolting blank face routes, they were rappel bolting next to perfectly good cracks that had been led free without bolts.

But back then, even though Alan's ascent was done in much better style than Todd's, it was still considered a travesty by Yosemite climbing mores. Alan's ascent was instantly discounted by the locals, including the few who had been lurking in the bushes below, watching, eager to report back to the denizens of Camp 4 that Alan had totally hangdogged the route, preplaced gear, pulled up on pins, chiseled holds, and all of that, most of which was entirely untrue.

"So, how hard is it?" I asked Alan as we coiled the ropes and packed our gear for the hike back to the lot.

"I don't know," Alan said, looking up at the crack, massaging his aching fingers. "All I can say is, it's not 5.14."

By the time we arrived back at the truck, the lurkers were gone but they had left their mark: a cute picture of a doggy drawn in the dust on the rear window, with some censorable commentary about Alan's sexual orientation. After a good laugh, we departed the Valley. It had been the shortest, strangest trip to Yosemite I had ever made.

26 THE VALLEY SYNDROME

"Are you sure you want me to print this?" Michael Kennedy asked over the phone. "It's going to generate a lot of controversy."

He was referring to an unsolicited opinion piece I'd written after returning home from Yosemite. After the shitstorm of controversy that arose over Todd Skinner's and then Alan Watts's ascents of *The Stigma*, I was, one might say, a little pissed off. People had written a lot of negative, untrue, and unkind things about Todd and Alan. Some of them had their facts right and expressed their opinions in a respectful manner. But some were arrogant assholes about the whole thing, so I decided I would be one, too. In the piece, I excoriated the Yosemite locals, calling them out for thinking themselves the best climbers in America when the facts demonstrated otherwise. Aside from some hard big wall routes, they hadn't done anything lately that matched the pure difficulty of what Todd, Alan, and all the foreign climbers were doing. Sure, John Bachar could still solo circles around everybody, except maybe Peter Croft, and Ron Kauk and a few other Valley climbers were no doubt as technically proficient as any of the foreign hotshots, but the whole lot of them seemed content to do hard boulder problems and repeat the same old routes. Both Jerry Moffatt and Kim Carrigan had said as much. So I took it upon myself to give the Yosemite contingent a kick in the pants to try to snap them out of it.

"Yes," I told Kennedy with only a little hesitation. "I'm sure."

"Okay," he said. "I'll run it in the next issue."

"THERE'S A PROBLEM GRIPPING PART of the American climbing scene," it began. "It's what's wrong with American climbing, plain and simple. It's called the 'Valley Syndrome.' The Valley Syndrome is a kind of creeping lethargy, a sedentary stagnation that cloaks Yosemite Valley in a shroud of complacency. . . . There are pockets of resistance, of course, but according to a number of recent visitors to the so-called Mecca of world rock climbing, the Valley scene is dead."

And so it went, bad-mouthing Bachar, Kauk, and every other Yosemite climber by implication, pointing out what everybody already knew: that visiting foreigners such as Moffatt, Carrigan, and Wolfgang Gullich were making a mockery of local standards, climbing our hardest routes, often on-sight, when the ethical elitists who proclaimed themselves the best climbers in the country would not even try them because they were "hangdog" routes. "Why are foreign climbers willing and able to do our hardest routes in excellent style when the 'Best of America' won't go near them?" I asked rhetorically.

The answer, of course, was that with only a few exceptions, the best American climbers were still climbing in an ethical fog, holding themselves back for the sake of purity of ascent instead of pushing the standards of gymnastic difficulty. For pointing out this obvious truth, I received death threats. I heard from more than one source that one of the leaders of the Valley tribe said, "I'm going to kill that asshole Smoot if he ever sets foot in the Valley again!" This surprised me a bit, since I had helped on a rescue with that particular climber the previous spring and he had seemed like a decent person, helping me fill out the paperwork to get paid for carrying some injured climber's pack down to the rescue van. But I guess I had it coming.

Because of my article, I was for a time the least popular person among the majority of California climbers—and ethically minded climbers everywhere, really. A war of words erupted; letters to the editor flooded in, some supporting my view and some opposing it, all vehemently. My critics were correct. "The Valley Syndrome" was a piece of crap ("bullshit" is what they called it), an overly simplistic "good guys" versus "bad guys" diatribe with jingoistic overtones. It lit a fuse, unleashing a stream of follow-up articles and debates, which further polarized the tricksters against the traditionalists. The schism in the sport of free climbing in America had been simmering for years, and now it was boiling over. I'd exercised the nuclear option, dropped the bomb, and it had exploded fantastically. Along with everyone else, I would have to deal with the fallout.

I don't know if "The Valley Syndrome" really was a catalyst for the shift that followed, a veritable shot heard round the climbing world that led to or at least precipitated the downfall of traditional climbing elitism and the uprising of youthful iconoclasm—a symbolic tearing down of the wall that had separated trickster from traditionalist. Maybe it was just a terribly written, juvenile rant that didn't make much of an impact other than to piss off a lot of climbers and further entrench them in their long-suffering stasis. In retrospect, I think of it as just one of many shots fired in a battle that had nothing to do with winning or losing a war.

Neil Cannon, a brash Colorado climber, wrote a response to my editorial he called "The Smoot Syndrome," which came out in the next issue of *Climbing*, along with a lot of the nicer letters to the editor. (The magazine received hundreds of mean, nasty letters in response to "The Valley Syndrome" that weren't fit for publication. "They called you everything you can imagine," Michael Kennedy told me, "and then some.") Although no one seemed to come to my defense outright, several readers chastised Cannon for being even more outrageously off base and mean-spirited in his diatribe. Then came Christian Griffith's "Manifesto," a declaration of complete revolution against the old traditionalist mores. "Climbing needs no shaggy watchdogs, whose low growl disguises their worn teeth, teeth worn through snapping in their own selfish interests," Griffith wrote. "Let the tyrants burn, the climbing dynamic must live!" Todd Skinner followed in *Rock & Ice* with comments in an interview titled "The Future Is Now," urging climbers not to wait to push their limits or be restrained by the naysayers lest they miss out on a once-in-a-lifetime opportunity. And later, Alan Watts wrote "Eurotrends," explaining how his approach at Smith Rock, which mirrored the European approach to establishing and climbing the hardest free climbs, was not only legitimate but preferable. The tricksters were in full revolt, flooding the magazines with their Euro-sport-friendly propaganda. Naturally, the traditionalists fought back. Interviews of Ron Kauk and John Bachar were published in *Climbing*, in which they presented their arguments against trickster tactics. For a long time, every issue of *Climbing* and *Rock & Ice* contained at least one article advocating or denouncing hangdogging and rappel bolting, and the letters to the editor bordered on vitriolic, full of "descriptive salvos of rhetorical diarrhea" and "mud-slinging" that "rivals that of the political arena" according to various correspondents. It was, in a small sense, a revolutionary war, and people were taking sides.

Ironically, many of the stalwart traditionalists who railed most vocally against me or against hangdogging and rappel bolting in general—including Kurt Smith and Ron Kauk and a whole host of other Yosemite locals—changed their collective tune only a few years later, adopting those despised tactics under the justification that the hardest routes could not be climbed without a rappel-placed bolt or two, or even preplaced gear in cracks. It was as if they had been repressed under a dictatorial, elitist regime. Before long, Kauk was rappel bolting new routes in Yosemite Valley and getting into fistfights in the Camp 4 parking lot defending his right to do so. And it was Kauk who eventually established Yosemite's first 5.14 route, *Magic Line*, a desperately thin crack that he protected with preplaced gear. Even Kurt Smith, for all of his vitriolic rage against hangdogging, was soon rappel bolting 5.13 face routes in Tuolumne Meadows in defiance of the local ordinance. He would become one of the leaders of the US sport climbing movement.

Not everybody changed sides, though. There still is, and will always be, a small group of zealous defenders of the faith, members of a highly persecuted religious minority who will forever rail against hangdogging, rappel bolting, and whatever other perceived climbing transgression they are compelled to object to. They are out there. If you don't believe me, read the message boards.

27 SMITH ROCK, USA

In the fall of 1985, I pitched an article to *Mountain* magazine about the hard new climbs at Smith Rock. *Mountain's* editor at the time, Bernard Newman, accepted it and wanted it right away. So before I knew it, I was driving back to Smith Rock. I must have driven down to Smith Rock six times in September and October to work on the article, take photos, and hang out and climb with Alan Watts and the usual cast of locals—Kent Benesch, Chris Grover, and Brooke Sandahl. Six hours down straight after my temp job on Friday, then six hours back late Sunday night, weekend after weekend.

Despite Kim Carrigan, Geoff Weigand, and Jonny Woodward's visit that spring, Smith Rock had fallen back into locals-only mode. There were a few more visitors than before—a German here, a Canadian there, a small swarm of Japanese climbers including Hidetaka Suzuki, a return visit by Woodward, who had stayed on in the States—but for the most part the same half dozen climbers seemed to be the only ones there. I became a semi-local that season, which meant I had hung around so much that the other locals would talk to me and allow me to belay them, and vice-versa, and I was permitted to hang out in and camp behind Mike Volk's trailer, with full kitchen privileges. But the true sign of acceptance into the tribe was that I was now subjected to near-constant verbal abuse by Alan, Grover, and Sandahl—mostly good-natured and well-deserved trash talk.

Most of the abuse resulted from the article I was writing, or more accurately, the article they were allowing me to write, contingent on their approval of the final manuscript, which was by no means assured. At first a couple of the locals weren't very excited about me, an outsider, putting together an article about their area, especially after I let them read my first draft. They ripped it to shreds, literally, after figuratively lighting it on fire and stomping on the ashes.

That kind of peer review is a good thing if you have the stomach for it. It was constructive criticism, better than the "thanks for your submission, but . . ." rejection letter that writers become accustomed to. At least the Smith Rock tribe let me rewrite the story, over and over again. Each time I made a trip down to Smith Rock, I handed them a new draft to rip into. After about the sixth draft laboriously typed on a new IBM Selectric typewriter, my article finally won their disgruntled approval. Of course it did. I was practically calling their little mud heap one of the greatest rock climbing areas in the world.

"Among those rock climbing areas famous for their excellent rock, sunny weather, or abundance of extreme routes," I wrote, "Smith Rock is about to take its proper place. If you haven't heard of Smith Rock before, don't let it bother you. Up until a few years ago, no one in America had heard of it either. And, although it still isn't a favourite destination of this country's climbers— that still being Yosemite—Smith Rock is rapidly earning a reputation as one of the premier free-climbing centres in America; and judging by an increasing number of foreign visitors, perhaps Smith Rock is among the best in the world."

In late October 1985, I scurried home and mailed it off to Bernard Newman with my best photos. The article was rushed to press and came out in the January/February 1986 issue of *Mountain*. I could not wait to see it. I envisioned a glorious spread of my photos accompanying the article. I'd sent in shots of various climbers in action on a bunch of the most photogenic routes: *Watts Tots*, *Slow Burn*, *Latest Rage*, *Sunshine Dihedral*, *Chain Reaction*, *Midnight Snack*, *Monkey Space*, *Moons of Pluto*, and more. I hoped one would make the cover.

Unknown to me, an Austrian climber, Heinz Zak, had visited Smith Rock for a week that fall after I had departed with my completed manuscript. In addition to being a climber of some repute, Zak was also a fair photographer, and had persuaded Alan to pose for photos on some of Smith Rock's finest routes. When my advance copy of *Mountain* 107 arrived, I pulled it out to see—much to my dismay—a shot of Alan nearly upside down on the golden sunlit arête of *Chain Reaction*, seemingly suspended by some magician's trick above the pointed crest of the Smith Rock Group. It was a beautiful shot, dramatic and brilliantly composed—and, disappointingly, not mine. Far better than any photograph I had submitted, it was deserving of the cover.

Inside the magazine, I found that Zak had submitted more photos: an upward sweeping shot of a climber on *Sunshine Dihedral* in full sun; a brilliant full-page shot of Alan leading *Close Shave*, a 5.12 route up the veritable chin of Monkey Face, showing the *East Face* in full sunlight; and a shot looking down at Alan leading up the crux of the *East Face*, looking *très* casual in his Wayfarer sunglasses. There were also a couple of shots by Kim Carrigan: one of Jonny Woodward making an on-sight ascent of *Split Image*, and one of Geoff Weigand on *Slow Burn*. Out of the ten photos that accompanied the article, three were mine. I couldn't be too disappointed about it, though; the article was gorgeous.

The combined effect was a postcard from a faraway land of sunshine and warm, golden rock, where a small group of misfit climbers had quietly developed the hardest free climbs in America. "Come to America!" it shouted to climbers everywhere. "Come to Smith Rock, where all your wildest dreams can come true."

IN THE SPRING OF 1986, instead of going to Joshua Tree where I had faithfully gone each spring for the past several years, I went to Smith Rock. As I drove south from Madras and Monkey Face came into view, I found myself looking forward to an evening hike through the deserted rockscape or a bouldering session among the basalt columns just off the picnic area, followed by dinner at La Siesta, either by myself or with any Smith Rock locals who happened to be lurking about.

Instead I found the parking lot overflowing with cars, trucks, and vans from seemingly everywhere: Washington, British Columbia, Idaho, Oregon, New York, Connecticut, Virginia, Utah, Wyoming, California. There were vehicles lined up on the side of the road nearly to Juniper Junction. Climbers were sprawled all over the picnic area and the rocks throughout the park, gaily festooned in gaudy Lycra tights, hangdogging on everything. Todd Skinner was there; the Wyoming plates on his white VW van gave him away. Russ Erickson, our local dirtbag savant, was there in his Opel station wagon parked in Mike Volk's driveway. British expat Jonny Woodward was there, hanging out at Mike's place. Current British upstart Mick Johnston was there. So were a contingent of Japanese climbers, a regiment of Colorado climbers, and a boatload of other talented climbers from other distant places. It was, to put it mildly, a shit show.

The locals seemed a bit stunned by the invasion. Not exactly displeased, just startled by Smith Rock's newfound popularity. They hadn't counted on this. The write-up in *Mountain*, and especially Zak's compelling photos, had overnight transformed this formerly obscure western-themed state park into a virtual Disneyland of rock. Clearly they were going to need a bigger parking lot.

I, too, was caught off guard, and frankly disappointed, in an admittedly hypocritical way. I had come to know Smith Rock as a place of quietude, a pastoral commons where, on some days, more dead cows might come floating down the Crooked River than human beings might scramble over Asterisk Pass, where more vultures could be seen circling overhead than climbers on the rocks, where one might disappear for an afternoon into the lonesomeness of the western frontier and feel miles away from everywhere. Not wilderness, but still a place bigger than all of the human activity it could muster. And now? Now everybody and their dog seemed to have come to Smith Rock, there was no space in the lot, and you had to wait your turn to get on the routes.

I parked in front of Mike's trailer and hiked down into the Crooked River Gorge and along the trail to the Dihedrals, where most of the climbers seemed to be concentrated. It was astonishing to see climbers simultaneously on so many routes: *Chain Reaction, Darkness at Noon, Heinous Cling, Last Waltz, Sunshine Dihedral, Watts Tots,* and *Latest Rage.* Not that anybody was sending any of these routes, mind you, they were merely occupying them: leading up, clipping a bolt, falling off, swearing profusely, hanging on the rope, practicing moves, and repeating until they managed to hangdog their way to the anchors, or just gave up and lowered off.

Todd Skinner still had Beth Wald and Bill Hatcher in tow. Todd was hangdogging his way up a 5.12 route in the Dihedrals like everybody else. As always, Todd greeted me enthusiastically, shook my hand, got chalk on my shirt, asked how things were up in the northern swamp, and insisted that I immediately give the route a try. I obliged, but failed miserably at the crux, as did everyone else.

I joined the throng and made a quick ascent of *Watts Tots.* My belayer, Chris Hill, a teenager from Colorado who had just put up a new 5.13 route there, followed me up without falling off. From what I observed, we made the only actual ascent of a 5.12 route at Smith Rock that day. I tried to muster enthusiasm to climb something else, but I wasn't into it. It was too hot; it was too crowded. Everybody was taking themselves too goddamn seriously, like they expected to just walk up each route on their first try, and when they didn't, they were whipped into a frenzy of profane outrage. Climbers were being highly territorial, leaving ropes on routes all day, clogging them up for hours as if these were "their" routes. Most of them didn't seem to be having any fun. Me neither. I was moping about how Smith Rock had changed into a noisy gymnasium filled with testosterone-addled, Lycra-clad, profanity-shouting punks out to prove to themselves and anybody else who might care that they were worth a shit. It was a position I was not morally permitted to assume, because along with that bastard Heinz Zak, it was pretty much my fault that all of these climbers had come to Smith Rock and were destroying everything I had loved about it.

"I'm out of here," I said to Todd that afternoon, packing up and preparing to leave.

"What, already?" he said, surprised. "You've only been here for a few hours."

"Yep. I've had enough."

"Well, then, adios, Pilgrim," Todd said, as he always did when I was heading for home. "See you along the trail somewhere."

"You should come up to Index," I said before leaving. "You have to get on *City Park* again, before Alan does."

"Jesus, Smoot!" Todd exclaimed, feigning exasperation. "I've already told you, my fingers will never go back into that accursed crack."

As always, I didn't quite believe him.

PART FIVE

THAT ACCURSED CRACK

A great deal, perhaps everything, will remain incredible and incomprehensible. One paradox, however, must be accepted and this is that it is necessary to continually attempt the seemingly impossible.

—Hermann Hesse, *The Journey to the East*

OPPOSITE: Todd Skinner on *City Park* (5.13d), Index, 1986

28 A WALK IN THE PARK

The first pitch of *City Park* is a steep, elegant, thin crack—a seam really—splitting a slightly overhanging granite shield on the right side of the Lower Town Wall at Index. Originally climbed in 1966 as a nail-up route, *City Park* got its name from the moss and ferns on the wall, which reminded the first-ascent team of taking a stroll through the arboretum in Seattle, following the name given to an earlier route up the wall, *Japanese Gardens*, another fern-and-moss-fest nearby. The pin scars that developed over the years of repeated piton ascents greatly enhanced the first pitch's popularity as an aid climb. Before climbers embraced clean climbing in the early 1970s, pin scarring left a legacy of ugly cracks across the country, but often made it possible to free climb a formerly "impossible" crack. It was believed, but yet to be proven, that the first pitch of *City Park*, which was similar to *The Stigma* but steeper and longer, could be climbed free. Its difficulty was anybody's guess. No one had given it a serious try.

One of my early mentors, Erik Thixton, always insisted *City Park* would go free. He and Russell Erickson had tried it on toprope way back in the 1970s. They were able to at least hang on at every part of the crack.

"If you can hang on, you can climb," Erik opined. "You just have to be strong enough to make the moves and committed enough to keep trying when you fail over and over for days or weeks or years."

After my first time up *Godzilla*, the classic 5.9 introduction to Index climbing just right of *City Park*, I rappelled slowly down the thin aid crack. Stopping often to slide my fingertips into the subtle pin scars, twisting and pulling downward, I became a believer. Fingers fit in here and there; ripples and nubbins would allow feet to stick on the otherwise featureless steep granite. It was obvious that each section of the crack could be climbed, but could it be done in a continuous free ascent? Could you let go to place protection from such tenuous finger jams? Would you have the balls to lead up above a series of tiny wired nuts hastily slotted into flaring pin scars? Some doubted the route would ever go free, at least not without many more years of nailing to "enhance" the pin scars. But others had faith and believed that someday, someone would free climb *City Park* and it would be the hardest free climb in Washington. During the heyday of Index free climbing in the early and mid-1980s, climbers plucked all of the low-hanging fruit, resulting in a plethora of 5.11 and 5.12 crack and face climbs. But the ripest plum remained mostly untried: *City Park* was still an easy aid crack. As a free climb, it was regarded as a project for the future.

Todd Skinner was of the opinion that the future was now, and during the summer of 1985 he secretly visited Index and made an attempt on *City Park*. He was there for only a couple of days, long enough to rappel down the crack, feel the holds, confirm he could hang on everywhere and even make most of the moves, and realize that it could go free and that it would be hard—damn hard. During that winter following Todd's ascent of *The Stigma*, he continued to send letters asking about *City Park* and whether Alan Watts knew about it, although he expressed doubts about coming up to try it. "Too hard on my fingers," he complained. "I'm still having trouble from Yosemite so I'm going to concentrate on face from now on. It's the future anyway."

NONE OF US KNEW THAT TODD had come up to Index. He hadn't been there long; the rain had chased him off. I only found out later when Todd sent me a letter to say he had tried it, it was too thin, his fingers still hurt, and he wasn't coming back. This was bullshit, of course. He would come back. He knew it would go free. He would never give it up without another try. Todd suspected that *City Park* might turn out to be his Holy Grail—a 5.14. And because of that, he was deathly afraid that Alan Watts would steal the route from under him.

Todd had reason to be afraid. Alan had just climbed the *East Face* of Monkey Face and repeated *The Stigma*—both steep pin-scarred cracks, both hard 5.13. Todd had made a bold and ridiculous proclamation about *The Stigma*: "If anything in America is 5.14, this is it." Alan had fired up the pitch with seemingly minimal effort after dispatching the *East Face* only a few days previously.

"Under penalty of death and then dismemberment and finally public scolding," he wrote to me that winter, "you must let no word of this crack reach the ears of Alan Watts!"

I replied that Alan had talked about it the last time I was at Smith Rock, thinking it might be "fun" to come up and give it a try. And after I visited Smith Rock in March 1986 and saw Todd there, I told him that Alan had mentioned something about driving up to Index to check it out. In reality, Alan had expressed amusement at the *idea* of beating Todd to the free ascent. Never mind that by this time Alan's fingers were toast, curled-up arthritic claws, and he was popping ibuprofen like candy. Despite his sarcastic demeanor, Alan was a gentleman; he would give Todd an appropriate amount of time to free climb *City Park* before giving it a try. Todd didn't know this, though, and my suggestion that Alan was thinking about trying it got Todd riled up.

Sure enough, Todd raced up from Smith Rock one weekend soon after, lying to everyone there about where he was going and what he was doing. He had some slide shows lined up, he said. He would be back in a week for more mud pulling.

Todd's arrival at Index in late March must have been a disappointment: it rained for two days, and the crack was dripping wet. He would have to come back another time. Stopping at the Index general store on the way out of town, Todd encountered a local youth. "Hey, kid, do you want to make some money?" he asked. Todd offered to pay him to go out to the Lower Town Wall every so often and look at the crack and post a note on the bulletin board outside the store to report whether it was wet or dry. Todd would then call the store periodically, asking the proprietor to read the note. "Wet," he was told. "Still wet." Then one day the proprietor said "dry" and Todd raced back up to Index from Smith Rock only to find water still seeping in the crack from the previous week's rain. Hopes dashed, he scuttled back to Smith Rock.

By the time Todd returned at the end of May, the crack was dry. I drove out to Index one Saturday morning and there he was, camped out with Beth Wald in a turnout beside the Skykomish River across the railroad tracks from the wall. They had arrived the night before, and Todd had not yet set to work on the climb. The business of the day was to put up a toprope and start working out the moves.

Todd went first, did the moves he could do, then allowed others a turn to work out the sequential boulder problem–type moves he hadn't been able to figure out. I got my turn, and I found the crack to be a pure joy to climb—except for the excruciating pain, that is. Once I made it above the bolt ladder and a couple of easier flake moves, the crack became thin and stayed that way. The first twenty feet or so consisted of fingertip layback and jam moves, with one good golf-ball-size knob for a foothold, then smears and little features—a tough section to lead while placing gear without pumping out or barn-dooring off. After that, it was all jams, thin thumbs-up finger jams and wrenching thumbs-down locks in pin scars, some deep, some shallow, some allowing two fingers, others barely accepting fingertips, all without much for the feet except little ripples and crystals in the vertical granite.

I pulled past one section that was much too thin and painful for me and continued climbing. About midway up, the crack jogged a little to the left, then continued straight up to a ledge. This section was more technical, requiring some sequential jamming and laybacking. It was a spot Todd had not figured out, and he hung there on rappel watching me work out an intricate sequence, taking mental notes for his next attempt. After that, it was all tiny pin scars, straight up, perhaps technically easier but no less difficult until the final section, which was only 5.11, a virtual cakewalk compared with the moves below. Russ Clune, an East Coast climber making a tour of West Coast climbing areas, had followed Todd up from Smith Rock with a contingent including Bob Yoho and Hugh Herr; he gave it a try as well. It was a regular hangdog-fest, something not at all familiar to or greatly appreciated by some of the Index locals, who quietly watched the assault as it progressed day by day.

If the crack had been intersected by ledges every thirty feet or so, it would have been a "reasonable" four-pitch route of 5.10, 5.13-, 5.13, and 5.11. Todd approached the route exactly that way. Each day, he free soloed *Godzilla* and set up a toprope, then worked *City Park* section by section, repeating each one until he had it wired before moving on to the next section. Later, when he had each section wired, he made a few tentative lead attempts, hangdogging his way up the crack while figuring out where to place nuts so as not to plug up the best finger jams. The route soon looked like a chalkboard, all circles and arrows marking the best footholds, jams, and gear placements.

Watching this day after day became tedious. To relieve the monotony, I went climbing with Clune, Yoho, and Herr, taking them on a tour of the area classics. Clune had done a lot of impressive climbing since we had met in

Joshua Tree the previous spring, including most of the hardest routes at the Gunks, and he would go on to free solo some of them—*Supercrack* included. I had not met Yoho before but knew him by reputation from his ironic, iconoclastic letters to the editor printed in *Climbing* magazine, missives like "Path of the Dastard," a hilarious, satirical send-up of Phil Bard's article about John Bachar, "The Path of the Master." I also knew Herr by reputation. In person, he was quiet and seemed shy. We would watch Todd monkey around on *City Park* for a while, take a turn belaying, or tie in and flail about on toprope ourselves, then we'd wander off to climb routes that were humanly possible, leaving Todd to tilt at his windmill.

After Clune, Yoho, and Herr went back to Smith Rock, I abandoned Index. Todd's quest to free climb *City Park* was dragging on too long. I had to make some money, and so retreated to Seattle and took a temp job. I kept track of what was going on at Index, which was not much other than Todd's usual toproping-the-crack-into-submission routine, day after day. Whenever it seemed like Todd was close to making a serious attempt, I would drive out to Index to bear witness. After one close effort, where Todd fell on the penultimate hard move, just short of the end of the difficulties, Todd and Beth had to depart for California for a series of slide shows.

"It is so hard to leave now," Todd said, shaking his head in resignation. "I know I would do it tomorrow. But the show must go on."

When Todd and Beth returned several days later, rain thwarted Todd's efforts once again. On rainy days, Todd and Beth would usually hang out in Index, or at their soggy campsite. On one particularly drizzly weekday, they abandoned camp and headed into the big city, where I treated them to dinner, hot showers, and a tent pitched in my living room. By this time, Todd had the route all but wired.

"I don't think it will be 5.14," he admitted. "It is as hard as *The Renegade*, though, maybe harder. If Alan says *The Renegade* is 5.13b, then this will be 5.13c."

WHEN THE RAIN STOPPED, TODD and Beth returned to Index. I drove out the next day to find them lounging in their camp, reading a newspaper. It was a clear, crisp spring morning, ripe with potential. After some more lounging around, the whole troupe headed over to the Lower Town Wall. Todd went through his pre-climb routine, then soloed *Godzilla*, his usual warm-up. He moved adeptly up the 5.9 crack-and-corner system, scarcely hesitating on even the hardest moves. He had that route so wired from so many ascents that summer he could have climbed it blindfolded. He trailed two ropes on the climb, and as soon as he reached the ledge at the anchors, he set up a rappel and lowered himself down *City Park* slowly, making sure each jam was dry, re-marking a critical foothold here and a pin scar there to be sure he hit his sequence perfectly.

Suddenly, a torrent of profanity rained down from above. We all looked up, startled, expecting to see Todd plummeting to his death, bleeding profusely, or fending off a vicious hornet attack, such was the suddenness and intensity of his rage. But no, he was still safely on rappel, only twenty feet or so down the crack, apparently intact but livid. Todd continued his tirade. We had no idea what was happening. Todd usually did not swear this intensely except when he fell on a route, as was *de rigueur* among the young punk climbers of the day. But this was a different kind of swearing. He seemed to really mean it.

"There's grease in the crack!" Todd roared. "Jesus Christ! Goddamn it! *Goddamn it!*"

We were incredulous. Grease in the crack? How would grease get in the crack? It did not register at first, but the bright ones among us soon figured it out. Even so, it was beyond belief that someone would carry out such a dastardly deed. We were at Index, not Yosemite. There were no Valley locals lurking about. Who could have done it?

Todd's disposition did not soon improve. He continued rappelling down the crack, cursing when he found that several more pin scars had been slathered in thick, dark grease. And then there was no more. The rest of the crack was clean and dry. Only the 5.11 finish had been vandalized. The saboteurs had apparently known that Todd was close to leading the crack and, taking advantage of his days away, had slimed the final section with grease collected from the railroad tracks. It would have been something for Todd to have led through the crux in fine style, only to stick his fingers into a hole full of grease and come sailing off just short of his moment of triumph. Index was no stranger to controversy—pins and bolt hangers had been stolen, bolts had been chopped, and even some trees had been cut down once or twice—but this was entirely unprecedented.

Because of the rain, nobody had been climbing at Index, so there were no witnesses to the incident. But there was much speculation over who did it. A few hard-core, traditionalist climbers topped the list of suspects, and through the grapevine, two were fingered as the likely culprits. Like the *Wings of Steel* shitters, they will remain forever unnamed by me. They know who they are, and so does everybody else in the climbing community. At least they didn't damage the rock or cause any death or disfigurement. Fortunately, a little grease didn't hurt anything, except maybe Todd's feelings.

After rappelling down the route, Todd was in a funk. He couldn't believe it. But he soon gathered his senses and did a most idiotic and brilliant thing. He went back to his van, grabbed a butane torch, and headed right back up there to burn the grease out of the pin scars. This seemed insane, of course: a wrong move with the torch and he could have burned through his ropes and fallen to his death. But Todd, like any right-minded zealot, was not about to let sanity cloud his judgment. He spent the next few hours hanging on the rope, carefully burning grease out of the crack.

Once the grease was burned off, Todd got back on the route late that afternoon. I'd spent nearly a month watching Todd climb the same 120 feet of rock every day, and it wasn't exactly a thrilling prospect to watch it all again. The grease incident had been far more exhilarating than Todd's efforts so far to free the pitch. But at the same time, a free ascent of *City Park* would be history in the making, perhaps the most exciting thing to happen at Index since they put the railroad through.

Todd ascended the face moves with ease to the base of the crack, then led cleanly up the first section of crack, to where it jogs slightly right and shoots up the shield. He placed only a couple of nuts and got halfway up the shield before falling off. In his usual fashion, Todd swore mightily when he fell. After a pull up the rope and a short hang to rehearse a move, Todd lowered off, pulled the rope, and rested. He was back on it again about ninety minutes later and got past his high point, only to fall off again, this time taking a thirty-footer. Todd was running it out about fifteen feet between nuts, which seemed crazy but was also quite reasonable. Stopping to place protection burned precious forearm strength, a rare commodity on such a strenuous pitch, and in a few places he simply could not let go to slot in a nut.

Todd had once theorized that climbs would someday become so hard that it would be impossible to let go to place protection. Here was his theory in practice. It was alternately fascinating and horrifying to watch him lead out so far above wired nuts in pin scars. I'd recently taken a short fall and sheared through the cable of an RP, nearly hitting the ground due to the additional twenty feet added to my fall. I'd also had a whole string of wired nuts zipper out of a crack, resulting in a ground fall. Even when aiding *City Park*, I did not fully trust half of my placements, but I took solace in the fact that I had so many nuts in the crack that some of them would probably hold a fall even if one or two blew out. To me, the idea of taking a fifteen-foot runout above a #2 RP on 5.12 moves, with the next piece fifteen feet below, bordered on lunacy. It was a gamble. If Todd fell and hurt himself, he was stupid; if taking such long runouts allowed him to free climb the route, he was a genius. So far, he was racking up points on the genius side.

After a long break, Todd made his third try of the day, getting even higher before just missing a move that would have all but assured success. After the obligatory bout of cursing, Todd lowered off, pulled the rope, and took another long break. He had one more shot that day. If he didn't succeed, it would be Sunday or Monday before he could try again. With the weekend coming, and the possibility of saboteurs lurking, ready to strike again, he wanted desperately to finish it. To calm Todd's paranoia, I offered to hang out at the base of the climb during his rest break to guard against sabotage. I had experience in this field, after all. Todd had one try left in him that day, and it would be a good one.

The crew returned in the evening, later than I thought prudent if Todd was going to have a shot at freeing the pitch in daylight. Todd took his time roping up and preparing for the climb. He was meditative and serious, not his usual jokester self. With his eyes closed, he pantomimed the moves, complete with clipping gear and chalking up, all the way to the top of the crack. When he was finally tied in and racked up, it was starting to get dark.

Todd climbed quickly up the 5.10 face to the crack, clipped a Friend, made a couple more moves to a good foothold, clipped an RP, then downclimbed to a ledge. After a short rest, he fired up the first part of the crack, a thin jam-and-layback section, to the first horizontal seam, where the crack kicked back to just over vertical. He clipped a nut. It was twilight now, really too dark to be climbing, but Todd was still moving up. He passed through the first crux beautifully, sticking the thumbs-up pinkie jam perfectly, the thinnest move of the route, and continued up another twenty feet to a fixed pin without another piece of protection. He clipped the pin, did the technical crux moves to establish in the upper half of the crack, and muscled his way up the tiny pin scars, his feet deftly finding purchase on ripples and crystals despite the impending darkness. Another fifteen feet up, just a few moves short of the end of the hard climbing, Todd placed a piece of protection and cranked up another move, then another, to reach the horizontal break at the base of the final crack section. He had all but done it. Just a few moves of easier climbing to go. There were shouts of encouragement and congratulations from below as Todd placed one last stopper, shook out his arms, and prepared to complete the climb.

Then suddenly, like before, a flurry of profanity rang out from above. "God-damn it!" Todd shrieked. "*Goddamn it!*" The woods echoed with obscenities. "I missed a spot! There's still grease in one of the jams!" He balanced there help-lessly, whimpering like a baby, having just completed the hardest moves on one of the hardest crack climbs in the country. We couldn't believe it.

"Can you skip that jam?" I asked.

He tried, reaching up and sticking his fingers in a lower pin scar, then reaching for a higher slot, but backed down. "No. Damn it!" His forearms were flaming. He couldn't hang on there for much longer and still have strength to finish the pitch. If he didn't figure out how to bypass that greasy hold soon, he was going to pump out and fall off. By the sound and looks of things, Todd was giving up.

"Todd, to your right is a ledge," I yelled up. "If you mantel up on that ledge, it's 5.9 to the top."

"What?" he yelled back desperately.

"Reach right to the ledge and mantel up. It's a 5.10c mantel, then it's 5.9 to the ledge."

"A mantel?" Todd shrieked. "I hate mantels!"

Quickly realizing he had no other option, except to let go and try again another day, Todd reached tentatively to the right to touch the ledge, then committed to it, shifting his weight over to the ledge and hanging from both arms. He pulled up, shifted his right hand and pressed down, and with a big groan muscled his way up, groped a flake, got a foot on the ledge and levered up. He stood there for a long time, shaking one arm and then the other. He did not have any protection left to place; he had carried only what he needed to protect the crack. It got darker and darker, to the point where we could barely see him against the fading sky. Finally, he started moving again, slowly climb-ing the flake, and in darkness he did the final thin crack moves and pulled unceremoniously up onto the ledge to complete the first free ascent of the first pitch of *City Park*. It had not been pretty, but it had been done.

UNFORTUNATELY, TODD DID HIMSELF and his reputation no favors by getting back on the route the next day, a Saturday. All dressed up in a red shirt and his flashiest Lycra tights and his sponsor's rock shoes, he hangdogged his way up the route, posing so Beth could take pictures. Todd needed photos of himself free climbing the route, to go with the articles about his ascent and for his slide show and to give to his sponsor for advertising. But a lot of local climbers were out at Index that day and they saw him preplacing gear and hangdogging around for photos. Naturally, when they read later how he had free climbed *City Park*, they had some doubts. It didn't help that Beth wrote in *Rock & Ice* that Todd had ticked the route and they had gotten out of there the next day, waving at Alan Watts, who had just arrived to try it. In fact, Todd had climbed it on Friday night, hangdogged on it on Saturday for photos, and then departed—a small detail that, when misconstrued by a skeptical audience, easily led to the wrong conclusion.

It could be accurately said (and has been many times) that Todd hadn't free climbed the entire crack—that the true first free ascent still awaited. Instead of executing the 5.11a finish to the crack proper, Todd had, out of necessity due to the villainous actions of others, taken a variation to finish the pitch. But as I see it, the mantel was probably harder than the crack under the circumstances, considering Todd did it on-sight and in the dark, when he was fully blown from having just done a hundred feet of 5.13 climbing to get there. In fairness to his critics, however, I concede that Todd had not climbed the traditional first pitch of *City Park*. It was a shame that one crucial pin scar was still greased—and that the crack had been greased at all, really—because Todd would easily have finished the crack and there would be no doubt about it. One thing is certain: he did free climb the pitch, variation or not.

Jokingly, Todd suggested renaming the pitch *Grease Monkey* in honor of his would-be saboteurs. Disappointingly, he rated it "only" 5.13c, probably to avoid having Alan Watts cruise in and downgrade it as he had *The Stigma*. Alan arrived at Index with a trio of Smith Rock climbers in tow the day Todd was posing for pictures and gave *City Park* a fair shot, coming close to flashing it on lead. "I remember giving it one heck of a good go," Alan recalls. "It fit perfectly into my wheelhouse, and the higher I got, the more I thought I was going to do it." But one move short of the end of the hard climbing, he slipped out of a pin scar and tore a ferocious flapper. Alan's finger injury thwarted any further attempts, forcing him to give it up and head back to Oregon.

History is a semifluid thing, as storytellers well know. The story that is remembered is the story that is told, which may or may not be what happened. And it doesn't matter anyway. Todd free climbed the route and got the hell out of there, racing back to Smith Rock and then eventually to Wyoming to check out some limestone cliffs he had heard tell of, glad to be done with the whole *City Park* affair. Although it was harder than anything Todd had yet climbed, and about as hard as anything done in America to date, Todd was disappointed. It wasn't the hardest route in America; it wasn't 5.14. Hell, Alan Watts had almost flashed it! Todd would have to keep searching. His 5.14 was out there somewhere, out where the potatoes and tuna fish play.

29 THE HATCHET JOB

Hugh Herr hadn't liked climbing at Index. He had come up from Smith Rock with Russ Clune in June 1986, while Todd Skinner was working on *City Park*, tried to climb a few routes, then pretty much gave up. An East Coast climber more accustomed to thin face climbing at the Gunks and Cathedral Ledge, Hugh did not adjust well to the sometimes smooth, featureless rock, which required a lot more finesse. Or, perhaps more correctly, Hugh did not *adapt* well to Index granite. But he didn't forget about Index, far from it. Back home after his West Coast trip, Hugh set to work preparing for his return, intent on repeating *City Park*.

I hadn't climbed much with Hugh Herr when he visited Index that spring. We had shared a toprope on *Iron Horse*, one of those Index "5.11d" routes that tended to repel any visiting climber who hadn't learned the nuances of Index granite. Hugh had seemed shy and kept to himself. Even so, we struck up something of a friendship, probably because we were somewhat alike—other than the fact that I had use of both of my feet and Hugh did not. We got to talking one afternoon in the Lower Town Wall parking lot, where he told me he would be coming back to the Northwest later that summer to meet a doctor in Seattle involved in prosthetics research. I invited Hugh to stay at my place and maybe do some climbing while he was in the area. He accepted.

Hugh's research trip evolved over the weeks into a full-on climbing trip. He would call me every couple of weeks to update me on his travel plans and itinerary. He'd be arriving the first week of August. He had to be in Seattle for a week or so, then he was free to climb for a few weeks before he had to fly home to start classes at MIT. He told me he planned to try to repeat Todd's free ascent of *City Park*. I had to suppress a laugh. The idea of Hugh free climbing *City Park* struck me as mildly absurd. It didn't seem possible that someone with two artificial legs would have any chance of free climbing the thin crack Todd had conservatively rated 5.13c. Hugh was a really good climber, there was no doubt about that, but he didn't have feet. To free climb *City Park*, I imagined, Hugh would have to muscle his way up on finger jams with his legs dangling uselessly behind. Hugh was deadly serious about *City Park*, though, as I would soon find out.

"I've been working on some special feet just for *City Park*," he told me on the phone before he flew to Seattle. "I think I have them just right. I'll be able to do foot jams!" he said excitedly. "It will be a piece of cake."

LET'S CALL IT A DAY, one wishes Hugh Herr might have said. It was Saturday, January 23, 1982. He and his partner Jeff Batzer had just completed an ascent of *Odell's Gully*, one of the popular ice climbs in Huntington Ravine, a glacial cirque on the southeast side of Mount Washington. The climbing had been easy, and they had topped out early despite high winds and snowfall. Rather than descend, they decided to continue to the summit of Mount Washington, another mile or so and a thousand feet higher—a mere hike in good conditions.

The previous day, Herr, then a seventeen-year-old high school student, and his regular climbing partner, Batzer, age twenty, had driven out from Lancaster, Pennsylvania, to New Hampshire for a weekend of ice climbing. Their plan was to climb all day Saturday and maybe Sunday, if the weather justified the extra day, then drive home late Sunday. Like most climbers his age, Hugh was not religiously bound to the idea of getting home in time to get to school the following morning. He had already skipped school on Friday, so if he was late to school on Monday, it wouldn't be the end of the world.

At first, everything went according to plan. The 500-odd-mile drive to Pinkham Notch had been long but uneventful. That night, the pair hiked in to the Harvard Cabin, the climbers' base camp for Huntington Ravine. Early the next morning, they hacked their way up *Odell's Gully*. Hugh had led the technical pitches quickly. With time to kill, they decided to continue on to the summit for no particular reason other than because it was there, but after a few hundred yards of trudging uphill through what was escalating into a raging blizzard, they quickly realized their folly. They turned back and started down what they thought was the *Central Gully* of Huntington Ravine, which would have led them back to the Harvard Cabin. By the time they figured out they were in the wrong gully, it was too late. Believing they had simply descended a different gully on the south side of Mount Washington, they continued downward, expecting to eventually come across the trail to the cabin. But no trail materialized, and no cabin.

Herr and Batzer were unaware that they had made a serious blunder. They were descending into the Great Gulf, a glacial cirque on the mountain's north side, moving farther from survival with every step. Still, it was cold and they had to keep moving, so they plodded hopefully downhill, expecting to find the trail at any moment. Hugh broke through the snow at one point and fell into a stream, soaking his feet and pants. Eventually they holed up in a cave under a boulder where they spent an uncomfortable but not quite desperate night.

By the next morning, the storm had intensified. They had to get out of there, fast, and so they continued their now desperate attempt to find their way to shelter. At some point, Herr realized his feet were frostbitten; he couldn't walk more than a few steps without falling over. They stumbled around for a while longer until impending darkness forced them to bivouac. In the morning, Herr didn't have the energy or, frankly, the will to go on. Convinced no one was looking for them, he decided to stay put. Batzer went off by himself, still hoping he could find his way to a road or trail and, eventually, a rescue; but he didn't get far and soon returned. The two boys huddled together in their primitive cave, slowly freezing, expecting to die.

Unknown to Herr and Batzer, a coordinated search and rescue effort was under way. The trouble was, it was focused on the area with the highest probability of locating the pair—the south side of the mountain, where they had been climbing and were presumed to have become lost in the storm or caught in an avalanche, the latter being a very real possibility. On Monday morning, two of the rescuers followed the pair's path, climbing *Odell's Gully* and then continuing to a shoulder of Mount Washington, looking for traces of them. Finding nothing except a carabiner and some footsteps in the snow at the top of the gully, the rescuers descended, and were caught in an avalanche on their way down. One was able to dig himself out enough to radio for help; the other was killed.

On Tuesday, another rescuer, who had decided on her own to snowshoe into the Great Gulf, came across tracks in the snow and followed them. She found Herr and Batzer huddled in their cave, still alive, but barely. The pair was airlifted out that night, hypothermic and frostbitten. Batzer would lose a thumb, some fingers, his left foot, and the toes on his right foot; both of Hugh's legs were amputated below the knee. The physical toll was only part of the story. Batzer and Herr were accused by some as being responsible for the death of the rescuer killed in the avalanche, morally culpable for being a couple of dumb kids out climbing in a storm in the first place. Their physical and emotional recovery from the incident promised to be long and difficult.

Herr had been something of a child prodigy as a climber: He had climbed 5.10 at age thirteen and 5.11 at age fourteen; by the age of sixteen, he had climbed *Supercrack*, the hardest route at the Gunks, with only one fall, and had free soloed a Gunks route rated 5.11+. He had also climbed *Astroman* and several other hard routes in Yosemite. After his amputations, Herr's future as a climber was in doubt. But whatever feelings of guilt he retained from the incident, his physical recovery was astonishing. The loss of both feet did not slow him down—not a bit.

As soon as he could, Herr was climbing again—literally climbing the walls of the hospital at first while he recovered from his amputations, later returning to the Gunks to try climbing with his prosthetic legs. The standard-issue prosthetic feet weren't ideal for climbing. They worked passably on easier climbs at the Gunks, which involved edging on horizontal ledges, but were heavy and awkward. Dissatisfied, Herr was soon designing his own prosthetic legs and feet, modifying them from the socket down. He replaced the clunky plastic "leg" with an aluminum pole, to which he bolted a block or wedge as a "foot." His first prototypes were Frankenstein-esque monstrosities, but he kept tinkering and improving his "legs" and "feet" to the point where he could not only climb again but climb hard.

By the time he returned to Index in August 1986, Herr had, post-amputation, put up some of the hardest face climbs in New England and the Gunks, cutting-edge 5.12 routes that made headlines in the Basecamp section of *Climbing* and even got him on the cover. Before long, Herr became the subject of countless news articles, profiles, TV shows, and books. People who had no interest in or affiliation with climbing whatsoever knew who Herr was. They were calling him the "Mechanical Boy." Hugh Herr was famous. And he was just getting started.

Despite his innate climbing ability and mechanical innovations, Herr had been stymied by Index climbing on his earlier visit because of the uniform verticality of its cracks and its general lack of positive edges. Gunks climbing was all edges—steep and overhanging climbing on horizontal and vertical joints, with the hardest climbs involving thin, crimpy edges and fierce roofs. Herr's climbing feet to this point had been designed for edging, and had worked perfectly, better than human feet ever had because they could stick reliably on dime-edge holds that normal rock shoes would slip off of. But Index climbing was devious: it required deft footwork such as thin toe jamming and adept smearing on divots, bumps, and wrinkles, an exercise in faith as much as skill on many of the harder routes and even some of the easier ones. Herr's rigid wood-block-and-rubber feet were not flexible enough for such intricate footwork and did not fit in thin cracks. It was a shortcoming he did not take lightly. After failing to climb anything meaningful at Index during his visit that spring, and knowing he would be coming back to Seattle oix weeks later, he improvised a solution.

HUGH FLEW OUT THE FIRST WEEK in August, the hottest August in Seattle in years. I picked him up at Sea-Tac Airport. Watching him walk off the plane, aside from a slight stiffness in his stride, you would never have guessed he was a bilateral amputee. And you would never have guessed he was one of the best rock climbers in the country if you hadn't tied him in to a rope and sent him up a route, which was exactly what I had in mind.

"Do you have your climbing gear with you?" I asked him.

"Of course," he said. "Why?"

"We're going climbing."

In honor of Hugh's visit, I had spent the previous day scrubbing moss and scraping dirt off of three potential routes on a little granite crag beside I-90: a clean arête, a thin arching crack, and a fingertip crack. Jet lag hadn't set in yet, so Hugh was game. I drove us straight there from the airport and proudly showed him the routes. I took the first lead, the middle flake, a poorly protected 5.11a pitch. Hugh switched out his walking feet for his face-climbing feet and followed the pitch easily.

"That was fun," Hugh said. "Now let's have a go at that thin crack. I want to try my new crack feet."

The crack was dead vertical and slightly offset, forming a shallow left-facing corner into which fingertips barely fit. It had been nailed once or twice (there was a faint pin scar where a good RP could be placed), and a line of dark, rusty bolt studs ran up the wall to the right, where somebody a decade or more earlier had apparently practiced bolting before heading up a big wall. Hugh sat down on a granite block and pulled out his secret weapon: a rubber-tipped acetyl wedge shaped like a small hatchet head bolted to an army surplus aluminum pole. He fastened it to his prosthetic leg and stood up.

"In theory, I can stick this into the crack and torque it like this," he said, demonstrating in a narrow gap between two boulders, "and it will lock in and I can stand on it. Let's see if it works."

Hugh climbed awkwardly up a series of short ledges to get to the crack, his prosthetic blades all but useless, like climbing in hockey skates. Then he jammed up the crack with his fingertips and stuck his right "foot" in the crack and twisted. He stood up on it and grinned down.

"Hey, it works!"

"That's cheating!"

"I'm a cripple. How can it be cheating?"

Hugh's "bionic" foot got him halfway up the crack, to where it got too thin for fingers. He had to rely on pure strength to pull up to a vertical flake of granite three inches thick that stuck out like a dorsal fin, requiring powerful pinching moves. Hugh grunted up a couple of moves but fell off. I took a turn, leading up the fingertip jams, finding little bumps and smears for my feet where Hugh had just whacked his plastic foot into the crack. I pinched the fin, did one move, realized I'd screwed up the sequence, and let go. Hugh climbed back up and after a couple of big grunts powered up the pinch moves to reach the easy crack above. It had been a good test of Hugh's "hatchet feet," and a likely first free ascent, at 5.11d, of some unknown climber's obscure aid practice crack.

THE NEXT MORNING, I DROVE HUGH to his meeting with Dr. Ernest Burgess, administrative director of the Prosthetics Research Study at Swedish Medical Center. Burgess was the inventor of the Seattle Foot, a new, cutting-edge prosthetic foot that was getting all kinds of press. We sat in a drab waiting area outside the PRS offices. Eventually, a white-haired, energetic man, half Columbo and half White Rabbit, burst into the room.

"Hello, hello," he said, coming over to us. "Which one of you is Hugh?"

Burgess was a nice but slightly mad scientist who was frantically but genuinely enthusiastic about all things prosthetic. He gave us a demonstration of his Seattle Foot, a spring-aided prosthetic foot that allowed amputees not only to walk but also to run efficiently. Hugh and Burgess talked for quite a while about the Seattle Foot, then spent a long while discussing prosthetic limbs in practice and theory, handling various prototypes and drawing diagrams on the whiteboard. While this was going on, one of Burgess's patients came in for a consultation, an old fellow in a white shirt, khaki trousers, and a cap with a logo of Mount Rainier on the front. Burgess greeted him as he shuffled in.

"Ome, I have a surprise for you. This is Hugh Herr. He's an amputee, and he's a climber, like you."

"Well hello there, young fella," the old man said, extending a shaky hand to Hugh. "It's a pleasure to meet you."

Ome Daiber was a Pacific Northwest climbing legend, a party to the first ascent of Mount Rainier's Nordwand in 1935 via the classic *Liberty Ridge* route. For a long while we listened to Daiber tell one tale after another, about *Liberty Ridge* and other routes, his medical problems, and his recent ascent of the Counterbalance, a long, steep walk to the top of Seattle's Queen Anne Hill. Given his advanced age, affliction with diabetes, and resulting amputations, a walk up Queen Anne Hill was quite an accomplishment.

Another PRS doctor, Al Rappoport, came in eager as all get-out to meet Hugh. Also an amputee (just one leg), Rappoport was fired up to try climbing. Hugh and I agreed to take him over to the UW practice rock so he could try out Hugh's climbing feet. After Hugh's meeting, we piled into Al's big white Cadillac convertible and went cruising down Broadway, over Capitol Hill, and down through Montlake to the Rock. We got some looks as we pulled up in Al's pimpmobile. Hugh and Al got even more looks as they pulled up their pant legs, removed their prosthetic feet, and screwed on climbing feet. It was the first time I knew of that an amputee had climbed at the Rock, and here were two of them.

Al, for all of his enthusiasm to try climbing, gave up after just a few minutes.

"This is hard," he said. "I don't know how you guys do this."

Meanwhile, Hugh spent an hour or so traversing and climbing, showing off his ability and strength. I was tempted to show him some of the hard problems, but falling off of boulder problems, even onto the loose gravel spread around the formation, didn't seem like a good idea for an amputee. Hugh's prosthetic feet were good for climbing, not so much for landing, so he contented himself with easier problems and low traverses, testing his new feet on thin crack problems. They seemed to work well, but Hugh wasn't satisfied.

That night and the next day, Hugh put his hatchet feet to the grindstone. He had packed along a grinding wheel in his luggage. He pulled it out, plugged it in, and sat there for hours grinding and reshaping his plastic feet, a bandanna pulled bandito-like over his face. Then he glued on a thin strip of rubber. After several hours of this tedious work, he seemed satisfied. He held up his fake foot proudly. He was ready to try *City Park*.

WE WENT OUT TO INDEX the next morning and Hugh set right to work on the route. He didn't bother to toprope it; he just racked up with a set of stoppers, RPs, and small cams and led upward. This wasn't exactly unknown territory for Hugh. He had prior information from me and from watching Todd and taking a turn on toprope two months previously, although this beta was not all useful since Hugh would be climbing in an entirely different style, using foot jams all the way up a crack too small for the feet of mere mortals.

For his first attempt, Hugh wore two hatchet feet, which were not exactly suited to the 5.10 face section at the start, but he tiptoed up it and was soon climbing the crack. Hugh 'dogged his way upward, using straight-in foot jams. The finger jams were no easier for Hugh, but the footwork was much less taxing. It seemed something like front-pointing with crampons—kick, insert foot, twist, stand up, repeat.

Amazingly, Hugh did every move free—albeit with many falls and hangs—on his first attempt. But in doing so, he trashed his feet. By the time he reached the anchors, the rubber had all peeled off, exposing the bare acetyl, which had absolutely no affinity for the weathered Index granite. It would be a few days before we returned to Index. Hugh went back to the grinding wheel, intent on perfecting his hatchet-foot design.

Over the next two nights, Hugh honed his feet, grinding them, applying a layer of rubber, ripping it off, and grinding them some more until he was satisfied. The next day we went out to Index for a photo shoot for the Patagonia catalog, during which Hugh hangdogged his way up the crack for the photographer and tested out his improved feet. They worked well, so well that Hugh took a night off from the grinding wheel.

We were back at Index the next morning. Hugh used only one hatchet foot this time. He had learned through trial and error that using both blades at the same time made the climbing more difficult because he couldn't use any of the footholds, whereas with one of his regular climbing feet on, he could toe in on a few of the edges and bumps. He gave it a good try on his first effort of the day, climbing halfway up the crack before taking a twenty-foot fall. After lowering off and resting for a few minutes, he got back on and sent it, and that was that. In the course of three days, one of which was spent posing for photos, Hugh had free climbed *City Park*. And he'd done the direct finish that Todd Skinner had skipped because of the greased hold.

"That was fun," Hugh said, smirking, "but I want to climb something hard. Are there any *hard* climbs around here?"

THE CRITICS HAD A FIELD DAY with Hugh's ascent of *City Park*. Hugh wasn't human, he was a machine, they said, a robo-climber. He hadn't free climbed the route; his was a glorified aid climb. Hatchet feet were cheating; he had practically front-pointed up the route, they said. Would it be a free climb if another climber used special shoes with a stiff-pointed tip that could be wedged into the pin scars like front-pointed crampons? What if you cut off your hands and used a prosthetic hand that had a range of RPs wired to it instead of fingers, they wondered. Would that be legitimate? Not that anybody wanted to try any of those things. And not that anybody was particularly dismissive of Hugh's energy, enthusiasm, or ability. They just thought his use of specially designed artificial legs was unfair.

I am sure Hugh would have preferred to have climbed *City Park* with his real feet rather than his adaptive feet. But that wasn't possible, and he wasn't about to quit climbing because of it. Adaptive climbing wasn't a "thing" yet; although Hugh wasn't the first amputee to adapt a prosthetic foot to climbing, he was the best at it, and would continue to get better. Whether Hugh's adaptations really gave him an advantage over other climbers was a fair question, though—a question he was determined to answer.

"Let's go to Yosemite," Hugh blurted out on the ride home from Index. "I want to climb *The Stigma*."

"Seriously?"

"Yeah!"

"No way," I said. "They want to kill me. Seriously!"

"Think about it," Hugh said with that smirk of his. "Todd Skinner climbed *The Stigma*, then Alan Watts did it. Think how much it would piss them off if an amputee came in and climbed it! Hell, I climbed *City Park*, and it's harder than *The Stigma*, right?"

"That would be something."

"It would. It would. Think about it. It would be awesome! Oh, man."

Hugh laughed himself silly at the thought of it, but he was serious. So I thought about it. He was right—it certainly *would* piss them off. It would be the ultimate insult. An amputee climbing *The Stigma* in better style than Todd Skinner or Alan Watts, belayed by that asshole Jeff Smoot. This time they wouldn't just write graffiti on the dusty windows. They would break the windows. There might even be physical violence.

Hugh's idea had merit, though. It *would* be hilarious to sneak into the Valley, have Hugh fire off *The Stigma* in an hour or two, and then drive off before anybody realized we had been there. Maybe he would even flash it because he could jam his hatchet foot in where Todd and Alan had only been able to smear or toe on an edge or layback. But I couldn't shake the fear that I'd run into somebody in the Valley who was still so completely outraged about "The Valley Syndrome" that they would go apoplectic, beat me up, and hang my mangled corpse off the Cookie Cliff. It would be confrontational, to say the least.

"How about the *East Face* of Monkey Face?"

"It's a face climb," Hugh said. "I want to climb a crack."

"*Fallen Arches*?"

"It's only 13a. And it's got a bunch of sideways jamming and laybacks."

"Has anybody climbed that roof problem in Little Cottonwood Canyon? What's it called?"

"Yeah. It's 12c or something. I want something *hard*."

"*City Park*'s the hardest crack you're going to find, I think."

"I want to climb something amazing."

"Let's free El Cap. Hudon and Jones freed all but ninety feet of the *Salathé*. Maybe you can free the *Nose*."

"Yeah, right," Hugh chided me. "You want to go to Yosemite now?"

"Never mind. How about *Sphinx Crack*?"

"I don't know. Maybe."

It went on like that for a while, but time was running short. Hugh had to get back to Boston in a couple of weeks for school, and he had some friends in Boulder he wanted to hang out with beforehand. After ruminating for many hours over what to do, Hugh finally resigned himself to giving *Sphinx Crack* a try. He made a couple of phone calls to let his Boulder friends know we were headed their way.

30 RIDDLE OF THE SPHINX

We left for Colorado early the next afternoon. Before we pulled out of my driveway, I plugged *Zenyatta Mondatta* into the cassette player and cranked it up. I knew how much Hugh liked the Police; he'd been randomly busting out Police lyrics all week. Out of the blue he'd bust out with the chorus from "The Bed's Too Big Without You." As we drove eastward on I-90, Hugh babbled along with Sting, singing the lyrics of "De Do Do Do, De Da Da Da" over and over. When I got sick of it, I turned off the cassette player. That did not stop Hugh. We'd be driving across a mountain pass or along a snaking river in complete, blissful silence, and all of a sudden he would wail out a line from "Roxanne" that would startle me out of a trance.

Darkness fell as we headed south, crossing from Idaho into Utah. The interstate became the domain of trucks, big illuminated tractors hauling single and double trailers, all driving eighty to ninety miles an hour from one end of the country to the other. One blazed past me and pulled into my lane. I floored it and caught up and felt the car get pulled into the draft. The trucker tapped his brakes and backed me off. I kept trying, and eventually caught some drafts. I continued south on I-84 into Ogden, then cut south onto I-15 to Salt Lake City.

Hugh had been sleeping most of the way since eastern Oregon, but he woke up as we drove into Salt Lake City, about twelve hours after leaving Seattle. "I'm hungry," he said. "Let's get something to eat."

"Denny's?" I said, pointing to the highway sign that said there was a Denny's off the next exit.

"Again?" Hugh said. "We just ate at Denny's in Pendleton."

"It's probably all that's open," I said. "It's one o'clock in the morning."

"Okay."

The Denny's parking lot was nearly full and there were kids everywhere, unruly Salt Lake City teenagers sitting on cars, running around the parking lot, having a good time on a Friday summer night. I pulled in slowly, waiting for the crowd to let us pass, and parked in the back of the lot. There were hardly any customers inside. Still, the sign told us to "Wait to Be Seated." We waited, and nobody came.

"Let's just sit down," Hugh said after a few minutes.

I shrugged my shoulders. Why not? We went and sat at a booth by a window. A surly waitress saw us and came straight over.

"You're supposed to wait to be seated," she said curtly.

"I had to sit down," Hugh told her. "My feet are killing me."

"Where you from?" she asked, still surly.

"Boston," said Hugh.

"Sorry," the waitress said, softening. "I thought maybe you just came in from out there." She pointed in the direction of the parking lot. "What can I get you?"

We both ordered Grand Slam breakfasts with chocolate milkshakes. While we waited for our orders to come, we pondered the situation in the parking lot. Salt Lake City was the last place we would expect to find a crowd of out-of-control teenagers. This was Mormon country.

"Every culture has its rebels," Hugh said. "Maybe they want to be bad, so they come to Denny's and smoke cigarettes in the parking lot. Look at us! We're bad kids! We're smoking at Denny's!"

Our food came and we ate greedily. Suddenly there was a loud *boom*! from out behind the restaurant. The window rattled fiercely and the whole restaurant and parking lot went dark.

The manager called the police. "There's been an explosion," he said excitedly. "Somebody set off a bomb!"

"Let's get out of here," Hugh said. I nodded in agreement.

We sucked down the last of our milkshakes, tossed some money on the table, and walked out. There were wild kids running all over the place. We looked around the parking lot to see what had happened. A transformer on a utility pole was shooting flames and sparks and dark smoke. A police cruiser arrived, blue lights flashing. An officer got out and started chasing a group of kids around behind the restaurant. Others were pointing and laughing. Someone was jumping up and down on the roof of a car. We could hear sirens. We got in the car, drove slowly through the parking lot and out onto the street, and turned toward the freeway. Two fire trucks came roaring past, sirens wailing.

"What a riot! You'd think somebody won the Stanley Cup," Hugh said. "We got out of there just in time."

THE DRIVE ACROSS COLORADO TOOK us over Independence Pass, 12,095 feet high, my first crossing of the Continental Divide. We followed the highway through a labyrinth of passes, canyons, and valleys to a spot on the map marked Pine, which consisted of little more than a general store, a post office, a few widely spaced houses, and a two-lane highway heading right on through. We turned up the road marked "Sphinx Rock" and there it was, looming on the hillside across the canyon. I parked at the first turnout, and we hiked up to the rock to check out the route before it got dark.

To those with generous imaginations, Sphinx Rock could be said to vaguely resemble a sphinx. Slight undulations in the curved golden granite might be seen as humanlike eyes and perhaps a nose, the jutting lower shelf as the paws of a lion in repose. But there was no mistaking the jagged lightning-bolt fissure that sliced through solid rock as if cleft by Thor's hammer itself.

Sphinx Crack had a curious history. During the 1940s, two yokels thought it would be a grand experiment to try to blast a huge granite outcropping sitting on a ridge above Pine in half, apparently so they could watch the blown-off half trundle magnificently down into the canyon. They scrambled up to the top of the rock, drilled a hole deep into the dome, dropped in some dynamite, reeled out some wire, pushed the plunger, and *boom*! After the smoke and dust cleared, they were nonplussed to see the rock entirely intact. They plugged in some more dynamite and hit it again: *boom*! Again, nothing happened, except that they had wasted a lot of time and dynamite. They gave up and went on their way, much to the relief of the townsfolk.

But the rock *had* been split. The dynamite had produced a hairline fracture, at first invisible to the casual observer, but that over time with the help of frost wedging and gravity expanded to form a crack ranging from microscopic at the base of the rock to three inches wide at the top. Once rock climbers noticed the crack and started trying to climb it, they approached it as an aid problem. That was challenging enough, the crack being so thin at the base that no piton could be hammered fully into it, and so wide at the top that no available piton would fit. Tied off pitons with just the tip pounded in allowed tenuous passage up the first thirty feet of the crack, at which point it widened sufficiently to take pitons that were not in danger of popping out under body weight. From there, it was a fairly straightforward aid climb up a short dihedral, out a six-foot overhang, and up the angling crack splitting an overhanging headwall. The final section, too wide for pitons, was passed with wood blocks hammered into the crack. For the most part, placing pitons wasn't difficult; the challenge was finding enough pitons of the same size to make it to the top.

Although it became a routine aid route, the crack was ill-suited for free climbing. Generally sharp edged and painful for jamming, it was almost uniformly too wide for finger jams, too narrow to fit hands, and too thin for toe jams. It angled to the left and overhung slightly the entire 130 feet from the ledge to the summit, with absolutely no good footholds anywhere on the upper 100 feet of the route. But it was not impossible. The first thirty feet of the route, to the alcove under the roof, could be freed via 5.11 fingertip jams and face climbing. From there, 5.12 underclinging and thin jamming led out the roof and onto the headwall, which marked the start of a seemingly endless sequence of overhanging wide finger jams and thin hand jams with virtually no positive footholds. No single move was particularly difficult, but the cumulative effect of the continuously awkward, strenuous jamming made the route a technical endurance problem that few had been able to solve before our visit.

Steve Hong, a thin crack technician from Utah, free climbed *Sphinx Crack* in 1981. A tireless rock athlete who, like Tony Yaniro, trained obsessively on a self-designed crack machine, Hong spent countless days over a period of two years working the route before finally pulling it off. His efforts included multiple toprope attempts, lead attempts with preplaced gear, and hangdogging. He broke the route into two pitches, climbing the 5.11 start to an existing hanging belay, then launching into the final ninety feet of 5.13 jamming. Yaniro made the second free ascent later in 1981, after only four days of combined effort. He climbed the entire crack in a single free yo-yo lead, eliminating the hanging belay.

Because he skipped the hanging belay, Yaniro has been credited by some with the first all-free ascent of the route. No offense to Hong, whose ascent was certainly legitimate in that he free climbed the entire route, but a hanging belay is a rest point on aid that Yaniro was able to bypass. This is a stylistic conceit, of course, because on multipitch free routes, especially on big walls where hanging belays are unavoidable, a route is deemed free even if you hang at the belay. However, there's a big difference between a hanging belay of necessity and one of convenience. It seems unassailable that a hanging belay on a single rope length of climbing is a point of aid screaming for elimination, and the person who eliminates such an aid point has to receive credit for the first free ascent. None of that matters, though. In 1985, a visiting Japanese climber, Yuji Hirayama, put all stylistic squabbles about the route to rest when he free climbed *Sphinx Crack* on his first try, with no falls, placing all protection on lead. Hirayama's ascent may well have been the hardest on-sight of a free climb at the time, and for many years to come.

Fresh from his free ascent of *City Park*, Hugh Herr entertained delusions of flashing *Sphinx Crack*, too. And why not? Hugh was a skilled crack climber with incredible upper body strength, great endurance, and prosthetic feet that could be adjusted to fit in any size crack. He had what seemed like twin advantages: with his hatchet feet, he could conceivably use foot jams where others could not, and without the "inconvenient burden" of the weight of two lower legs, his strength-to-weight ratio was off the charts. If anybody was going to repeat Hirayama's on-sight flash, Hugh had the best shot. He was excited to try.

The next morning was glorious. The air was crisp, the sky was light blue, and there was not a cloud in sight. Before the sun hit the tops of the pines, we were hiking back up to the top of Sphinx Rock and rappelling down the crack to see what Hugh was in for.

"That's going to be hard," Hugh said as he unclipped from the rope after rappelling down the crack, looking pensively back up.

I scrambled up and retrieved the rope. When I returned to the ledge, Hugh was laying out a rack, which consisted of mostly the same size of TCU and Friend, 1 inch to 1.5 inches, as well as a couple of wired nuts and smaller cams for the first forty feet of the route and a couple of larger cams for the finish, Hugh being optimistic he would get that far without too much difficulty. However, he had already decided that a flash ascent wasn't going to happen. The first thirty feet to the alcove consisted of thin, marginally protected face and shallow pin-scar climbing, ill-suited to Hugh's hatchet feet. Looking at the route from below, he'd figured out that he would need to use his face-climbing feet for the first section, then switch into one of his hatchet feet for the upper crack. He would have to use the hanging belay, thus negating any hope of his flashing the route.

I offered to lead up to the alcove to establish advance camp for Hugh's summit assault. There were a couple of tenuous moves, but I was soon clipping the anchor bolts. I would leave the upper crack for Hugh. Hugh lowered me off, then tied in to the toprope and climbed to the alcove in his face-climbing feet. He fired right up the 5.11 start and was soon at the anchors, where he switched out one of his face feet for a crack foot, intending to jam his right foot into the left-leaning crack and find ripples or crystals in the rock for his left foot. Hugh pulled up a rack of cams, arranged from smallest to largest, front to back, then chalked up and was ready to climb.

"Watch me," Hugh said.

"I've got you. Fire it."

Hugh climbed a few feet to the top of the alcove, where the crack jutted out horizontally about six feet beneath a triangular overhang. He placed a cam. Climbing past the roof required grasping the crack with your fingers and pulling while walking your feet along the wall, an already strenuous technique made even more difficult by the fact that Hugh's prosthetic feet were not at all suited to the type of footwork required—especially his hatchet foot, which was all but useless when not jammed in a crack. Despite this additional hand-icap, Hugh grunted his way to the lip of the roof, where he was able to pull up and clip a bolt. After Hugh surmounted the roof and got his first good foot jam, he placed a cam, clipped it, then said, "Take me." I pulled in the slack and Hugh let go and hung there, shaking out his arms.

"That was damn hard!" he called down. "It's probably two grades harder with prosthetics. I'm already pumped."

Hugh hung there for a while, resting, then started climbing again, leading up from where he had left off.

Hugh climbed up to where his feet were even with his last piece of protec-tion, placed another cam, clipped it, and let go. He rested a few minutes then repeated the process until he was about twenty feet above the roof.

"Hangdogger!" I yelled up at him.

"This is hard," Hugh called down. "It's just the wrong size for jamming. I can't do a finger lock, but can't get my hand in there. It sucks."

"You're doing fine. It's just your first try."

Hugh hung there for a while, then spontaneously busted out with a refrain from "Roxanne" that could be heard all the way down in Pine, I was certain, judging by the number of dogs that began barking at that very moment.

31 THE SMOOT SYNDROME

Hugh gave up on *Sphinx Crack* after a few days. It was just too hard, a different style of climbing than he was prepared for. Todd Skinner came out one day and gave it a few tries. John Sherman tagged along to heckle him. A couple of Hugh's friends from back East, Jeff Gruenberg and Jimmy Surette, also showed up to give the route a try. Everybody put in their best effort, but nobody was willing to devote weeks to it. Hugh and I retreated to Boulder, where George Bracksieck, the editor of *Rock & Ice* at the time, invited me to stay in his basement guest room. Hugh and his friends stayed at Christian Griffith's house.

I didn't see much of Hugh after we arrived in Boulder, except at Wendy's practically every night for the salad bar, which was apparently the preferred grazing ground for every young male climber in town. He went off climbing with his friends most days. I hung around with George, helping him put together the upcoming issue of *Rock & Ice*, only occasionally going off climbing. One night, Hugh and I went out to dinner with Neil Cannon, my archenemy, or so it seemed based on his "The Smoot Syndrome" editorial in *Climbing*. I had heard Cannon was badmouthing me up, down, and sideways, and that he had suggested I wear a bulletproof vest because the traditional climbers were "gunning" for me—in jest, I hoped. I had also heard he was a firearms buff, so I was a little apprehensive about meeting him. He turned out to be a nice guy, a little opinionated, but I couldn't complain about that, could I? He even brought me a gift, a used Kevlar vest into which, he told me proudly, he had personally unloaded a clip from his 9mm Glock. He handed it to me across the table after showing me where the bullets had hit the vest.

"This Kevlar is amazing," he said. "It's so light, but none of the bullets went through. See?"

I put the vest on. It was just my size.

"You should wear it while you're in town," Neil said.

"I will," I said, and I wore it proudly for the rest of the evening and the next day when I went climbing in Eldorado Canyon.

I WAS SITTING ON TOP of the big boulder below the Whale's Tail in my new Kevlar vest, alone, looking out for snipers on top of the Bastille and wondering what to do. There were a few climbers bouldering around. I watched them for a while, marveling at their collective inability to climb anything, except for one guy who free soloed a route up the most overhanging part of the Whale's Tail cave. It was a muscular route with big edges, a sideways fist jam, an athletic traverse at the lip of the cave to a thin crack, and a fingertip layback followed by more gymnastics to pull over the top.

The route, *Horangutan,* was an old aid pitch first climbed in the early 1970s. Dick Cilley toproped it free in the late 1970s, and Bob Horan was the first to lead it free in the early 1980s. He then free soloed it a number of times, eventually even barefoot. As it turned out, the climber I had just watched soloing the route was Horan himself. I chatted him up, after which he led me on a tour of some boulder problems, then took me up on *Rainbow Wall*, at my insistence, so I could get some photos of him on Eldorado Canyon's first 5.13 route.

Horan had bagged the first free ascent of *Rainbow Wall* in the summer of 1984, practically stealing it from Christian Griffith according to some. Not so according to Horan, who saw it as a community project. Griffith was the one who had installed a few bolts along the short aid line in spring 1984, and soon he and two other locals—Horan and Harrison Dekker—were vying for the coveted first free ascent. Griffith and Dekker each came close before leaving Eldorado on a trip to Yosemite, abandoning the route for the time being. Horan continued working the route in their absence and finally pulled it off.

Despite the rappel-placed bolts, *Rainbow Wall* wasn't particularly controversial. Nobody was out protesting the route by chopping the bolts. That wasn't the case with another route, Griffith's *Paris Girl*, which became a lightning rod for controversy. Griffith had spotted the potential line, toproped it, rappelled down to place eight protection bolts, then led it in the spring of 1985, establishing the second 5.13 route in the area. The next year, someone chopped the bolts. The problem with *Paris Girl* wasn't so much that it had rappel-placed bolts; other routes in Eldorado had rap-bolts and they weren't getting chopped. It had more to do with Griffith's flamboyant and abrasive bad-boy Euro-punk style. Griffith had taken an aggressively iconoclastic approach to his looks, actions, and climbing that rubbed a lot of climbers the wrong way. His new route had rap-bolts, sure, but on *Paris Girl*, Griffith had spaced the bolts far apart, with hard climbing in the long runouts. He'd done so as a statement against the anti-bolting crowd: If he placed bolts sparingly and left sporting runouts that scared away critics of rap-bolting, who would have standing to complain? Some viewed this as elitist. When a photo of Griffith making the first ascent in his best Lycra tights ran in *Climbing* magazine, some believed it was a move designed to attract climbers to a potentially dangerous route. While Griffith was away in Yosemite in 1986, someone removed the bolts on *Paris Girl* with a crowbar. When Griffith returned, he replaced them. They were chopped again, replaced, chopped, replaced—so many times that people lost count.

This kind of negative feedback didn't stop Griffith. If anything, it emboldened him. He embarked on a series of controversial rappel-bolted projects, establishing several more hard routes including *Lakmé* (5.13b), a harder variation to *Genesis*; *Desdichado* (5.13c), an overhanging face left of the arête on *Lakmé*; and *Verve* (5.13c), a face climb in Boulder Canyon. These first ascents established Griffith as the best, or at least the most aggressive, free climber in Colorado during the mid-1980s, although Horan was no less active in establishing hard new routes in Eldorado and Boulder Canyons.

Horan gave *Rainbow Wall* a good effort for the camera, then turned it over to me. I managed to climb to the third bolt, which was okay because that's as far as Horan got that day. We had a lot of good excuses. It was August, it was hot, our rock shoes were oozing off the little edges. In truth, we gave up easily. We had no intention of actually climbing the route; we were just playing around.

I HUNG AROUND BOULDER a few more days before heading home, waiting for George to cut me a check for some of my photos he'd published in a previous issue. I needed the money desperately. My bank account balance was dwindling fast, and I had a car payment due and no job. Hugh was already on a plane back to Boston and would be attending classes at MIT in a week, on his way to fortune and fame as a developer of robotic prosthetic limbs for amputees. I had no idea what I was returning to, or escaping from, but I felt I had to get out of Colorado—fast.

Actually, I did have one job offer: a couple of days earlier, George had offered me an assistant editor position at *Rock & Ice*. I had turned him down.

"This is too much for me to do by myself anymore, so I need to hire somebody to help," George had said. "Think about it."

I thought about it all the way back to Seattle, mulling over the reasons I had declined the offer, stupid reasons to turn down what was pretty much my dream job. But in the endless hours of a road trip driving straight through from Boulder to Seattle by myself, past the innumerable buttes and prairies and Wall Drug signs, I had a lot of time to think, and I thought I had made the right decision. Boulder was an expensive place to live, I had convinced myself, and what George was offering to pay wasn't enough unless I found a cheap place to stay. Staying in George's spare basement bedroom wasn't a realistic long-term option. Everyone I had talked to in Boulder agreed: you couldn't afford to live in Boulder unless you could afford to live in Boulder.

And, to be honest, I was more than a little homesick. After two years of being almost constantly on the road between temporary jobs, and now broke and with summer coming to an end, I wanted to get home. The fall climbing season was coming up, and I was eager to get back on Index granite and the boulders of Icicle Creek Canyon, maybe head down to Smith Rock to see what was happening there. I had to get a job first, though. I had no money except the check George had given me, which would be gone the minute I got home and sent off the car payment. I had to get back to school, see about getting on some career track. This freelance writing for the climbing magazines just wasn't cutting it.

PART SIX
CHURNING IN THE WAKE

Change, as much as anything, is what tradition in climbing is about.

—Alan Watts

32 TO BOLT OR NOT TO BE

About the time I was having my existential crisis while driving home from Boulder, two Frenchmen, Jean-Baptiste (J.B.) Tribout and Jean Marc Troussier, were on their way to Smith Rock, where, as Alan Watts put it in his 1992 guidebook to the area, "they blew the place apart." I had been idling in Colorado—hanging out at the pool, playing tennis, and living the life of luxury in George Bracksieck's basement guest room, delaying the inevitable return to reality. If I had not gone on the trip to Boulder with Hugh Herr, I probably would have gotten a full-time job and spent every weekend hanging out at Smith Rock, and so I would have been there to witness the latest French invasion. Instead, I was moping home along the freeway, wondering why I didn't just take the goddamn job at *Rock & Ice*. I missed the whole show.

During their five-week tour de force, Tribout and Troussier blasted up most of the hardest Smith lines in record time, including Alan's long-standing project *Rude Boys* (5.13c). They also put up several new routes, including an unrelentingly thin, steep face climb up the dead-vertical wall left of *Sunshine Dihedral* that Alan had been calling the "Sunshine Wall." Alan had rappelled and cleaned the line in 1984 and had attempted it on toprope, working out the moves section by section. He knew it would go; he had even placed bolts in preparation for leading the pitch. "I was probably good enough to do it in 1985 if I had believed I could," Alan recalls, "but I couldn't see myself being able to link the thing. At least for me, breakthroughs first occur in the mind, not on the rock. Until I imagined I could do it, I couldn't." Alan had a mental block about the route in part because he was placing his bolts far apart. "Foolishly, I was going through a phase where boldness seemed as important to me as pursuit of difficulty, leaving runouts between bolts that were super scary, so I couldn't get up the motivation to try it much."

The other thing was, Alan knew the route was going to be 5.14.

ALAN HAD MET TRIBOUT at a climbing competition in the French Pyrenees in early September 1986. To his surprise, Tribout had heard about Smith Rock, and he along with Troussier and Corrine LaBrune had already booked a flight to Oregon for that fall. Alan told Tribout about his Sunshine Wall project and encouraged him to work on it.

Tribout arrived at Smith Rock that October and, in a ten-day effort, succeeded in leading the Sunshine Wall free, establishing *To Bolt or Not to Be* as the hardest free climb yet done at Smith Rock, and completely altering the landscape of American rock climbing. The *East Face* of Monkey Face was confirmed 5.13d, hands down the hardest free climb in America at the time. Tribout's route was at least a letter grade harder. It was easy to do the math. Tribout had won the race; 5.14 had arrived in America.

"If I had been possessive, perhaps I could have fought him off and done the first ascent a couple years later," Alan says. "But if I had, Smith Rock climbing, and US sport climbing, wouldn't have evolved the way it did. I wanted Smith Rock climbing to succeed more than anything else. Any ascent that moved Smith climbing forward felt like a victory to me, whether I did it first or not. We were all excited about his ascent," he added. "We had no choice but to be excited. I mean, class was in session. What else could we do?"

The Smith Rock climbers threw a party for Tribout a few days after his ascent of *To Bolt or Not to Be*, and someone had the idea of having a pull-up contest. Alan knew better and sat it out. But Chris Grover took up the challenge and did sixty consecutive pull-ups. It looked like Grover was going to win, but then Tribout stepped up to the bar. He flew past Grover's total without even slowing down, and didn't stop until he'd cranked off eighty pull-ups. To celebrate his victory, he ripped off his shirt and chugged a can of beer that someone handed him. "J.B. was super competitive," Alan recalls. "Whatever it was, J.B. could not—and would not—be beat."

Tribout later confessed to Alan that the pull-up contest caused his elbow tendonitis to flare up so badly he couldn't climb for a couple months. There wasn't any lasting damage, though. The next time J.B. Tribout visited Smith Rock, he was climbing better than ever.

BY FALL OF 1986, IN THE SHORT TIME since my visit in the summer of 1983 when I had found the place vacant, Smith Rock had gone from bucolic backwater to overcrowded theme park. After Tribout's ascent of *To Bolt or Not to Be*, it only got worse. The locals were worked up over *To Bolt or Not to Be*, feeling Tribout had pretty much swooped in and stolen it out from under Alan, Alan's invitation notwithstanding. Even more upsetting, though, was that none of the locals was good enough to do it, even Alan, and they knew it. But they were pragmatic. Rather than sit around whining or give up climbing for a career in stock trading or law school or something equally stupid, they answered the call. They worked hard to repeat the routes that Tribout and Trousseau had established, and they set out to establish their own new routes that they hoped would match or at least come close to the new standard.

Like the Invasion of the Route Snatchers just two years before, Tribout's ascent of *To Bolt or Not to Be* served as a catalyst for American climbers to push free-climbing standards. It was the clearest signal yet that rappel bolting was the most expedient way to get the job done. Smith Rock climbers, having already embraced the Euro-climbing ethic, soon upped the game. A few days after Tribout and Troussier departed Smith Rock, Chris Grover, aptly described in a 1986 *Outside* magazine article as Smith Rock's "guardian troll," bought himself a Bosch Bulldog—a compact, relatively lightweight cordless hammer drill—and immediately got to work rappel bolting a new route down a steep, pocketed wall on the right side of Morning Glory Wall. With the Bosch, he could place bolts in a matter of minutes; the drill was an innovation as important to the rappel-bolting crowd as Friends had been to free climbers a decade earlier. Sean Olmstead soon led this inaugural Bosch-bolted route at Smith Rock, *Churning in the Wake*, and rated it 5.13a—not quite 5.14, but a start. Before long, several other machine-bolted routes were ready to go, including *Vicious Fish*, which at 5.13c/d was right up there with the *East Face* of Monkey Face in the race for second-hardest route at Smith Rock. With the aid of Grover's Bosch Bulldog, the Smith Rock climbers quickly upped the local standards.

American climbers weren't quite on par with the French by the end of 1986, but within a year, an American climber would break through the ceiling, not only repeating *To Bolt or Not to Be*, but establishing a new, even bolder 5.14 route at Smith Rock. It wouldn't be Alan Watts or Todd Skinner, or even Christian Griffith.

33 THE GREAT DEBATE

In December 1986, several of the most influential rock climbers of the day convened in Denver, Colorado, at the annual meeting of the American Alpine Club to take part in a panel discussion titled "The Great Debate (Or, Is 5.14 Worth It?)." It was a somewhat stuffy affair rife with old-guard mountaineers, as AAC meetings tended to be, although this meeting marked an effort by the club to be more inclusive—to acknowledge rock climbers as legitimate climbers, too, and possibly encourage them to become paying members.

John Gill, the iconic boulderer, was invited to deliver the keynote address; legendary Colorado rock climber Layton Kor was fêted as the guest of honor; and the "Great Debate" was included in the program under the pretense of providing a forum to arbitrate the current rift in the rock climbing community over style and ethics. In a crowded venue with an estimated four hundred onlookers, the proponents of the conflicting styles took their seats and presented their views—Todd Skinner, Alan Watts, and Christian Griffith on the side of the hangdoggers; John Bachar, Ron Kauk, and Henry Barber for the traditionalists; and Rob Robinson, Randy Vogel, and Lynn Hill representing the gray area in between.

The highly touted "debate" was actually an orderly and mostly polite discussion, with each panelist getting a chance to express his or her opinion and ideas about the current conflicts in the sport, chiefly over rappel bolting and hangdogging. New AAC president Jim McCarthy then grilled them, and at least one panelist likened his questioning to trial interrogation: "The court found me guilty of hangdogging," Lynn Hill later wrote about McCarthy's examination, "but I didn't feel guilty." After the McCarthy inquisition came an open question-and-answer session, where panelists were subjected to pointed questions from the decidedly conservative AAC crowd. This included Yvon

Chouinard, who fueled anti-hangdogging sentiment by handing out "The Devil Is a Hangdog" T-shirts, and those members of the audience who had showed up wearing T-shirts that proclaimed "Sport Climbing Is Neither."

In an editorial, *Climbing* magazine suggested a more appropriate title for the forum would have been "Great Opinions—For Those Who Don't Know Already, Or Can't Guess." A writer in attendance referred to the "Great Debate" as being as effective at resolving the conflict as "ditch digging with a plastic spoon."

"Truth be told, there was no debate," Watts recalls. "Each participant had three minutes to present their position. It was just a show; it changed the opinion of no one. But," he adds, "sport climbing was such a polarizing issue at the time, I think there were genuine concerns a riot might break out."

Henry Barber, the senior member of the debate panel, was perhaps the staunchest traditionalist present. An East Coast climber from the old school, Barber refused to use Friends or sticky rubber shoes, viewing them as cheating. Even other so-called traditionalists, Kauk and Bachar included, had no qualms about improvements in technology that made climbing easier so long as the rock was not damaged and the spirit of traditional climbing persisted unscathed. Kauk and Bachar, the demigods of Yosemite Valley, were the current generation's traditional climbing icons, Bachar perhaps more so than Kauk. ("I *am* the debate!" Bachar was quoted as saying about the forum.) After all, Kauk had climbed *Supercrack* "Phoenix style" (i.e., with hangdogging), but in Yosemite he toed the line. In Bachar's view, routes should be started from the ground to maintain both the risk inherent in climbing and a sense of adventure. He had no qualms about chopping bolts on routes that did not adhere to the traditional ethic.

During the debate, Bachar complained about climbers who had rappel bolted routes to bag a first ascent, believing they had "copped out on the challenge by walking around the back." Bachar explained: "I don't really believe bolts should be placed on rappel. It offends the guys who are out to do first ascents [from the ground up]." When asked about his own placement of bolts from hooks, as on *Bachar-Yerian*, Bachar agreed that it was aid climbing, but defended the practice on the grounds that it preserved the sense of adventure of climbing from the ground into the unknown. "The only way to bolt is on the lead, on-sight, without prior knowledge of the route," he said. "And if you can't do it, leave it for someone else."

On the other side of the coin, the "New Wave" climbers—or "Euro-dogs," as they were derisively called at the AAC meeting—embraced everything the traditionalists despised: hangdogging, rappel inspection, toprope rehearsal, and rappel bolting.

Watts identified himself as a strong proponent of European tactics, a sort of anti-Bachar. "Hangdogging is essential to acquire the skills necessary to succeed on today's hardest climbs," he argued. "Traditional tactics, as commendable as they are, simply are not a means to succeed on 5.14."

On the subject of rappel bolting, Skinner said, "Ethically, drilling bolts on the lead, bolts however they are drilled, it doesn't matter. The performance is the end."

Watts agreed. "Bolting on rappel is the only way to protect futuristic routes," he said. "Denying the validity of hangdogging and preplacing bolts closes one's eyes to one of the best tools available to improve. Simply put, they allow a climber to do a hard route faster, and I feel that the more hard routes you do, the better climber you will be. Time is spent facing new challenges, rather than wiring the same old problem. But if this fails to convince you, I suggest a trip to Smith Rock to attempt America's first 5.14, the Sunshine Wall [*To Bolt or Not to Be*], a route recently pioneered by Frenchman J.B. Tribout. This one route does more to show the benefits of European tactics than any amount of debate."

The more moderate traditionalists, Vogel, Robinson, and Hill, blended the traditional and European styles into an almost "anything goes" ethic. They accepted individual stylistic approaches so long as they did not affect other climbers directly, such as by dictating how others climbed a route or by altering the rock. In their view, rappel inspection, toprope rehearsal, and hangdogging weren't anything to get too worked up about because they did not affect others' ability to climb a given route in their preferred style. However, rappel bolting and manufacturing of holds were not okay, because they changed the character of the route for everyone.

Although presumed to be a traditionalist, Hill had hangdogged at the crux of *Vandals*, the first 5.13 route in the Gunks, a minor breach of local ethics. At the time of the debate, she was coming off a season of sport climbing in France that had further broadened her thinking on how to approach hard free climbing. "With my background as a gymnast, I view hangdogging as a technique for training, not climbing," Hill told the crowd. "Clearly, it has produced some very hard routes. I don't see anything wrong with it. It doesn't hurt anyone else."

Vogel, a vocal Joshua Tree climber, agreed, casting it as a moral issue of importance only to the transgressor. "Hangdogging and previewing may erode a climber's personal integrity," he said, "but once that person is gone, I can still experience the rock the way it was before."

On the subject of rappel bolting, Hill expressed a "when in Rome" attitude. "I don't look down on people who place bolts," she said. "There are obviously different types of rock, limestone in France, welded tuff in Smith Rock, and I have enjoyed doing routes that have been bolted on rappel. . . . Each area is unique and it is the responsibility of the local climbers to organize themselves and decide what should be done."

The issue of competition was brought up—in particular, whether the race for higher grades was worth it. Watts took the lead in expressing the sentiments of the tricksters. "Many critics of European tactics feel that high numbers are not everything—they point to adventure, danger, and inner growth as vital components of the sport," he said. "Indeed, numbers are not everything, but difficulty has always been an important part of climbing tradition. The Europeans are way ahead of us in the free-climbing game. The world's hardest routes, the boldest solos, and the most remarkable flashes have all been accomplished by Europeans. Throughout the 1960s and 1970s, the US was on top of the rock climbing world, and I've always been proud of this. Frankly, it bothers me when I hear the top French climbers referring to US climbing as a 'myth.' The only way for us to improve enough to climb their hardest routes is to adopt their style. Climbing the hardest routes is not important to everyone, and there's no reason why it should be. But for those of us who have made it our goal to put the US on top again, the path to take is clear. Among these individuals, there is no debate."

Kauk responded: "To truly raise the standards of free climbing," he said (ironically, because he would soon be going against his own words), "you can't sacrifice style or purity for a higher number."

All sides almost unanimously agreed that the creation of holds—chipping, chopping, enhancing, whatever you called it—was absolutely unacceptable. "People think, 'Well, nobody really chops holds,'" Vogel said, "but there are some very revered climbers who have been known to participate in this activity. What those climbers were saying is that they were the best climbers in the world, and that nobody would ever be any better. People are justifying what they're doing because of the extreme level of climbing they're participating in. They're doing a 5.13, therefore it is justifiable to do something a little quasi-ethical. However, five or ten years from now, dozens of people will be doing 5.13s every day. To think otherwise is very naive."

Griffith, who had seemingly embraced the concept of creating holds in his opinion piece "Manifesto" (*Climbing* No. 98), seemed to agree, but left room for the possibility that it might become necessary to the future advancement of the sport. "Most people up here consider chipping holds as being completely disadvantageous," Griffith said. "I really agree with that right now. I consider extreme difficulty as being relatively unnatural. You have to have just enough that you can climb it but not so much that it is easy, and the variation in between is very, very limited. There may come a time when there isn't a natural place for a 5.15, or 5.16."

"Chiseling [in Buoux] is commonplace," Bachar countered. "Some 7cs that were the hardest routes of the time were chiseled, manufactured to make them go. Now 7cs are commonplace, and they're looking for 8bs and 8cs to do. They had them—they chiseled them to make the 7cs—and now the new 8bs are [being] manufactured."

On this point, Skinner sided with Bachar. "That is the point where you admit the route is too hard for you."

"I think that style matters in life," Barber told the audience. "I think that tomorrow is another day. We should leave some of these gems of climbs and real challenges for climbers who will be really inspired to do them in the best possible style."

Although the Great Debate didn't do anything to change anyone's opinion, after the event ended a small group—Watts, Skinner, Kauk, Bachar, and Pat Ament, who was covering the debate as a journalist—continued the conversation in Bachar's hotel room. "Bachar stood firm," Watts recalls, "but Kauk was willing to see our point of view."

A few months later, Bachar, along with Kauk, would visit Smith Rock for the first time and give hangdogging a try.

34 CAN'T KEEP HER DOWN

In 2017, thirty years after the Great Debate, *Climbing* magazine published an article called "Can't Keep Her Down: A Consolidated History of Women's Climbing Achievements." The article hit some of the highlights: Liz Robbins becoming the first woman to climb a Grade VI big wall route after climbing the *Regular Northwest Face* of Half Dome in 1967 with her husband, Royal Robbins; Bev Johnson and Sibylle Hechtel making the first all-female ascent of El Capitan in 1973; Molly Higgins and Barb Eastman making the first all-female ascent of the *Nose* in 1977. And then the article jumped ahead to 1985, briefly mentioning the European competition-circuit rivalry between American free climber Lynn Hill and French alpinist Catherine Destivelle, as well as a couple of 5.13 routes climbed by European women. Reading the article, you might assume that female climbers did nothing of any importance between the late 1970s and mid-1980s. Lynn Hill, I am sure, would disagree.

Hill was not included in the Great Debate as a token woman climber. She was no joke. A gymnast and track athlete as a child, Hill was athletic and strong, able to do fourteen pull-ups in sixth grade. She started climbing in her early teens, mostly at Joshua Tree, and within a couple of years, by the late 1970s, she was hanging out and climbing with the likes of John Long, John Bachar, Ron Kauk, Jim Bridwell, and John Yablonsky in Yosemite. At age eighteen, she was leading 5.11 and climbing big walls, including ascents of the *Nose* and the *Shield*. She and Long soon became an item, possibly the best boyfriend-girlfriend climbing duo ever at the time, although you could drop the boyfriend-girlfriend part: they were one of the best climbing teams period.

Hill was a rarity in the early 1980s: a woman who climbed hard, independently of men (her many climbs with Long notwithstanding). Around

Hidden Valley Campground and Camp 4, most female climbers seemed to be attached to male climbers. Todd Skinner, for example, always seemed to have a girlfriend along on the tour, a decent climber, sure, but not one who was pushing the standards independently of her male counterparts. It was rare to see an all-women climbing team, even rarer to see a woman leading anything very hard.

"Climbing was a radically boy-centric sport back then," recalls Kerwin Klein, now a happily retired history professor living near Joshua Tree, a short drive from many of the favorite bouldering grounds of his youth. "In hindsight, it was probably the most male-dominated it had ever been. We started climbing at what was probably the nadir of women's participation. We thought it was normal," he adds, "but it was just fucked up."

Hill commented on this gender imbalance in her 2002 autobiography, *Climbing Free*. "[Climbing] back then was directed by a fraternity of men, and there was little encouragement or, frankly, inclination for women to participate," she wrote. "Yet women climbers were out there."

Many of the women climbers active in the early 1980s were holdovers from the 1970s. Hill was inspired by her predecessors, especially Bev Johnson, who made a solo ascent of the *Dihedral Wall* on El Capitan in 1978. And Hill did big climbs with women, including ascents of the *Nose* and the *Shield* on El Cap with Mari Gingery, who along with Hill was one of the few women among the ranks of the Stonemasters. But there were very few female climbers in the early 1980s, at least in America, who were doing climbs you heard about.

Catherine Freer was a notable exception. I used to see Freer, a Seattle native and "hardcore climber chick," bouldering at the UW practice rock; she was stronger than most of the men, and tougher—someone I would have been hesitant to go climbing with out of fear of not measuring up. A 5.11 climber who did hard aid routes in Yosemite and elsewhere, Freer was invited to attend the International Women's Rock Climbing Meet in Britain in 1982, and the following year she traded leads with Todd Bibler on the second ascent of *Zenyatta Mondatta*, a 5.9 A4 route on El Capitan, perhaps the hardest big wall route then climbed by a woman. In 1984, she joined a team that made the first ascent of the north face of 21,129-foot Cholatse, a 4,500-foot wall of rock and ice in Nepal, and she was a member of expeditions to Dhaulagiri, K2, and Everest in 1985 and 1986. She perished on an attempt to climb Mount Logan's Hummingbird Ridge in 1987.

Lynn Hill was another exception. Though just shy of five-foot-two and a mere 110 pounds—a full foot shorter than Long and half his weight—she was Long's equal on the rock, sometimes his better. She adopted Long's fanatical training regimen, got strong, and pursued hard free climbing with a passion. In 1979, the pair took a trip through the western United States, establishing and repeating hard routes wherever they went. On a cliff near Aspen, Colorado, Long led an aid route that had a few bolts but looked a little dangerous for a free lead. "For sure 5.12," Long recalled, "and you'd probably have to on-sight it or deck. Lynn said I'd have to be a pea brain to even try it." Long took that as a challenge and led the pitch without falling. "It was basically a solo," he said. Hill followed the pitch, also without falling.

"I had a really hard time making some ridiculously long reaches," Hill recalled in her essay "The Stone Masters." "Somehow I was able to use holds that John didn't even recognize as such."

It's a feat Long still can't believe. "I have no idea how Lynn followed," Long said. "Must have been 5.13 the way she did it." They had made the first free ascent of the route, rated 5.12c, which they named *Pea Brain*.

The pair continued on to Telluride, where they established many new routes including a free ascent of an overhanging aid crack called *Ophir Broke*. The route involved what Hill described in "The Stone Masters" as "a series of ridiculously thin, desperate moves" to reach the crack, which was too thin for Long's hands but perfect for Hill's, allowing her to complete the climb. At 5.12d, it was one of the hardest free climbs in the country at the time, and the hardest yet done by a woman.

In 1983, after an amicable breakup with Long, Hill moved to the East Coast and started climbing at the Gunks. There, she joined a team of locals including Russ Clune, Jeff Gruenberg, and Hugh Herr to establish *Vandals* as the area's first 5.13 route.

"I was the first person to go up since I was the lightest and had the best chance of being protected in case of a fall onto the marginal gear that was available at the start," Hill said in a later interview. She flashed the boulder problem start, which gave access to the crux of the route, a thin crack through a fifteen-foot overhang. "We took turns going up as high as we could, placing gear where possible." Sticking with the local ethic, the climbers lowered off after a fall, until Hill decided not to. "At a certain point I got sick of going up and down, so I began to hang there. Even though I knew it wasn't acceptable style, it made a lot of sense to me. It was a more enjoyable way of climbing."

In 1986, I interviewed Hill for a magazine article I wrote called "Altered States," an updated version of Mark Hudon and Max Jones's influential "States of the Art." In my Hudon-esque survey of some of the hardest new routes being done in the United States, Hill revealed her hangdogging on *Vandals*. Some climbers took her admission that she had hung on gear as proof that the route had not been climbed legitimately. But in the end, despite all of what Clune called the "jiggery-pokery" on the first ascent, each member of the group led the route from bottom to top with no falls.

Hill's experience on *Vandals* led her to "[throw] out years of climbing philosophy," as she put it in *Climbing Free*, and reevaluate her approach to climbing. "The old style of climbing," she decided, "suddenly seemed rigid, limited, and contrived."

She and Long had yo-yoed on *Ophir Broke*, but had lowered to the ground after each attempt. "From my experiences in gymnastics, I realized at a certain point that was not helpful if you wanted to push into the higher grades," Hill said in a 2016 interview with the *TrainingBeta* podcast. "Why go back to the beginning of your routine and repeat all the moves back up to that point . . . ? You should just practice that move that you're having trouble with and then link your routine together and everything's smooth."

Hill would soon view rappel bolting as a perfectly legitimate approach to establishing hard new routes, though only where needed and if accepted as local practice. Still, she did not abandon her traditional climbing roots. In 1984, Hill made one of the most impressive ascents yet done at the Gunks, leading *Yellow Crack Direct*, a poorly protected 5.12c route, on her first try. Her no-falls, on-sight first ascent was the technical equivalent of Jerry Moffatt's first-try ascent of *Equinox*, but more impressive given the difficulty, lack of protection, and element of uncertainty. No one knew whether a free ascent was even possible. In 1987, Hill climbed a new route at the Gunks called *Girls Just Want to Have Fun*. She rated it 5.12X. Some climbers think the route is 5.13; mostly, they toprope it.

During two trips to Europe in 1986, Hill participated in two competitions, winning one—the Grand-Prix d'Escalade in Troubat, France. She soon embarked on a career as a full-time competition climber, and before long she was dominating the Women's World Cup division, winning competition after competition from 1987 through 1990. She sometimes outperformed even the best male competition climbers.

While in Europe in 1986, Hill went sport climbing at the local crags. She liked it, and soon adopted many of the Euro-dog techniques, which she started practicing in the States, earning herself a place on the panel at the Great Debate—and a role as a leader in the women's movement in climbing.

It was a role she embraced. "I've always believed that being active is a good thing and that women were not really encouraged to do such things, especially in a male-dominated sport like climbing," Hill said in the *TrainingBeta* interview. "I was told that a woman could never do a 5.14, a woman can't do this and can't do that, and I'd just look at these guys and say, 'What?' It only happened a few times, and when it did I was shocked that that would be their true belief, that women could not do that. It's a very closed-minded attitude."

While climbing in Joshua Tree as a teenage girl, Hill was surprised when a man expressed astonishment that she, a mere girl, could climb a route he could not. In Europe, some male climbers treated her as second class. One asserted that it was "impossible" for a woman to flash a 7c (5.12d) route. Another laughed at her for failing to flash a 7b+ (5.12c) route, then mocked her for wanting to try a 5.13. Even John Steiger, who interviewed her for the "Women's Issue" of *Climbing* in 1987, expressed amazement at seeing Hill make an on-sight flash of a 5.12b route. "Never had I seen a woman climb so well." Clearly, Steiger needed to get out more.

Hill would soon put to rest any thought of male dominance in the sport. In 1990, after J.B. Tribout famously declared that no woman would ever climb 5.14, Hill became the first woman to redpoint a 5.14 route, sending Tribout's *Masse Critique* (5.14a) in Cimaï, France. That fall, at a World Cup final competition in Lyon, France, she was one of only three competitors to complete the superfinal route. The other two were men: French climbers François Legrand and Didier Raboutou. It was significant that men and women were competing on the same route, instead of women having a separate "easier" route, which was usually the case. Unlike the two men, who took a variation around the route's roof problem, Hill climbed it directly—the hard way, leading one commentator to proclaim that "at that moment Lynn Hill was arguably the best climber in the world, male or female."

However groundbreaking and impressive these events were, establishing Hill as one of the best rock climbers in the world, man or woman, they are not what she will be most remembered for. She had something bigger in mind.

35 PUNCHLINE

In the wake of the French invasion of 1986, climbers swarmed to Smith Rock to try to repeat *To Bolt or Not to Be*. Smith Rock was the place to be—and be seen—for every aspiring or established hardman. Even such stalwart traditionalists as Ron Kauk and John Bachar visited in the fall of 1987, to the amusement of some and the consternation of others. Kauk and Bachar's visit seemed to legitimize the top-down tactics that Alan Watts employed: two of the staunchest proponents of traditional climbing had traveled to the center of the sport climbing universe to hangdog on a bunch of rappel-bolted routes. To many climbers, me included, this disappointingly marked the beginning of the end of an era.

Bachar gave *To Bolt or Not to Be* a try. He was seen and even photographed hangdogging on it wearing Lycra tights, apparently trying to fathom just how hard 5.14 might be, an exercise that no doubt made him keenly aware that the sport had eclipsed him in terms of pure gymnastic difficulty. Bachar did not spend much time on the route, just enough to confirm that this 5.14 sport climbing business was, as he suspected, bullshit. "He didn't really see the point," Alan recalls. "He was a brilliant climber, but his mind was made up."

Kauk was another story. He succeeded in climbing *Darkness at Noon*, a 5.13a testpiece on the Dihedrals, and was intrigued by the possibilities that sport climbing presented. Kauk would return to Smith Rock and eventually repeat *To Bolt or Not to Be*. "He never would have done that if he had followed Bachar's path," Alan believes. "Kauk had a huge impact on sport climbing's eventual acceptance. He was tremendously influential and well-respected."

At Smith Rock, and soon elsewhere, Bachar's nightmare had come true. The European ethic he'd witnessed during his 1981 visit to Germany had, in six short years, infected the majority of American climbers, who, judging by

their antics on the sport climbs of Smith Rock, had embraced rappel bolting, hold chipping, and toprope and hangdog rehearsal as legitimate means
of ascent. Rather than liberating Bachar from his staunch ethical stance, his
visit to Smith Rock seemed only to entrench him further. Bachar returned to
Southern California with a renewed zeal, continuing to exorcise his frustra-
tion with the ethical demise of the sport he loved by putting up death routes
and making bold free-solo ascents, especially in Tuolumne Meadows. This
aggravated a lot of climbers, including his former allies—Ron Kauk among
them.

Unlike Bachar, Kauk adopted the new paradigm after his visit to Smith
Rock. The following year, he went over to the dark side, rappel bolting a new
5.12b route on Arch Rock in Yosemite Valley with Mark Chapman. This did
not sit at all well with Bachar, especially after he found out that one of his
ground-up projects in Tuolumne had been rap-bolted, with Kauk being the
primary suspect. Bachar immediately chopped the offending bolts on the
Arch Rock line, hoping to send a message. Predictably pissed off, Kauk and
his wingman, Chapman, confronted Bachar in the Camp 4 parking lot. This is
how it went down, according to published accounts:

"What gives you the right to take someone's route out?" Kauk demanded.
Then, according to Bachar, Kauk faked a punch, pulling back at the last minute.

"I didn't flinch," Bachar said later. Kauk disputed Bachar's version, claim-
ing he had just walked off while Bachar yelled, "Why don't you hit me? Why
don't you hit me?"

Chapman stepped up. "If you ever chop my bolts again," he was reported
as saying, "I'll kick your ass!"

"There's no point in waiting," Bachar replied. "Go ahead and punch me.
Go ahead."

At which point Chapman lost it. "A switch just went off and I hit him," he
admitted later. He punched Bachar in the neck, sending him to the hospital
for evaluation and landing himself in the Yosemite jail to cool off.

Bachar later dropped all charges and apologized for chopping the route,
which Kauk named *Punchline*. A more contrite Chapman wrote up a report
for *Mountain* magazine.

"I wish it had never happened," wrote Chapman. "[Bachar] was a friend
of mine, but he rubbed a lot of people the wrong way. I like to think that we've
all grown up a lot since then, and still admire John for all of the great things

he's done." According to Chapman, though *Punchline* was the first rappel-bolted route in Yosemite in eighteen years, it was "accepted by nearly all locals as an instant classic, [and] enjoyed a brief and celebrated life before John Bachar returned to the Valley and chopped the route." He noted that the route had since been rebolted, and that there were other rap-bolted projects in the works. "While at this point both Bachar and Kauk have their followers, it seems the majority of climbers couldn't care less about how routes are established. What they do care about is the flagrant misuse of bolts regardless of how they are placed. Most climbers feel the main criteria for judging a route's validity should be the finished product and whether it is a worthy addition to the Yosemite climbing community, not how the route was established.

"Putting these ethical dilemmas aside," Chapman continued, "Yosemite seems to be finally awakening from the big sleep that has engulfed it for the past eight years and is poised to retake its traditional position at the forefront of world climbing. [Watch this space!]"

Chapman's apology did not end the drama; it was just getting started. Kauk rap-bolted *Crossroads* (5.13b), the arête just left of Bachar's traditionally established *Phantom* (5.13b), with *Crossroads* joining *Phantom* halfway up. Bachar didn't chop *Crossroads*, but two of his followers, Scott Cosgrove and Dave Schultz, tried to. They failed because Kauk had used larger bolts that resisted their efforts. Just trying, however, was enough to give them a round in the "boxing ring" with Kauk, as *Climbing* magazine editor Michael Kennedy put it. Kennedy facetiously suggested that Kauk and Bachar "duel to the death so the rest of us can get back to actually climbing rather than arguing about it."

The drama did not abate. By midsummer, all of the hangers on recently rap-bolted lines in Yosemite had been flattened by "unknown parties." And so it went, not only in Yosemite but in climbing areas across the country. Bolts were placed and removed, replaced and chopped. Angry letters were written and rebutted. Tempers flared; cars were vandalized; fights broke out.

Bachar took it all very hard. He retreated from Yosemite to Owens River Gorge, a then relatively unknown canyon on the eastern flank of the Sierra Nevada south of Yosemite, a sanctuary that he and a handful of climbers had mostly to themselves. Few people, no conflict, no drama, just rock. But it did not take long for the hordes to invade the Gorge with their Bosch Bulldogs, rappel bolting line after line. Bachar lost it. One day he arrived at the Gorge with his boom box, popped in a gangsta rap cassette tape, cranked it up to full volume to the annoyance of the hangdogging throng, and started soloing a 5.12 route.

"This climber chick came over," he said later, "and asked me if I could turn the music down. I said, 'You know what, you guys got rap-bolts, I got rap music.' I was pretty pissed off. I'd just been through the same thing in Tuolumne. I was like, 'Where do I have to go, Mars?'"

WHILE CLIMBERS WERE FIGHTING each other over rappel bolting in Yosemite, another 5.14 route was going up at Smith Rock—this one by an American. Scott Franklin was a brash young East Coast climber with an ego to match his technical ability. By the time he first visited Smith Rock in the fall of 1987, he had pushed Gunks climbing to near world-class standards with his first ascents of *Cybernetic Wall*, a bouldery 5.13d route that had shut down Jerry Moffatt, and *Planet Claire*, which he rated 5.13d but was later upgraded to 5.14a. Franklin had even soloed a 5.13a route called *Survival of the Fittest*, making him the first American to solo a route of that standard. Upon his arrival at Smith Rock, he started tearing through the harder routes, repeating *Churning in the Wake* and *Rude Boys* "without hardly breaking a sweat," according to Alan Watts. He set to work on *To Bolt or Not to Be* next. After a month of effort, he sent it, becoming the first American to climb 5.14.

"At the time I didn't realize what kind of mental barrier it had become not just for me but a whole generation," Franklin said in an interview for the Rock and Snow shop's blog. "5.14 was this whole mythical level; getting through it was a big deal. I think what opened my mind there was overcoming what was seemingly impossible."

Having broken the 5.14 barrier, Franklin sought a new challenge. He returned to Smith Rock in 1988 and bolted an unlikely line up the most overhanging section of the east wall of the Christian Brothers formation, where the rock rolled up like the underside of a bowling ball and appeared to be strafed by machine-gun fire. His resulting route, which he called *Scarface*, started with a powerful 5.13 sequence of overhanging finger pockets that led to a hollow flake, above which loomed another 5.13 crux passing an overhang. In its natural condition, the route promised to be perhaps 5.13d, but not 5.14. The hollow flake provided a good rest, inconveniently making the route "too easy." Looking to be the first American to establish a 5.14 route, Franklin decided the flake had to go. No one really objected to its removal; after all, loose flakes were routinely snapped off new Smith Rock projects during the rappel-bolting process. But this one was a lot bigger and more stubborn than the usual taco-chip flake. It was the kind of flake that would kill someone if it ever pulled off.

Franklin first tried to lever the flake off, but it wouldn't budge. He took a hammer to it. It still didn't come loose. Next he tried to blast it off with M-80s. When the smoke cleared, the flake remained, evidently solid and not a safety issue. But Franklin wasn't about to give up, not with a potential new 5.14 route on the line. He enlisted the help of Mark Twight and Randy Radcliff, freshly arrived from an ice climbing jaunt in Canada. Twight tried to pry off the flake with an ice ax shaft. The ice ax snapped; the flake did not. Still, they persisted. Finally, with the aid of a borrowed sledgehammer, they succeeded in dislodging the flake. They were eager to see what was behind it: Would the route still go? Luckily for Franklin, a crucial finger pocket was revealed, allowing him to link the existing crux sections. The connection was hard—hard enough to raise the rating from 5.13d to 5.14a. Franklin sent the pitch in April 1988, establishing Smith Rock's second 5.14a route.

The 5.14a standard was not surpassed at Smith Rock until 1992, when J.B. Tribout returned and succeeded in climbing *Just Do It*, an open project on the overhanging wall left of the *East Face* of Monkey Face that had resisted attempts by many climbers, including Alan Watts. Alan had bolted the line and tried it, but he ultimately gave up on it, realizing it was beyond his diminishing abilities. Tribout rated it 5.14c. For many years, Smith Rock had the highest concentration of 5.13 and 5.14 routes in the United States. And aside from the routes first climbed by Alan Watts, most of them had been established by French climbers, primarily Tribout.

"I don't know what it is," one Smith Rock local complained. "Smith Rock just lifts its skirt every time Air France unloads in Bend, Oregon."

36 PUMPING PLASTIC

"Richard, I seem to have misplaced my climbing pants." Rich Johnston looked up to see Stimson Bullitt. "Stim," as he preferred to be called, was a well-known scion of a prominent Seattle family—a lawyer, author, political candidate, activist, and former president of a Seattle media empire. He was also a member of the new climbing gym in town, the Vertical Club. Bullitt had taken up mountaineering in his fifties, and by age sixty-two he had made solo ascents of many peaks in the Cascade Range and had even summited 20,310-foot Denali. Four years later, at an age when most people were retiring from active pursuits, Stim took up another new sport: rock climbing. So it was that he found himself standing at the check-in counter at the Vertical Club, wondering what had become of his beloved pants.

"What do your pants look like?" Johnston, the owner of the gym, asked.

"Oh, they're blue," Bullitt said, regretfully.

"Let me check the lost and found."

Bullitt, Johnston recalls, was very concerned about his pants. "They were his favorite pants. He climbed in them for years. Whenever he came to the gym, he was wearing them. He was really bummed about losing them."

Johnston checked the lost and found box and there they were, a pair of dirty blue sweatpants with holes in them. "Real dirtbag stuff," Johnston recalls. "You would have wanted to throw them in the wash, or the trash."

"Are these your pants?" Johnston asked Bullitt, holding them up for Stim to see.

"Oh my gosh! Yes!" Bullitt said, lighting up like a five-year-old reunited with his lost puppy. "Thank you very, very much!"

The point of this story is not that Stim Bullitt was reunited with his favorite pants. It is that he lost them in a climbing gym, a venue that did not exist in the United States prior to 1987. That, and the fact that a sixty-eight-year-old veteran mountaineer had become one of its most enthusiastic members from the day it opened its doors.

THERE IS NOW A WHOLE GENERATION of climbers who can't imagine a world without climbing gyms. Before the Vertical Club—the first gym of its kind in the country—opened in October 1987, Seattle climbers had the University of Washington practice rock, which was completed in the spring of 1976, and Schurman Rock, built at Camp Long in West Seattle in 1939. Otherwise, if you wanted to practice climbing, you had to climb on buildings, retaining walls, freeway overpasses, or do pull-ups in your basement like everyone else.

Schurman Rock (originally "Monitor Rock") was a primitive structure consisting of rocks stacked up twenty feet high and cemented together to form a large boulder-like heap. Designed to teach climbing skills to Boy Scouts and other youth groups, Schurman Rock was mostly used for climbing instruction. The Mountaineers conducted their basic climbing courses there, and many young climbers, including Fred Beckey and Jim and Lou Whittaker, cut their teeth on the formation.

The UW Rock was something completely different, a series of concrete slabs tilted up at various angles like a Calder stabile, slabby on one side, overhanging on the other, all embedded with a sparse assortment of rocks and intersected by parallel-sided cracks, even a couple jutting across a roof. It was a nearly perfect structure for hanging out and bouldering on a sunny afternoon or evening. After the UW Rock was built, you could go to Schurman Rock almost any day and have the place to yourself. Not so at the UW Rock. On any given weeknight or weekend day, several dozen climbers would congregate there, bouldering, training, hanging out, being part of the scene. A whole generation of Seattle-area climbers grew up at the UW Rock during the late 1970s and early 1980s. It was the place to be if you were a rock climber in Seattle.

And then in the late 1980s, the UW Rock suffered the same fate as Schurman Rock: climbers mostly abandoned it in favor of the latest artificial climbing venue.

WHILE CLIMBING ACONCAGUA IN 1986, Rich Johnston and Dan Cauthorn, two Seattle climbers known to frequent the UW Rock, spent a rest day tent-bound at 18,000 feet. Naturally, they got to talking, and the discussion eventually came around to business. Johnston, a paralegal tired of his desk job and looking for a more entrepreneurial venture, wondered if opening an indoor climbing gym in Seattle could be a good idea. At that point he was open to anything that would get him out from behind his desk and make money.

"What do you do in the winter to stay in shape?" Johnston asked Cauthorn.

Cauthorn laughed. "Drink beer and do pull-ups in the basement," he answered.

"What do you think about a rock climbing gym?" Johnston asked.

Cauthorn gave him a funny look. "A *what*?"

Despite Cauthorn's initial reaction, the idea of a rock climbing gym stuck in Johnston's head. "I wasn't thinking about taking climbing indoors so much as just creating an alternative type of health club for the after-work crowd," Johnston says. "There was no real vision, it was just an idea."

Indoor climbing walls were nothing new in 1986. By then, they were already well established in England. Although the British had not invented the artificial climbing wall concept (Clark Schurman had; his "Monitor Rock" was the first), they had adopted it wholeheartedly in the 1960s as an effective means of improving strength and technique rather than just teaching fundamentals. A prime example was the Leeds Wall: in 1964, Don Robinson embedded small rocks in a brick wall in a hallway at the University of Leeds, not merely filling existing recesses with holds but removing bricks and placing natural rock holds in the gaps. It was a simple wall, primarily used for traversing, but climbers were soon making up contrived problems and naming some of the particularly difficult moves, such as the notorious "balance move." One student, John Syrett, proved the efficacy of learning and training on an indoor climbing wall when he fired up the hardest route in the area on his first day out on gritstone. Two decades later, there were dozens of indoor climbing centers and walls across Britain, part of a burgeoning industry and thriving culture.

When Johnston returned to Seattle from Argentina, he shopped his climbing gym concept around. Everyone he talked to told him he shouldn't do it. "They said it was a stupid idea," Johnston recalls. Despite the opposition, he thought he was on to something and decided to go for it. He offered Cauthorn 15 percent of the company if he would build out the gym; Johnston would provide management and funding. Cauthorn wasn't being asked to put up any money, just his time and labor. Cauthorn agreed. What did he have to lose?

Johnston found a space for the gym: a cold, dreary, abandoned cinder-block warehouse that had once served as a Sprite bottling plant along the railroad tracks on Elliott Avenue. "It was just down the hill from my aunt's house on Queen Anne," Johnston recalls. "I used to go down the hill and play there as a boy. When I found that space, it felt like it was meant to be."

With a suitable space under lease, Cauthorn brought in his crew, which included Cal Folsom, Greg Child, Tim Wilson, Greg Collum, and Tom Hargis—pretty much all of Cauthorn's climbing pals who needed work. They started by building an overhanging plywood-panel wall at one end of the space and framing out a pea-gravel crash pit below it. Cauthorn and Johnston figured out what to do about holds.

In their research, they came across a picture of a wooden wall with wood blocks nailed to it, but it seemed too primitive. If they were going to charge people money, they needed to do better. "We should use real rocks," Cauthorn suggested. His idea had merit. The Leeds Wall and other popular climbing walls in England had real stones cemented in the brickwork. Plus, there was an inexhaustible supply of free rocks lying about pretty much everywhere in the Seattle area. They searched the market for bolt-on artificial handholds but found little available. "Entre-Prises was making handholds at the time, but only in Europe," says Johnston. "We tried to order some, but nobody would bring them into the States." The only ones they could get were prototypes from Metolius—plastic polyurethane blobs that poorly mimicked Smith Rock finger pockets and were murder on the hands. They were, in Johnston's words, "the shittiest handholds you can imagine." Johnston bought some anyway, but nobody liked them. Thankfully, Metolius kept experimenting and was soon producing better-quality holds.

For the time being, given the lack of options, they went with rocks, but they couldn't figure out how to glue them to wood. "We didn't want the rocks just popping off when climbers were pulling on them," Johnston says. They did some research and found that a certain brand of construction-grade epoxy called Hydro-Ester Trowel was "the best stuff you could get." Johnston spent two weeks searching "all over the country" for it, only to find it in abundant supply at a store right across the street—another bit of synchronicity that convinced Johnston his climbing gym idea was meant to be.

"We glued rocks to the plywood panels that we'd painted with an epoxy-and-sand-textured paint mix and also glued rocks to the cinder-block walls and punched holes in the cinder blocks to make finger pockets," Johnston recalls. "Really primitive stuff. We asked people to bring in rocks that we could glue to the walls. Somebody brought in a bunch of rocks from Joshua Tree, so we had a Joshua Tree wall. Of course, we got a lot of rocks from Index, but we also had a Buttermilks wall and a Cookie Cliff wall made of rocks people brought from those places. People really loved those walls."

Perhaps *love* is too strong a word. The dead-vertical cinder-block walls were tough, with a predominance of small rocks glued on and only a few big ones, requiring a lot of thin edging and crimping, and the pockets were sharp edged and rough on the fingers. If you didn't rip the skin off your fingers, you were likely to end up with tendonitis in a hurry. "Yeah, we injured a lot of people," Johnston admits, stifling the urge to laugh. "We didn't know what we were doing."

In addition to the wood-panel and cinder-block walls, they created what they called the "anthill," an amorphous reddish-brown blob composed of gunite, a concrete and sand mix, sprayed onto a chicken-wire frame. It looked more like a freestanding turd than anything. "It was awful," Johnston concedes. "Nobody would climb on it. We had to tear it out."

Johnston funded the gym project with $14,000 from his savings, a huge commitment at the time. Despite his optimism for the project's success, he didn't immediately quit his day job. The gym didn't make any money in its first year, but didn't lose any either; it grossed $68,000, just enough to cover rent, salaries, and overhead. "I went two years without making any money from it," Johnston says. "I had to live off of my savings." The gym's initial lack of profitability had a lot to do with its shortsighted marketing plan: Johnston fully expected climbers to pay money to climb indoors. "We thought people who were into climbing would do this," Johnston says, and they were, but there was a problem. "God, they were cheapskates," he says. "I thought I was going to have to file bankruptcy." Being a climber himself, Johnston should have known better. He'd climbed at the UW Rock and knew the local climbing community already had a climbing gymnasium. It was outdoors, sure, but it was free. Luring them indoors was going to be a tough sell.

"Memberships were a hundred twenty-five bucks a year and climbers were pushing back," Johnston recalls. "Everybody was trying to get a deal." So he offered them a deal: the first twenty-five climbers who paid $500 could buy a lifetime membership. "I don't think we sold any," says Johnston, laughing. "They were thinking, no way, this isn't going to last."

The turning point for the Vertical Club came a few years in, when climbers started bringing their kids, then their kids' friends. "It was pretty rough-and-tumble back then," recalls Johnston. "It was dirty, there was the gravel, the old couch, and all the dirtbag climbers hanging around basically. It was kind of a sketchy place to be bringing kids, but it was great. They loved it."

Once the friends came in, their parents started bringing them, then the parents started coming in to climb. Before long, the climbers had been supplanted by a new type of clientele: people who liked the idea of an alternative to the usual health club atmosphere and were willing to pay for it.

WE HAD ALWAYS JOKED ABOUT PUTTING a roof on the UW Rock so we would have somewhere other than our collective garages and basements to practice climbing during Seattle's rainy winters. If anything, the Vertical Club co-opted the Rock's popularity, siphoning climbers indoors to enjoy a new kind of fake climbing experience without the inconvenience of bad weather. This wasn't intentional, not entirely.

"We did model it after the UW Rock a little," Johnston admits. "It was the same concept, but it was intended as a social place to go after work. Maybe the rain did influence it, bringing people in out of the Seattle rain, but it wasn't the determinative factor. I think it could have been successful anywhere." And it was. In 1988, a climbing gym opened in Portland, and before long they were popping up across the country. Dozens of gym climbers became hundreds, hundreds became thousands, and eventually thousands became millions as the popularity of indoor climbing gyms exploded.

In some ways, the change in climbing culture as a result of climbing gyms is ironic. "Tommy Caldwell did a slide show at an American Alpine Club dinner held in Seattle in 1999," Johnston recalls. "At the end of his show, he asked if there were any questions. Sally Jewell [then a board member of REI, later to become secretary of the interior] was there, and she asked him, 'What's the best way to get youth into the outdoors?' 'Climbing gyms,' Caldwell answered."

37 RADIO FREE *SALATHÉ*

In 1961, after their second ascent of the *Nose*, Royal Robbins, Tom Frost, and Chuck Pratt ventured up a new route on El Capitan, following a line of ledges, cracks, and chimneys up its great southwest face. Robbins had prophesied that a future generation would pioneer such a route. Just one year after the *Nose*, perhaps feeling the need to outdo even himself, he and his partners gave it a go.

After fixing ropes up the first thousand feet of the route to Heart Ledge, they discarded their fixed lines and continued to the top alpine style. Instead of forcing a direct line as Warren Harding had done on the *Nose*, they exploited El Capitan's weaknesses, committing themselves to an intricate route linking a series of ramps, chimneys, and crack systems up the vertical and sometimes overhanging wall, completing some of the most difficult free and aid climbing yet done. They placed only thirteen bolts on the entire route, which they named the *Salathé Wall* in honor of early big wall pioneer John Salathé.

The *Salathé Wall* is regarded as El Capitan's "most natural line," according to Robbins, "thirty-six rope lengths of superb, varied, and unrelenting climbing on a near-vertical wall in one of nature's most masterful canyons. Is it any wonder climbers from all over the world have come to try the *Salathé Wall*?" The route begins with ten pitches of moderate climbing to Heart Ledge, formerly mixed free and aid, now going all free (*Free Blast*, 5.11, first free climbed in 1971). From Heart Ledge, the route traverses down and left to and then goes up the infamous Hollow Flake, a serious, unprotected offwidth pitch that still gives pause to most climbers. It provides only a hint of what comes next: The Ear, a flake of rock jutting out from the main wall that forms a bombay chimney, an upside-down V, also difficult if not impossible to protect. It makes the Hollow Flake seem like a Sunday stroll.

Once past these mostly mental obstacles, the route becomes more sensible, climbing steep cracks and chimneys leading to the top of El Cap Spire, a detached pinnacle with a flat summit large enough to pitch a tent. Here the route's real difficulties begin. Robbins, Pratt, and Frost dangled and whacked their way up the thin, overhanging, and increasingly difficult pitches leading up to the headwall and then the headwall itself, from which retreat became increasingly unlikely without fixing ropes. Once the leader had completed a pitch, the second would prusik up the rope and remove gear, after which the third would prusik up a free-hanging line to join the others. (Prusiking up a free-hanging Goldline rope 2,500 feet off the deck must have been a memorable experience.) The final headwall pitch proved to be one of the most difficult on the route, but Pratt prevailed in completing the lead. Robbins and Frost followed, and after some easier climbing, the team topped out on the summit of El Capitan, having completed, according to Robbins, "the greatest rock climb in the world."

Like every other major big wall route in Yosemite, a series of one-up ascents ensued over the following years as subsequent parties vied to climb the *Salathé Wall* in better style, a faster time, or both. After the first ascent of the *Salathé Wall* in semi–alpine style, the next logical progression was to climb the entire route in one push. Yvon Chouinard and Steve Roper tried it and failed after Roper balked partway up the route. Weather and illness thwarted a strong effort by Robbins, Frost, and TM Herbert. After Robbins and Frost eventually made the first alpine-style ascent in the fall of 1962, the usual cavalcade of "first ascents" followed: first solo ascent, first clean ascent, first female ascent, first all-female ascent, first female solo ascent. Eventually the route was climbed in under twenty-four hours, followed by increasingly faster speed ascents. At some point, the only real "first" that awaited was a first free ascent, if it was possible, which was widely doubted.

Mark Hudon and Max Jones were not among the doubters. They made a rapid ascent of the *Salathé* in May 1979, free climbing all but about 300 feet of the route. A dynamic duo who climbed and publicized a number of hard free routes across America during the late 1970s and early 1980s, Hudon and Jones weren't necessarily trying to free climb the *Salathé Wall* during their 1979 ascent; they were just trying to climb the route as quickly and in as good a style as possible—"as free as can be," as they put it. Their concept was the precursor to modern speed ascents of El Capitan and Half Dome, where climbers free what can be freed quickly, aid the rest if required, pull up on gear when expedient, and do not fool around too long to try to free a pitch. Where a pitch wouldn't go free after a few tries, Hudon and Jones would resort to aiding past the hard moves and continue on, unconcerned with whether their ascent was done in perfect style.

Their ascent was groundbreaking stuff. They had pushed free climbing on El Capitan to new heights, literally and figuratively. Every El Cap route already had some free climbing; much of the *Nose* already went free, and most of the *Salathé Wall* had been free climbed prior to Hudon and Jones's ascent. But no one had previously made a serious or even half-serious attempt to free an El Cap route other than the *West Face*, which went at an underwhelming 5.11c, or the *East Buttress*, at 5.10d, neither of which counted as a major "big wall" free climb. No, the real challenge would be freeing a route up the 3,000-foot-high central section of El Cap, either the *Nose* or the *Salathé Wall*. Hudon and Jones had shown the *Salathé* might go, and in 1980 Ray Jardine made a serious effort to free the *Nose*. Trouble was, Jardine had chiseled a line of holds to create a "free" traverse, thinking this would open the route to a free ascent. It didn't, at least not right away. And ultimately, Jardine would not be the one to free the *Nose*. Lynn Hill would eventually do that in 1993, though in 1979, such a thing could scarcely be imagined.

IF YOU STAY IN YOSEMITE long enough, you end up climbing a big wall: the *Nose*, the *Salathé Wall*, the *Regular Northwest Face* of Half Dome. It happens, even if you aren't a big wall climber. So it didn't surprise me to hear that Todd Skinner had climbed the *Salathé*. Why wouldn't he?

What I didn't know, because Todd was keeping it a secret, was that starting in 1985, after he'd climbed *The Stigma*, he made a series of reconnaissance trips up the *Salathé* to scope out the route for a possible free ascent. John Sherman, who often referred to Todd as "Tard" and viciously chided him for being a hangdogger, had suggested the *Salathé* wouldn't be any more technically difficult than *The Stigma*. Sherman offered to join Todd on a free attempt on the route. But Sherman was a staunch traditionalist. "I'll go up there with you," he told Todd, "but no hangdogging." Not surprisingly, Todd sought out other climbers to try the route with him. He invited his old friend Paul Piana to come along on the first attempt.

"Todd called me up one day, out of the blue," Paul recalls, "and said, 'Hey, we're going up on the *Salathé*. Want to join us?'"

The pair had often talked about trying to free climb the *Salathé*. "We'd looked at pictures of the wall together. We'd see a crack and say, 'If that crack was at Vedauwoo, we could do it.'" Paul was excited about the invitation.

"Sure," Paul replied. "When?"

"Tomorrow."

"I told him, 'Maybe in a couple of weeks,'" Paul says. "But he couldn't wait that long."

The remaining aid on the *Salathé*, what had not been free climbed already by Hudon and Jones and others, consisted mostly of overhanging, thin, pin-scarred cracks on the headwall. Or so Todd thought, until he tried to figure out how to free the traverse to the Hollow Flake. The usual way of getting to the Hollow Flake was to pendulum over. Unable to pass the entrance exam to a free ascent, Todd and his partner went into "as free as can be" mode. They didn't waste a lot of time searching for a free alternative to the pendulum pitch or any of the other remaining aid pitches. But because of Todd's utter incompetence at aid climbing, they made slow progress. Aid climbing on the *Salathé* was scary for Todd; he called it "fraiding." He and his partner didn't reach the headwall until after dark, too late to scope those pitches for future free-climbing attempts.

Even though he had not been able to evaluate key sections of the route, Todd, the eternal optimist, was still convinced that the *Salathé* would go free. A lesser climber, such as myself or anybody else, really, would have given up on the idea. It was too uncertain, too speculative. The amount of effort that would be required would be tremendous, and the odds were that Hudon and Jones were correct: all but ninety feet of the *Salathé Wall*—the distance you might walk to your mailbox and back—would go free. Todd had spent thirteen days of effort free climbing *The Stigma*, a single seventy-foot 5.13b pitch at the base of the Cookie Cliff, and another thirteen days on *City Park*, a 120-foot 5.13c pitch at the base of the Index Lower Town Wall. There were still 300 feet of aid climbing remaining on the *Salathé Wall*, much of which promised to be at least 5.13; mathematically, based on his past performance, it would take Todd at least forty-five days to free the remaining aid pitches. That is, if they could be free climbed, and the climbing would be no harder than 5.13c, which was not at all guaranteed. Despite his college education, Todd did not seem to understand statistical probabilities, and he definitely did not know when to quit. Todd Skinner was exactly the climber for what promised to be an unprecedented, tenacious effort.

"After his first recon, Todd called me again," Paul recalls.

"Hey, we're going up on *Salathé* tomorrow," Todd said. "Want to come?"

"Darn it, Todd," Paul replied. "I can't go on one day's notice. If you want to go again, let's plan it."

Following a second foray up the wall in 1986 that went much like the first, Todd retreated to Boulder, where he compared notes with Paul. They reviewed photos, drew topos, and evaluated free-climbing options off the standard route based on the photos and Todd's recollection of those options, which was sometimes poor—all in absolute secrecy.

"Fearful of rival teams, we allowed no one to sit in on these planning sessions, even girlfriends," Paul wrote in the October 1988 issue of *Climbing* (No. 110). "The knowledge was committed to memory and the topos we drew were shredded and burned. The ashes were mailed to parts of the world where English isn't spoken. To the outside world, we hoped it would appear that the *Salathé* was not free climbable."

Why all of this secrecy? "We were really worried about a few other groups of climbers we thought might beat us to it," Paul recalls. "We thought Mark Hudon and Max Jones could have done it, although we'd heard they had moved away and were into mountain biking now. Randy Leavitt and Tony Yaniro, who were also phenomenal climbers, seemed like climbers who could pull it off, but they were also apparently doing other things. And Wolfgang Gullich and Kurt Albert, the German climbers, who we were really afraid of because they'd actually mentioned it to us as something they were thinking of trying."

According to Paul in his *Climbing* article, they had also learned "from the grapevine" that German climber Stefan Glowacz, who was tearing it up in Europe, had joined "a little-known fraternity of Europeans," including the Austrian Heinz Mariacher and Italian Maurizio Zanolla (better known as "Manolo"), to secretly explore free climbing the *Salathé Wall*. (One could never quite "secretly" try to free the *Salathé*; there were always other climbers on the route who could see what you were up to and report back to whomever you reported such things back to.) After spending ten days on the route in 1987, Glowacz had come away convinced it would not go free, especially the pitch above the Great Roof, which he believed would resist attempts for at least ten years—if it could be done at all. This was exactly the kind of challenge Todd Skinner could not resist.

During the competitions in Europe in 1987, Todd milked Glowacz for information about the *Salathé*. I imagine Todd playing the part of the aw-shucks hayseed from Pinedale, Wyoming, perhaps lulling his victim into spilling the beans with a story of gutting an elk during a hunting expedition in the Wind River Range—which type of knife was used and which parts of the elk were roasted over the smoky pinewood fire that everyone had huddled around to survive the snowy night. Having dismissed the route as impossible, Glowacz was no longer secretive about it and told Todd everything he wanted to know. Crucially, Todd learned that Glowacz had discovered a way to bypass the pendulum to the Hollow Flake via a 5.12b traverse sixty feet lower. This was just the information Todd needed to commit himself to a full-on free attempt at the *Salathé Wall*. The race was on, against whom no one really knew, but in any case, Todd and Paul made a pact to show up together in Yosemite Valley on May 1, 1988.

"When we first arrived in the Valley," Paul recalls, "we debated going into Camp 4, afraid somebody would give us guff about going up on the *Salathé*. I had this wig that my mom had given me as a joke, so Todd put it on. It made him look like Bob Dylan. I put on an old cowboy hat and dark glasses." Thinking their disguises would conceal their identities, they walked through the campground, trying to be inconspicuous. It didn't work. "We came up to a campfire and were sort of lurking in the background, and somebody says, 'Hi, Todd. Hi, Paul.'"

As subterfuge, Todd and Paul embarked on a series of so-called camping trips to scope out the route, test the most difficult terrain, find potential free variations, and become accustomed to life high off the ground. Their strategy was to spend a week at a time working different sections of the wall, disguising their free-climbing efforts, if possible, from the rest of the climbing world. To cache supplies for a later all-out attempt, the pair humped huge loads of food, ropes, and gear over twelve miles of hilly trail to the top of El Capitan, which was easier and less time-consuming than hauling everything up the vertical face. Rappelling down from the top allowed them to work on the route by day, then jug up the ropes and spend the night on the summit, complete with a blazing campfire.

Although the climbing was difficult ("harder than anything we had ever imagined," according to Todd), the pair's biggest obstacle to a free ascent of the *Salathé* was a lack of funds. They were nearly broke, and couldn't afford to stay in Yosemite much longer. Paul had "survived the past two weeks on 47 cents and Todd was the rich man of the team with 12 bucks still in his pocket," Paul wrote in his *Climbing* feature. They responded to this challenge by having a "yard sale" in the Camp 4 parking lot, selling off everything they had that was not vital to their continued quest to free climb the *Salathé*. They sold "virtually everything except our souls," according to Paul, which got them enough money to fund one more trip up the wall. It would either be another "camping trip" or a full-on push to free the route. They chose the latter and went for it, *Salathé Wall* or bust.

By this time, Todd's and Paul's fingers were trashed, as tends to happen on major big wall free ascents. "We were haunted by the specter of injury," wrote Paul. "Damage to a critical joint or tendon would finish our bid." To mitigate further damage, they agreed that only the leader would free each pitch and the second would jumar. It was not ideal style, but Todd and Paul were blazing a new trail and style was, for them, a secondary consideration at best.

Along with Bill Hatcher as team photographer, the pair recruited a veteran of Todd's 1985 recon, "Mad Dog" Bob Boehringer, to give them a daily weather report during their final assault. He would go by the handle "Radio Free *Salathé*." They had little to worry about; the weather cooperated fantastically. A thunderstorm or cold front could have thwarted their attempt, but conditions were ideal.

In early August 1988, Todd and Paul started up the route from the bottom, intending to get to the top or die trying. They quickly completed the *Free Blast* to Heart Ledge. Up next was the traverse to the Hollow Flake. After managing Glowacz's free variation just fine, they had a near epic on the Hollow Flake pitch. Todd led the unprotected 5.9 offwidth on a fifty-meter rope, which Paul realized too late was not long enough to allow Todd to get to the top of the pitch. Offwidth climbing was not Todd's forte, and he was struggling with the flake. Thinking quickly as they ran out of rope, Paul untied the belay and simul-climbed with Todd, without letting Todd know that neither of them was belayed. "I figured that only one of us needed to be freaked out," Paul wrote. Their luck held out; Todd reached the top of the flake and set a belay and all was well. For the time being.

Above the Hollow Flake and the Ear, an aid pitch presented the first real difficulty. The pair's original plan was to avoid it by climbing a 5.10d offwidth Steve Schneider had grunted up during the first ascent of a variation called *Bermuda Dunes*. But after their scare on the Hollow Flake, and lacking gear wide enough to provide even marginal protection, neither of them wanted anything to do with a completely unprotected 5.10d offwidth. So they tackled the aid crack, most of which had been led free by Max Jones in 1979. It had protection but promised to be difficult. It was. They split the pitch in two, using a belay above the initial 5.10d roof, from where Todd freed the remainder of the pitch at 5.13b. In inspired hyperbole, Paul described the thin corner crack as requiring "[s]earing, fingertip pin scars, laser-precise edging, and post-doctoral skills in body English."

The first 5.13 pitch behind them, the pair continued up to El Cap Spire without difficulty and pitched their sponsor's tent on the spire's summit for all to see. The "secret" was out: the two desperados were on a full-on mission to free climb the *Salathé*.

Although they were now halfway up the route, the pair was having doubts. The climbing was difficult and unpleasant. Little injuries were starting to take their toll. They took forced rest days to allow their fingers to heal just enough to try climbing again. "We decided that if ours had not been the first free ascent," Todd told me later, "we would have gone down."

Two pitches above El Cap Spire, the pair reached an A1 pitch that they had previously spent days trying to toprope via one of several promising face variations. It had so far thwarted their efforts to climb it free. But to their surprise, Todd managed to lead the pitch without falls at a relatively modest grade of 5.12d. One more "impossible" pitch in the bag, the pair continued to The Block and prepared themselves for the dreaded headwall.

As on the 5.13 pitch above the Ear, the pair broke the first headwall pitch into two, sinking in two bolts to create a hanging belay. Skinner led the first headwall pitch from the stance above the roof, beginning with a fifteen-foot runout above the belay to a fixed pin that he pulled off without falling, much to Paul's relief. He then tried, but failed, to free the next headwall pitch that day. "Todd couldn't crank the last few moves, or even swear during the inevitable thirty-foot plummet," lamented Paul. "The *Salathé*'s headwall remained, taunting and smug in its glorious position." The pair rappelled back to their portaledge in darkness, unsure of what the next day would bring.

Todd took a rest day, while Paul worked out the final headwall pitch. The next morning, Todd fired up the penultimate hard pitch without falling. Paul was up next on the final headwall pitch, the key to the free ascent, his torn-up hands barely holding together. After spending an hour cleaning his hands with alcohol and applying superglue and tape, Paul was ready. He failed on his first attempt, then pulled through on his second.

They rappelled down, packed up their camp below the Great Roof, and hauled it up to Long Ledge. Then, with some daylight left and impatient to finish the job, they climbed the final easier pitches to the top. It was in the bag; they had completed the first free ascent of the *Salathé Wall*. The pair rappelled back down to Long Ledge for a final bivouac, radioed to their support team on the Valley floor, and settled in for the night, drinking their fill of water, finishing off their supply of Pop-Tarts, quoting Louis L'Amour, and singing ribald songs about other climbers.

The next morning, Todd ate part of a carrot and tossed the rest off the ledge, an orange stub that was soon hurtling earthward at terminal velocity. Dropping a half-eaten carrot from high on El Capitan was bad form—a negligent act, inconsiderate of the fact that there may be hikers or climbers below who could be injured or even killed by anything tossed off a 3,000-foot-high cliff.

In fact, there were climbers below, approaching El Capitan at the very moment Todd tossed the carrot. They heard the carrot whirring through the air above them like incoming artillery and then explode in the talus dangerously close by. They moved away, thinking it was a rock, expecting more to follow. The timing could not have been more fortuitous. Had Todd not tossed the carrot, somebody probably would have been killed.

First over the rim, Paul started hauling their bags while Todd jumared up behind him. The pair's ropes were anchored to a large block. "It was an eight-foot-high boulder shaped like a right-handed mitten, leaning up against the wall," Paul recalls. "Other climbers had used it as their sole anchor. We just threw a loop of rope over the top of the block and plugged a #2 Friend under it. It seemed solid." He got their haul bags up to the rim by himself, but could not get them both over the lip, so he decided to wait for Todd to arrive to help him. While he waited, for added security, Paul clipped in to a fixed pin he spotted off to one side. "I was standing there while Todd was coming up, and saw a crack over to the left with a ¾-inch angle piton driven sideways into it," he recalls. "It was a stupid placement, but there it was, and for whatever reason, I went over and clipped one of the ropes into it. Just to be really safe. It didn't hurt to back up an anchor. You never knew."

Todd arrived at the rim, smiling, relaxed, pleased with the team's success. After Todd was done posing for the obligatory Layton Kor shot, he and Paul shook hands, congratulating each other on their successful climb.

"Let's get these bags up," Paul said to Todd, and they started hauling. Paul wrestled the first bag onto the ledge, but the second bag got hung up at the lip. "I couldn't get them both over the lip," Paul recalls, "so Todd went over and reached down to pull the second haul bag up, and we heard a grinding sound like a pallet of concrete blocks being dragged across a floor. We looked up and saw the block moving, sort of scooting toward us in slow motion. We were both tied to a short rope and couldn't get out of the way."

Neither had time to react other than to yell out in disbelief. Paul put his hands out to try and stop the block, but could not. They were like deer in the headlights, at the mercy of whatever was about to happen. "I heard a *crack!* like a rifle shot," Paul recalls. "The rope broke and Todd disappeared off the ledge and I thought, 'Well, there goes Todd. He's dead. I'm next.'"

The boulder ground over Paul, breaking his leg. "First I thought it was going to crush me," he recalls, "and while this was happening all I could think was, 'My parents are going to think they were right, climbing is stupid.' Then I just laid there waiting for it to drag me off into space, but part of it must have already been hanging over the ledge, because it just toppled off."

When the dust settled, Paul was dangling partly over the edge. "I was laying there feeling sick, in terrible pain, thinking Todd had already hit the talus," Paul remembers, "when I heard a breathless voice say quietly, 'Get the rope.'"

Paul helped Todd back onto the ledge, where they lay quietly for several minutes, dazed and injured, assessing the situation, afraid to move until they were sure that they were securely attached. Apparently, the block had scraped over an ascender that had prevented Todd's rope from being cut. The rope clipped to the block had been severed. Paul's last-minute decision to clip that "stupid" fixed pin with a separate tether, coupled with a healthy dose of dumb luck, had saved him from a fatal fall.

The block and haul bags plummeted earthward and exploded in the talus. Fortunately, the area was clear, the carrot having scared everyone away. It was a miracle that no one was killed, either above or below.

ALTHOUGH THEY HAD SURVIVED, THEY were seriously injured. Among other injuries, Todd had broken ribs, Paul a broken leg. After taking a moment to assess their situation, they topped out and made their way, slowly, to the top of the *Nose* route, hoping to find climbers who could help them. "We yelled and

EPILOGUE

When the legends die, the dreams end; there is no more greatness.

—Tecumseh

I have somewhat arbitrarily chosen Todd Skinner and Paul Piana's free ascent of the *Salathé Wall* as the ending point of the "hangdog days" era, since it nicely closes a chapter on the controversies that had begun a decade earlier, when Ray Jardine was hangdogging and chiseling his way up *The Phoenix* and the *Nose*, Tony Yaniro was establishing *Grand Illusion* as the hardest free climb in the world, and Mark Hudon and Max Jones were making their "as free as can be" ascent of the *Salathé Wall*. The controversies didn't conveniently end in 1988, of course. But by the time Todd and Paul dragged themselves to the rim of El Capitan in August 1988, the war was over. In a sense, the hard-line traditionalists had lost. Not that they were defeated, mind you; they had simply failed to hold their position against an unstoppable wave of rebel forces.

In 2001, there was another incident on *Paris Girl*, Christian Griffith's 5.13a route in Eldorado Canyon. By then, the bolts on *Paris Girl* had been crowbarred out and replaced countless times. This time, they weren't chopped; the first bolt was secretly sawed halfway through, leaving what one observer referred to as "an anonymous death trap for any climber who fell while attempting the route." Fortunately, the sabotage was discovered before anybody fell on the compromised bolt. The police were called in to investigate, but no one was arrested. It's frightening to think someone would be so enraged over a few bolts that they would endanger another climber's life.

Perhaps the ultimate bolt war was waged in 2012 on Cerro Torre, the famed Patagonia spire that mountaineering blogger Mark Horrell has called "the world's most controversial mountain." Cesare Maestri, an Italian mountaineer of considerable repute, had established a route up its southeast ridge in 1970 by using a gas-powered compressor drill to install a line of bolts straight up the rock. At the time, Cerro Torre was considered the most difficult mountain in the world, owing to a combination of steep rock, frequent antarctic storms, and an overhanging ice cap sitting on its summit that many assumed to be unclimbable. In fact, Maestri's so-called *Compressor Route* ended at the top of the rock face; he did not climb the ice cap. On the way down, Maestri pulled some of his own bolts to prevent others from repeating his route. This all caused considerable outrage in the international climbing community. How dare Maestri force a bolt line up one of the most iconic peaks in the world! And with a compressor drill! It was sacrilege! Any rock wall could be climbed with enough time and bolts, and here was proof.

In January 2012, American climbers Hayden Kennedy and Jason Kruk ascended the southeast ridge of Cerro Torre without using any of Maestri's bolts. It was an impressive climb, touted by the climbing media as the first "fair means" ascent of the route. On the way down, they removed 125 of the bolts. "Maestri's actions were a complete atrocity," wrote Kruk in a statement released later that month. "His use of bolts and heavy machinery was outrageous, even for the time. The Southeast Ridge was attainable by fair means in the '70s, he stole that climb from the future."

Reactions were predictably mixed. Some congratulated the pair as heroes for restoring the route to something resembling its pre-Maestri condition—for removing bolts that had been criticized for forty years as a mockery of all things sacred to alpinism. Others were less than supportive. "They fucked a historical route that was put up before they were born," complained one Yosemite veteran. "Kids have no clue." If Kennedy and Kruk's actions were deemed acceptable, some wondered, would a couple of foreigners come in and remove all the "unnecessary" bolts on El Capitan?

One of the most thoughtful responses to Kennedy and Kruk's erasure of Maestri's line came from Jim Bridwell, the godfather of Yosemite climbing. In 1979, he and Steve Brewer had ascended Maestri's route and reached the summit to make the third successful ascent of Cerro Torre. Using Maestri's bolts and a rack of Friends, the pair quickly climbed the rock face to the ice mushroom, then hacked their way to the top. "I assume that these two climbers believed they were making right that which they considered a wrong using anarchical, vigilante justice," Bridwell wrote in his op-ed piece published in 2012 on Planetmountain.com. "This eye for an eye biblical justice of equalization has a habit of never quite balancing."

Whether Maestri had been right or wrong in bolting Cerro Torre in the first place did not matter to Bridwell. He wondered if anyone had the moral right to pass such judgment on another's expression. "It is not a right to change or destroy someone else's creation," he wrote. "It only takes away the right of all others to repeat Maestri's route."

But perhaps Werner Braun, another Yosemite veteran, said it best: "What a freakin' drama. We scream when we put 'em in and we scream when we take 'em out."

In the end (whenever the end may be), the Cerro Torre incident will probably be seen as only proving that when it comes to placing and chopping bolts, it doesn't matter much which side you're on. Something is always lost.

AFTER HIS FREE ASCENT of the *Salathé Wall*, Todd Skinner told me he was finished with big wall free climbing. "The *Salathé* was worth it for the first ascent," Todd said, "but I wouldn't do that again."

As always, I didn't quite believe him. So it didn't come as a surprise to hear that, in 1990, Todd and Paul Piana, along with Tim Toula and Galen Rowell, had made a free ascent of the 2,000-foot-high north face of Mount Hooker, a Grade VI 5.12a route in Wyoming's Wind River Range. They'd followed the line of the 1964 first ascent by Royal Robbins, Dick McCracken, and Charlie Raymond.

Then in 1992, the Skinner-Piana team was back on another big wall, the 2,000-foot southeast face of Mount Proboscis in the Cirque of the Unclimbables in the Northwest Territories. Galen Rowell accompanied Todd and Paul for what Rowell thought would be an attempt to free the original line up the wall, which Robbins, McCracken, Layton Kor, and Jim McCarthy did in 1963. When they got there, Todd hatched a different plan.

"The rock is perfect!" Rowell quoted Todd as saying in his article published in the 1993 *American Alpine Journal*.

"But look at that hideous slime in the crack," Rowell remarked, noting water running down an inside corner.

"Not that," Todd said. "*That!*" He was eyeing the knife-edge arête that ran over a thousand feet straight up the face.

"But there are no cracks," Rowell responded, dubious.

"That's the point!" Todd exclaimed. "This is just what we've been looking for."

Todd and Paul started up the line, free climbing and aiding as the rock allowed. At the top of each pitch, they sank a bolt anchor and then rappelled down, cleaning and bolting as they went along. After two weeks of effort, they were ready for a final push to the top. Rowell joined, leading a key offwidth and insisting, like the true mountaineer he was, that the trio go all the way to the summit. Paul and Todd were leery; after their experience on the *Salathé*, they wanted to get down. According to Rowell, Todd asked Paul if he thought the climb would be a success when they got back to camp. "Not till we're back in Wyoming alive," Paul replied. They made it back to camp, and then back to Wyoming. Their route, *The Great Canadian Knife* (VI 5.13b), is regarded as the first big wall sport climb, Rowell's offwidth notwithstanding.

Todd and Paul were back in Yosemite in 1993, free climbing another big wall, the *Direct Northwest Face* route on Half Dome. This route, too, was first climbed by Robbins and McCracken in 1963, and it turned out to be harder than the *Salathé*. After twenty-four days, Paul gave up, but not Todd. He conned Steve Bechtel into joining him for the final push. Bechtel was "strong, tough and good on granite," Todd wrote in his 1994 *American Alpine Journal* article, "never complaining about danger and death." He also recruited Chris Oates, a Canadian climber. "I like to have a Canadian on my team," Todd wrote. "Lots of people aren't afraid to die, but Canadians, in particular, aren't afraid to live."

The trio pushed the route through to the top, tackling five pitches of 5.13 climbing, including the crux pitch, which Todd rated 5.13+. "We were met on the top by beautiful women, who gave us candy and lemonade as payment to be in our summit photo," Todd wrote. "We laughed loudly, kissed women we had never met before, lamented not having pistols to shoot in the air, and generally acted as Cowboys ought to after completing the first free ascent of the most difficult Big Wall in the world!"

He wasn't finished. Not even close. In 1995, Todd organized an expedition to free climb Trango Tower (Nameless Tower), a 20,500-foot granite spire in the Karakoram Range. British climbers Martin Boysen, Joe Brown, Mo Anthoine, and Malcolm Howells made the first ascent of Trango Tower in 1976. A German team composed of Wolfgang Gullich, Kurt Albert, and

Hartmut Munchenbach had made a free ascent of the peak in 1988 via the *Yugoslav Route*. Todd planned to make the first free ascent of the *East Face* route. He assembled a team for a "secret" meeting in 1994, and in 1995 the Cowboys on Trango team composed of Todd, Mike Lilygren, Jeff Bechtel, and Bobby Model, with Bill Hatcher along as expedition photographer, set upon Trango Tower. (Paul had to bow out because of a broken leg.) As Todd and Paul had done on Mount Proboscis, they aided the route to the summit, fixed ropes on most of it, placed some bolts, and worked each pitch. On the final ascent, each climber took some of the pitches, and as Model reported in the 1996 *American Alpine Journal*, "[a]t least one person on the team free climbed each pitch." The route, which they called the *Cowboy Direct*, was a Grade VII 5.13a. Todd and the team were criticized for bringing sport climbing tactics to the Himalaya, but, as always, they didn't much care. Todd's article about the climb was featured in the April 1996 issue of *National Geographic*. "Through luck and sheer stubbornness we had succeeded," he wrote of their successful climb. "But by the time we finished, we felt less like rodeo heroes than battered bronco riders who'd grabbed hold of something wild and held on just long enough to go home with the big prize."

You'd think Todd would eventually have had enough of big wall free climbing, and of the controversy that dogged him wherever he went, but he never did. He kept chasing his dreams, which always waited for him high on some godforsaken rock. Something drove him to higher, steeper walls. Whatever he was looking for, it was like that mishmash of misquoted lines from *The Terminator* that Todd had recited so often back in Joshua Tree in 1985: "That's what he does! That's *all* he does! You can't stop him! He can't be bargained with. He can't be reasoned with. He doesn't feel pity, or remorse, or fear. And he absolutely will not stop . . . ever, until he is dead!"

LYNN HILL RETIRED FROM FULL-TIME competition in 1993, but she was far from done with climbing. That same year, she threw herself ardently into another project—the biggest, most sought-after project out there: a free ascent of the *Nose*.

Hill was no stranger to El Capitan. Seeing El Capitan for the first time during an early 1970s family camping trip to Yosemite inspired Hill to try climbing. She first climbed the *Nose* in 1979 with Mari Gingery and Dean Caldwell, but she credits John Long with inspiring her to try to free it. "Lynnie,"

Long told her, as Hill recalled in a 2011 interview with *Climber* magazine, "you should go up and try to free climb the *Nose*."

She made her first attempt to free the *Nose* in 1989 with British climber Simon Nadin, whom she had met while on the European competition circuit. On that attempt, Hill became the first to free the Great Roof pitch, a supremely thin corner and roof crack that had rebuffed all free attempts since Ray Jardine tried it in 1981. This left only one aid pitch that had not been free climbed, the Changing Corners pitch, which had a reputation as a reachy boulder problem that would be difficult if not impossible for a shorter climber like Hill. Hill tried it but could not find a way through a ten-foot section. Eager to finish the climb, she and Nadin aided past this short crux and continued to the top.

In 1992, Hill made a speed ascent of the *Nose* with Hans Florine in a leisurely eight hours, during which she had a fresh look at the Changing Corners pitch. Something must have clicked, because she returned the next year with Brooke Sandahl on an all-out mission to free the route. First, she rappelled in to work out the Changing Corners pitch, which ascends a pair of shallow, pin-scarred dihedrals up an otherwise blank wall. Upon removing an old, broken piton from one of the dihedrals, Hill exposed a flare where she could get two fingertips in. She tried the moves on toprope and, after three days of rehearsal, worked out a convoluted sequence of stemming, smearing, jamming, and other creative techniques that suited her small stature. Back on the wall, she led through the Great Roof and Changing Corners pitches without falling and was soon leading the final difficult pitch up the headwall in style. When she topped out, completing the first free ascent of the *Nose*, she famously exclaimed, "It goes, boys!"

Hill's free ascent of the *Nose*, which she originally rated 5.13b but was later upgraded to 5.14a, came as a shock to those who assumed that one of the many men who had been trying to free the route would be the first to prevail, and who generally thought that a 5.14 big wall climb was not women's work. After all, J.B. Tribout had proclaimed that no woman would ever climb a route rated 5.14. Those who were surprised by Hill's ascent had not been paying attention.

"Ironically," Hill wrote in her 1994 *American Alpine Journal* article about the climb, "what initially appeared a pitch that would be desperate for a small person turned out to be a unique expanse of rock that almost seemed custom-designed for someone of my body dimensions and background in climbing." As Long had predicted, Hill had the perfect combination of strength, height, balance, and dexterity to solve the physical problems presented by the route, as well as an acute sense of intuition, determination, and perseverance learned through her years of competition climbing. An unlikely heroine in a long-running, testosterone-addled drama, Hill had fulfilled a prophecy of Mark Hudon and Max Jones: that not only the *Salathé Wall* but perhaps even the *Nose* would someday go free when 5.13 became established and climbers realized the possibility of 5.14. She also proved Hudon and Jones's assertion that body size and genetics can play a role in determining how hard a given climber can climb.

"I've always thought that Lynn was an awesome climber," says Hudon, "and I've never been too surprised that women are such good climbers. Lynn's determined as hell and talented beyond belief. It didn't surprise me too much that she freed the *Nose*. I was more like, 'Wow, that went free?' But 5.14 is 5.14."

"I'M GOING TO CLIMB FOR THE REST of my life," Bachar once told a reporter who was interviewing him for a news story about his soloing lifestyle.

"You sure about that?" the reporter asked.

"Yeah," Bachar responded, smiling.

And he did. John Bachar died in 2009 after falling off a 5.10 route at Dike Wall near Mammoth Lakes, California, while free soloing. When I watched him free solo in Joshua Tree and Yosemite in the early 1980s, he appeared to have impunity from the force of gravity, as if he could not and never would fall. He climbed with seeming effortlessness, moving fluidly on rock with absolute calm and focus and without apparent emotion. He was a Zen master of rock, a Yosemite god—in a word, perfection. I, like many others, nearly worshipped Bachar, or at least the image he embodied.

Immediately after seeing Bachar free solo for the first time, I went off alone and free soloed for my first time and was hooked. Like so many other climbers of my generation, I aspired to follow his path, and in my own way I did, enough to understand the quiet mastery that the free soloist must feel, to know the acceptance of death he must embrace and simultaneously put out of mind before stepping out over the void. Many times I have looked down beneath my feet at an eternity of air, at talus and shadows lurking below, well aware of the gravity and implication of the situation.

John Bachar's death did not surprise me. I accepted it with grim admiration. I had imagined it a thousand times before, as I am sure he and every other soloist had. It was part of the game he chose to play. He was supposed to die that way; an ordinary death would not have befitted his legend.

IN 1988, PETER CROFT MADE a first-try, no-falls ascent of a 5.13 pitch called *The Shadow* on the University Wall at Squamish, his home crag in British Columbia. In 2017, someone posed a question on the online SuperTopo discussion forum: "Does anyone know if Peter Croft's on-sight of *The Shadow* has ever been repeated?" Typical of discussions on the message boards, it quickly devolved into a debate about whether Peter's ascent was a true "on-sight"— done without prior inspection or knowledge of the route—or merely a "flash," a first-try ascent done with prior information about the route or after inspecting it. It was decided, by those who cared, that Croft had not truly "on-sighted" *The Shadow*, though his first-try flash of the pitch was certainly commendable. This distinction doesn't matter much, though; no one else has ever flashed the pitch, with or without prior inspection or beta.

"I knew how good he was," John Long says of Croft, "but his solo of *Astroman* still blew me away. It was amazing to hear he'd done it. There were a few sections that, to me, just seemed too sketchy. The boulder problem pitch was so thin. The Changing Corners pitch had stemming where you'd free-fall forever if you fell. The last pitch had loose rock. I'd done a lot of soloing, but I couldn't imagine doing those sections unroped.

"Peter had another level of competency and commitment," Long adds. "John [Bachar] and I would go out and climb twenty pitches in a day, stuff like that, but Peter was doing hard stuff all day. Doing actual mileage. That was something new to us. He had another level of dedication and perseverance."

Many believed Croft probably could have climbed 5.14 routes if he had wanted to. Maybe even freed the *Nose*. He was good enough. But he never did. It wasn't his style.

In 1990, Croft joined Dave Schultz to make the first one-day link-up of the *Nose* and *Salathé Wall* routes, climbing more than a mile of vertical granite in just over eighteen hours. Their ascent of the *Nose* that day in 6 hours, 40 minutes set a new record for the route, which didn't last long. In 1991, Hans Florine and Andy Puhvel climbed the *Nose* in 6 hours, 3 minutes, to which Croft and Schultz responded with a jaw-dropping time of 4 hours, 48 minutes. In 1992, Peter teamed up with Florine and lowered the mark to 4 hours, 22 minutes, leading to speculation that someone might someday climb the *Nose* in under four hours. Also that year, Peter, with Jonny Woodward, made the first free ascent of *Moonlight Buttress*, a 1,200-foot-high sandstone prow in Zion National Park. Originally rated 5.13b, which would have made it one of the hardest big wall free climbs in the country (at least until Lynn Hill freed the *Nose*), the route was later downgraded to 5.12d. No matter. Peter didn't really care about ratings, he just wanted to climb.

Peter put his speed-climbing ability to the test in 1998, making one of his most amazing climbs: a first ascent of a route up Spansar Brakk, a rock spire in the Charakusa Valley in Pakistan. He and partner Conrad Anker completed the 8,000-foot-long knife-edge ridge traverse that included 5.11 climbing in twenty-three hours round-trip. Peter's love of granite ridge traverses is unquestionable; it is where he seems most in his element. He soloed a traverse of the entire Stuart Range in Washington's Cascade Range in 1986, summiting six peaks up to 5.9 in difficulty over two miles of traversing. In the High Sierra, he made a one-day traverse of the Minarets in 1992; soloed the Evolution Traverse in 2000, with more than two miles of traversing on a high granite ridge crest; and made an enchainment of the four Celestial Arêtes on Temple Crag, linking four 2,000-foot routes up to 5.10b in difficulty. Peter has remained active to this day, establishing numerous long, hard routes in the High Sierra up to 5.13 in difficulty.

The last time I saw Peter, I was soloing halfway up a 5.10 pitch at Castle Rock in Leavenworth, Washington. He showed up at the base of the crag and started soloing after me. I continued up by a different route, and I looked down every now and then to see where Peter was and what he was climbing. The sun came over the canyon rim just as I reached the top, and there was Peter, picking his way deliberately up another route not far below. I waited for him to arrive.

"Nice day," I offered as Peter topped out on his first lap.

"Sure is," he replied. "Doesn't get better."

Then he turned around and climbed down the 600-foot face. I took the trail.

By the time I called it a day, Peter had vanished. He was like that, a ghost that people would see in the most remarkable places, appearing and then disappearing in the middle of a high granite wall or remote alpine ridge, or on a rarely visited summit. One moment he would be there, climbing quietly alone up some ridiculous route, the next moment, gone.

MARK HUDON WAS CLIMBING at Smith Rock with his wife one day in the mid-1990s when they were approached by another climber.

"Are you Mark Hudon?" the climber asked.

"Yes," Hudon said.

The climber stuck out his hand. "I'm Todd Skinner."

"Todd was a really good guy," Hudon recalls. "He really impressed me. The whole time he was talking to me, he was making sure to include my wife in the conversation. 'What are you climbing? Are you having fun?' Most climbers as well known as Todd wouldn't have done that."

"Do you remember soloing *Kamps Crack*?" Todd asked him.

Hudon remembered. He and Max Jones had stopped in the Needles of South Dakota in 1979. They were roping up to climb a 5.10 route called *Kamps Crack* when Hudon said, "You know what, Max, I think I'll solo this." Halfway up the route, he saw a group of five younger climbers sitting on a boulder, watching him climb.

"They had big eyes, and were quiet as mice," Hudon recalls.

"Hey," he said to them casually, continuing up the crack. When he got back to the base of the route, they were gone.

"Who were those guys?" he asked Jones.

"Beats me," Jones replied.

"I was one of those guys," Todd told him. "I saw you solo *Kamps Crack*, and it made me decide I would try to become a good climber."

"I'm glad I inspired people to take steps," Hudon says, forty years after he and Jones did their "as free as can be" ascent of the *Salathé Wall*, which had inspired Todd and Paul Piana to try it. "We were building on the accomplishments of those who came before us, always taking steps, trying to move forward. We always thought someone would come along and take the next step. So when Todd and Piana did the route all free, we felt they had taken the next step."

Although he had predicted the coming of 5.14, Hudon had not foreseen sport climbing, or what would happen at Smith Rock. Jones had visited Smith Rock in 1984 to participate in *Survival of the Fittest*, a made-for-TV endurance competition. "[Smith] has lots of great-looking faces," he reported to Hudon, "but I don't know how you'd protect them."

"I never imagined such a place would exist," Hudon says of Smith Rock. "I didn't see that coming." Although he has done some hard sport climbing,

Hudon would still rather hang out on a big wall. "I didn't really enjoy routes like *The Phoenix*," he says. "What I really wanted to do was free climb on the big walls." He's been hitting the big walls again lately. He climbed the *Nose* in a day in 2009, at age fifty-three, leading every pitch and finishing the route in 15 hours, 5 minutes.

Although he's past sixty now, he would still like to free climb the *Salathé Wall* via the *Freerider* variation. He has a trip to Yosemite planned already. He's going to climb El Capitan again.

"Would you join me on *Astroman*?" I asked him, still hoping to fulfill my goal of climbing it.

"I'd love to climb *Astroman* again!" he replied.

"AS YOU CAN SEE, MY LEGS are bionic," Hugh Herr told the audience during his 2014 TED Talk. Dr. Herr, as he is known these days in academic circles, was wearing pants hemmed at the knees, his shiny, high-tech plastic-and-metal artificial legs on full display. "I made sure to shave my legs last night, because I knew I'd be showing them off," he joked.

He wowed the audience by walking and even running on the stage to demonstrate the functionality of his bionic legs. Far from the slightly stiff-legged "pathological" gait he had displayed back when he was wearing the clunky Seattle Foot, he moved gracefully. Then, as if that was not enough, he brought out ballroom dancer Adrianne Haslet-Davis, who danced a graceful duet with Christian Lightner, her partner for the occasion—Haslet-Davis's first performance since she lost her left leg in the 2013 Boston Marathon bombing.

To say Hugh's research and development accomplishments in the field of biomechatronics have been significant seems an understatement. He is a professor at MIT, where he founded the Center for Extreme Bionics and also directs the Biomechatronics group of the MIT Media Lab. He has founded or directed several bionics research firms including BionX Medical Technologies, Inc., which developed the BiOM computerized ankle-foot system, the world's first leg prosthesis that allows amputees to walk as if they had biological legs; he wears two daily.

Clearly, Hugh has been busy since he boarded that flight from Denver to Boston and started his first class at MIT in the fall of 1986. He earned a master's degree in mechanical engineering at MIT, a PhD in biophysics at Harvard, then returned for postgrad work in biomedical devices at MIT, where he achieved full professorship in 2004. "He wasn't sitting around thinking, 'Gee, I wish *they* could come up with a better gadget,'" said William Gadsby in a 2014 *Smithsonian* magazine article about the future of prosthetic legs. A marine who lost his right leg in combat in 2007, Gadsby received a BiOM ankle-foot system, which he felt gave him back the life he had before his leg was blown off in Iraq; it had, physically and emotionally, fixed him. "[Dr. Herr] got those degrees so he could fix himself," Gadsby said, "and fix everyone else."

Hugh has radically changed the playing field, developing prosthetic devices that enable heavy lifting, stair climbing, rock climbing, and cross-country skiing. His aim is to normalize, to eliminate barriers, to raise the ocean so all boats rise. Hugh has been this way ever since his accident in 1982—refusing to feel sorry for himself, intent on turning setback into opportunity, tinkering, adapting, improving things, not only for himself but for every disabled person out there. The "Mechanical Boy" has grown up to become the "Biomechatronic Man."

Hugh is an inspiration to amputees who had difficulty adapting to traditional prosthetics and who hoped to walk normally again. Because of Hugh's work, they can.

He's been an inspiration for climbers, too, including Brittany Goris, who redpointed *City Park* on July 10, 2018—the first woman to accomplish the feat. Goris takes offense at those who argue Hugh cheated because his specially designed prosthetics were artificial aids that somehow negated the legitimacy of his 1986 ascent.

"I think those who don't consider Hugh's ascent of *City Park* a true ascent are perhaps lacking in an understanding of disabilities," says Goris. "He turned a tragedy into a genius and visionary life of accomplishments. I hope to one day meet the guy."

BRITTANY GORIS HAD BEEN WORKING on free climbing *City Park* since May, but this day in early July she wasn't liking her chances. It had rained in the morning, and she was worried the crack would be wet. Her fingers were still trashed from her attempt three days earlier, and her rock shoes were about worn out. Her elbows were sore from training, and her back hurt from heavy lifting at work. To top it off, her climbing partner was late to pick her up. Everything seemed to be going wrong.

"Basically my mental game was shit," she wrote in a blog article about that day. "Nothing was right, but nonetheless I had to try."

Goris, twenty-five at the time, discovered climbing in fifth grade, when she walked into a climbing gym in Fort Collins, Colorado, and insisted her mother sign her up. When she was seventeen, Brittany received a copy of Lynn Hill's autobiography, *Climbing Free*, as a Christmas present. It changed her life.

"Up until that point I had been a gym rat," she says. "I was passionate about climbing, but I had yet to fully immerse myself in the lifestyle."

Goris was particularly inspired by how Hill overcame obstacles, including the sexist attitudes of male climbers. "Her stories about how men would tell her that no woman would ever free climb 5.14 and how it lit a fire in her hit home right away," she says. "How she wouldn't accept when people said the *Nose* would never go free, or go free in a day. Her stubbornness, grit, determination, and passion are things that I read about and wanted to find in myself." Goris's grit and determination won out over the day's frustrations, which included waiting for a group of aid climbers to finish with the pitch.

"No problem," Goris thought. "I needed lots of rest anyway, and how long could they possibly take?"

A long time, it turned out. She returned at 8:45 p.m., thinking they'd be gone, but they were still there. One aid climber was still following the pitch, cleaning several stuck nuts. Minutes went by. The sun was setting. Daylight faded, along with Goris's hopes that she would be able to get on the pitch before it got too dark.

Fifteen minutes later, the aid climber was still working to remove the last stuck nut. Realizing the piece was not blocking any jams or gear placements, Goris asked that the climber abandon it so she could give the route one more try. The climber agreed.

Goris flowed up past her high point and soon found herself above the break, pinkies slipping out of the pin scars but feet sticking improbably to the wall. She was starting to pump out, but still cruising, so relaxed she even started singing to herself.

"With each move I became more and more certain that this was it, the moment that *City Park* had finally deemed me worthy," she wrote. "I placed each hand perfectly, each foot perfectly, and made not a sound until I was standing on the ledge below the final 5.11 section."

But she wasn't finished. There was still that final twenty feet of 5.11 climbing to the anchors, easy compared to what she'd just done, but still no gimme given the pump factor and fading light. Her composure vanished. She started rushing, climbing on pure adrenaline—stuffing her fingers into the crack, sticking her feet anywhere, racing to the top in the last light of the day. She held on, made the final moves, clipped the anchors, and felt instant release.

"As I latched the final hold," she wrote, "I let out a scream and felt tears immediately form and begin to fall."

The current consensus grade for *City Park* is 5.13d—not quite 5.14, but tantalizingly close. A lot of climbers have tried it, but aside from Todd Skinner's and Hugh Herr's ascents in 1986, the route has only been led by five other climbers—all locals. "It's sort of a locals-only kind of project," says Goris, "unless you're just that damn good that it could be bagged in few attempts."

Because of her limited trad experience, Goris is unwilling to offer an opinion of *City Park*'s grade. Mikey Schaefer, who bagged the first redpoint in 2006, told her he didn't know what to rate it either, but speculated that anywhere else it could be 5.14.

Some climbers have suggested that the route is better suited for women, a sort of dis that Goris doesn't take lightly. "If you ask me, it's suited for anyone with a vision," she says. "The rest is just a set of personal obstacles that must be overcome. Everyone has strengths and weaknesses," she adds. "I'm the tallest person to have sent the route [she's five-foot-eleven], but does that matter? No. It's all just personal strengths and weaknesses and learning to use what we've got to our advantage."

To anyone who tries to diminish her accomplishment, Goris points out that the route hasn't gotten any easier just because she did it. "I just tell them to go send it themselves and then get back to me with what they think the grade should be," she says. Half joking, she adds, "Maybe we should just call it 5.11d like everything else at Index."

ONE DAY IN APRIL 2013, Drew Ruana decided to do a work burn on *To Bolt or Not to Be*. If you had seen him off the rocks back then, you'd think Drew was just some fresh-faced preadolescent kid, a slightly nerdy eighth-grader who hadn't hit his growth spurt yet and still wasn't embarrassed to be seen in the same area code as his parents. At four-foot-nine and eighty pounds, Drew looked like he was ten years old, but he was thirteen. He didn't strike you as being a climber, but when he tied in, chalked up, and started up the rock, you realized you'd underestimated him. You might have thought a 5.14 route would be pretty stiff for a thirteen-year-old kid, but it was fair game for Drew, who had already dispatched four other 5.14 routes over the winter.

Drew's father, Rudy, started taking Drew out to the crags when he was three, his version of father-son time when he was pulling dad duty. Some weekends, Rudy would drive down to Smith Rock from the Seattle area on Friday night with Drew asleep in the backseat. Drew would wake up Saturday morning at Smith Rock and go climbing with his dad. "Sometimes we didn't climb," says Rudy. "We'd just throw rocks in the river, whatever, have a good time." But eventually it became about climbing. Drew did his first lead at age six, a 5.6 route at Smith Rock. "My dad said I could keep the quickdraws if I did the route," Drew recalls. "So I did it. Got the quickdraws."

Rudy brought Drew to the climbing gym for the first time when he was just two years old. When Drew was nine, the youth team coach urged Rudy to enroll Drew in the competitive program. Drew excelled and, that year, his dad drove him to a regional competition in Sacramento. His mom, Chris, wasn't too keen on the idea. "That's dumb," she said. "You're going to drive a nine-year-old to Sacramento for a competition? You're not going to Yosemite? You're climbing in a gym?" They went anyway, and Drew qualified for nationals. It wasn't so dumb anymore.

With his dad belaying, Drew flowed from thin edge to thin edge, making it look easy. The cruxes didn't feel that hard during his redpoint, Drew will tell you. It has a few hard sections but doesn't have any "stopper" cruxes that will spit you off over and over. It just starts hard and never lets up, stacking crux after crux most of the way up the 140-foot wall. Drew was at a disadvantage, though: he was a little kid, basically, and couldn't make the long reaches taller climbers could. He took that as a challenge. He struggled almost imperceptibly at the first crux, making impossibly long reaches between miniscule holds, his feet miraculously sticking to dime-edges. He muscled through even though he doesn't appear to have the musculature required to make such demanding moves. Above that, he was all fingers and toes, climbing up consistently thin edges and tiny pockets, clipping bolts five, six, seven, eight. He made it through the hardest of the climbing without falling off.

When you watch the video his mom posted to YouTube, you might think the kid has no respect for his elders, who struggled to climb routes this hard back in the day. Drew had spent only a handful of days on *To Bolt or Not to Be*. He was a short, skinny kid. "This isn't supposed to be happening," you might think. "It's supposed to be harder than this."

Drew did almost blow it near the top. His foot slipped off, but he dug in with his fingers, hung on, and recovered. He was way the hell up there, doing thin, technical moves on the steep slab, running it out between bolts, making his mom, who was filming him from below, nervous. "Come on, come on, come on," she whispers in the video, quietly urging him up the route. Drew was so close he could taste it. He started rushing, overcrimping, straining to pull up the hundred feet of trailing rope to clip in to the quickdraws as he climbed higher. Two bolts to go, then one. The chains were just a few moves away. He pulled hard and he was there. He let out a whoop and pumped his fist to the sky.

"Yeah!" his dad yelled as he lowered Drew to the ground. Rudy was excited, dumbfounded, and a little jealous.

"Holy cow," Chris, said to herself, astonished at her son's accomplishment. "Good job, Drew!" she yelled up, breathlessly. "Holy cow."

"DREW'S THE REAL DEAL," says American sport climbing's founding father Alan Watts, who put up the first 5.13 sport routes at Smith Rock thirty years earlier, bringing the area to international prominence. "Climbing *To Bolt or Not to Be* at age thirteen was unthinkable thirty years ago," he says. "It was something none of us could have imagined, but in the context of what youngsters are doing these days, it's totally expected."

It's the climbing gyms, Alan thinks, that have made the biggest difference. "We didn't have the gyms," he says, "and it was really hard to get into climbing when you were young. Today, kids start going to gyms shortly after they're potty-trained." Factor in the inevitability of each generation building upon the successes of past generations, Alan believes, and it only makes sense that today's young climbers are so good. "It would really be disappointing if it wasn't that way. It would mean our sport was fully mature and stagnating."

The sport is clearly not stagnating. It is thriving. In the past decade alone, Tommy Caldwell and Kevin Jorgeson free climbed the *Dawn Wall*, Caldwell and Alex Honnold speed-climbed the *Nose* in 1 hour, 58 minutes, fifteen-year-old Connor Herson free-climbed the *Nose*, and Margo Hayes became the first woman to climb 5.15. Possibly the most amazing ascent of the past decade—or maybe ever—is Honnold's 2017 free solo of the *Freerider* route up El Capitan. And Drew Ruana is coming down to Smith Rock practically every weekend, working on a project that, when completed, will be the area's first 5.15. All of this, Alan thinks, can be traced back to the controversies of the 1980s, perhaps as embodied in a single route: *The Stigma.*

"*The Stigma* may have been the single most polarizing route in the move toward sport climbing," Alan says, "which is ironic given that it was a crack climb. Of course, it had nothing to do with the nature of the route. The fact it was in Yosemite created most of the tension, given that Todd and I did the earliest ascents. The hardest single free pitch in the Valley wasn't done by locals and it brought the trad versus sport style issue to the national stage.

"I think everyone just assumed that I just preplaced nuts every two feet when I climbed *The Stigma*," Alan says. "I always saw irony in the fact that I did the route in a style that, apart from hangdog rehearsal, was very difficult to argue against. If Bachar had done the route on nuts, and I had placed bolts on a repeat, I would have been vilified.

"Oh, wait a minute," he remembers, "my ascent *was* vilified. It didn't matter how I did things back then. I was playing by a different set of rules and I wasn't popular in the Valley in 1985 no matter what I did."

Alan admits he hasn't always stayed current with climbing since he left full-time pursuit of the sport in the early 1990s. He got married, had kids, focused on a career. Still, he took notice of what was going on in the sport, especially Caldwell and Jorgeson's 2015 free ascent of the *Dawn Wall* and Honnold's *Freerider* free solo, the latter of which he considers the most outrageous single climb in the history of the sport.

"Where did the roots of these ascents take hold?" Alan wonders rhetorically. "They combined the strengths of the traditionalists and the sport climbers. The free ascent of the *Dawn Wall* borrows pretty obviously from the sport climbing movement. The hardest pitches were rehearsed endlessly before being freed."

One might miss the connection between Honnold's free-solo ascent and the sport climbing pioneers, Alan concedes. "It might seem that Honnold simply evolved from the remarkable solos of John Bachar and Peter Croft," he says. "This is true, but it goes deeper than that. Alex rehearsed *Freerider* extremely carefully, just like we used to do back in the day. He did whatever he needed to do to wire the hardest sections before he did his solo ascent. Imagine if he had been constrained by the 'no hangdogging allowed' ethic. Obviously he never would have succeeded. He probably would never have even tried."

Back in 1985, nontraditional climbers such as Todd and Alan were "cut zero slack," Alan recalls. "If we rehearsed a single move by hangdogging, we were criticized. If we preplaced a single piece of protection, we were ridiculed. The irony," Alan continues, "is that in making their climbs, Caldwell and Honnold used tactics that were, by 1985 standards, clearly taboo. But for good reason, their ascents are universally celebrated. The sport is so much better off now that everyone sees climbing through a broader lens."

In Alan's view, the battle was never about the superiority of sport climbing versus traditional climbing. "All we were fighting for was legitimacy," he says. "In that regard, we clearly won. There doesn't seem to be much of a debate anymore, with hundreds of thousands of sport climbs in the US. But traditional climbing didn't lose—it's still here and more popular than ever."

Alan now views the controversies of the 1980s as petty and unfortunate. "We should have spent less time bickering and more time enjoying the rare opportunities we had to be part of a changing sport," he says. "At the time, I was so caught up in the middle of it, it is only with hindsight that I recognize how fortunate I was to spend so much time with the luminaries of our sport. I regret that I sometimes couldn't look past the bitterness and controversy. Looking back, it's obvious that even those I clashed with the most were truly my peers. I shared more in common with them than ninety-five percent of the people I've met in my life. We were all climbers, and we all enjoyed the exact same thing, with only a few minor stylistic differences."

"That's the wonderful thing about where climbing is today," Alan says. "The battle we fought during the 1980s is over. The sport climbers didn't win. The trad climbers didn't win. Instead, climbing won.

"The cast of characters has changed, and the grades have shot through the roof," he continues. "But the feeling of climbing until you're pumped out of your mind, fighting to hang on and somehow scraping through with barely enough strength to clip the anchors, hasn't changed at all. And that was always the best part, anyway."

Alan has no hard feelings toward his former detractors. "There is not a single character from back in the 1980s that I wouldn't enjoy spending a day with on the rocks," he says. Todd Skinner is at the top of his list. "More than anyone else, Todd was my partner in developing sport climbing in the US. We shared the same views on where we thought climbing should go, and we were both committed to breaking free from the oppressive ethical restraints that we faced."

Alan first met Todd at Joshua Tree in the early 1980s. I remember the two of them trying to toprope *Moonbeam Crack*, a vicious thin crack John Bachar had toproped and rated 5.13a. Alan was clearly having a better go of it. Todd could not believe how strong Alan was for such a scrawny-looking guy. Todd eventually made extended trips to Smith Rock, and they would invariably run into each other when Alan hit the road.

"Todd was a very engaging personality," Alan recalls. "He was tremendously friendly, but he was as competitive as any of us. There was definitely a rivalry between us. We paid attention to what each of us did." Alan recalls how, while Todd was camped out at Smith Rock during the spring of 1986, he would disappear every couple of weeks for a "business trip." Only later did Alan find out through the grapevine that Todd was secretly working on *City Park*. "Todd was savvy enough to see me as competition, and at the time I could have done the route faster than he could. So he worked the route in secrecy."

Alan denies the existence of a race to be the first to establish 5.14 in America. At least, he wasn't racing anybody. "It didn't seem that important for some reason," he recalls. "It was no more important to me than moving from 5.13c to 5.13d." If there was a race between Alan and Todd to be the first to climb 5.14, Alan won the race when he made the second ascent of *Scarface* in 1988. (Todd had come painfully close with his ascents of *City Park*, 5.13d, and *Lizzy Beams Desire*, 5.13d, but would not climb a confirmed 5.14 until 1991.) If Alan had wanted to win the race, he thinks, he would have worked harder to climb his Sunshine Wall project, and would not have been so quick to invite J.B. Tribout to try it. "I had no doubt that I would do that route," Alan says, and he did eventually make the fifth ascent of *To Bolt or Not to Be* in 1989. "But what I completely missed was how quickly everything would evolve. I had operated at my own pace at Smith Rock for years. I assumed that the future would be just the same.

"Todd had a bigger set of gonads than me," Alan admits. "I did what I did at Smith with almost no outside scrutiny. That was the number one reason I had success. I was sensitive to criticism, and since almost every top climber in America was a strict believer in traditional ethics, I opened myself wide to criticism. I was safe in my little haven at Smith. Todd was far more willing to step into the lion's den and do controversial first ascents in traditional areas.

"Todd had a very clear vision of how he planned to make a living as a climber, and he always did his hardest routes with a photographer in tow," Alan recalls. "He always had a strategy, not just for the routes he was working on, but how his career would develop. It paid off for him.

"Todd had a unique capacity to make a person feel special," Alan adds. "He was really just an extraordinary personality, outgoing and very likable. He had a magnetic appeal that just drew people to him. I miss that. I miss his smile and his laugh, and his 'aw-shucks, I'm just a cowboy from Wyoming' persona. But more than anything I miss the conversations about where climbing was going."

TODD WAS ALWAYS LOOKING for the next big thing, some as yet undiscovered climbing area that might become the next Hueco Tanks or Smith Rock, someplace where there weren't any local climbers hung up on ethics or rangers enforcing any damn rules to dissuade him from having his way. He was jealous of Alan Watts, I think, for having had Smith Rock to develop as he pleased, and disappointed that route development at Hueco Tanks was always being restricted. So whenever he heard reports of "miles of limestone cliffs" somewhere, he would check them out. Most of the rumors proved unfounded; there were cliffs out there, but they were remote, or choss, not the sort of area he could develop into a destination climbing area. But then, in 1989, Todd's sister, Holly—a gold prospector who spent a lot of time poking around in the mountains—told him she'd come across an area near Lander in the heart of Wyoming that had limestone cliffs just like the ones Todd had climbed on in Europe.

That summer, Todd was climbing in the Black Hills of South Dakota. Tired of "pinching crystals" in the hot weather, he and his girlfriend, Amy Whisler, went to check out Holly's report. Amy remembers dropping Todd off at one area and then picking him up later at another. "He'd walked along the base of the cliffs," Amy recalls, "and when he came out, he was speechless. He was so psyched he was just silent." It was exactly the kind of place he had dreamed of. "It was his Mecca for sure," Amy says. Todd decided immediately to set up camp in Lander.

"Pack up the house," he said when they got to Pinedale at the end of the season. "We're not coming back." Todd and Amy camped out near Lander for a while, then rented a house. They eventually opened the Wild Iris Mountain Sports climbing shop. Todd invited his friends to join in developing the area, including Paul Piana, Heidi Badaracco, Jacob Valdez, and Steve Bechtel. For the first year or so, this small group quietly developed dozens of routes. Then an article was published and more climbers started to arrive. Lots of them. Just as Todd had hoped, Lander had become a sport climbing destination.

The International Climbers' Festival has been held in Lander since 1993. "It was a sit-around-the-campfire idea," Amy says. "We wondered, 'How can we get Lander on the map? How can we get the town to realize that climbing can be a huge benefit?'" Todd was the "idea guy," but "Paul and Heidi made it happen." The festival just celebrated its twenty-fifth anniversary. Paul was there, giving a slide show about his climbing adventures with Todd.

Amy loved Todd's enthusiasm toward other climbers, how he would encourage and be so psyched for them when they repeated his routes—and even when they would send a route he had tried and given up on. "Todd left behind many unfinished projects, routes he had worked on but couldn't do," Amy recalls. "He knew they would be done someday, and left them for other climbers to do."

One day while exploring Wild Iris, Jacob Valdez discovered a huge boulder that overhung on all sides. "You've got to come see this thing," he told Todd.

"Sure, sure," Todd said, but he already had a lot of projects in the works and put off going. When he did finally go to see it, he came back wide-eyed. Before long, he was working on a route up a particularly overhung face, a technical, sequential, pumpy line with pockets so small only one finger would fit in. Finally, in 1997, Todd pulled it off, establishing *Throwin' the Houlihan* as his first confirmed 5.14 first ascent. Unlike *Lizzy Beams Desire*, a route in the Needles he climbed in 1989 and rated 5.13d, and *City Park*, which has been called a sandbag 5.13d, it has always been agreed that *Throwin' the Houlihan* is 5.14a. It is considered the first 5.14 established by an American climber that has never been downgraded.

ALTHOUGH AMY CONSIDERS HERSELF "a girl who loved to be out there climbing with my friends," she was also active in developing routes at Wild Iris. Among her first ascents is a 5.13a route called *When I Was a Young Girl, I Had Me a Cowboy*, just a couple of routes down from *Throwin' the Houlihan*. But she's most proud of—and sentimental about—a route she called *Wind and Rattle-snakes*. It's only 5.12a, but it was a gift from Todd. "He bolted it and then took me out to it and let me do the first ascent."

Amy's father was a climber, and she joined him and his friends climbing and bouldering at Red Rocks in the late 1960s and early 1970s. She rediscovered climbing after high school and spent the next decade climbing, working odd jobs, and dropping in and out of college. She first met Todd at Hueco Tanks in 1985, just as Todd was leaving for Mexico. A year later, she ran into him at Smith Rock. Then in 1988, she joined Todd and Paul in Yosemite while they prepared for their *Salathé Wall* free attempt. "I dropped them off at the base of El Cap on my way out of the Valley," she recalls. "I got a call from Todd three weeks later. 'I'm alive,' he said. I said, '*What?*' I didn't even know about the accident."

Todd and Amy wed in 1999. Their first child, Hannah, was already a year old. In 2000, they had twins, Sarah and Jake. Being married with children didn't stop Todd from venturing out on climbing trips. Amy stayed home, running the store and raising the kids. It was part of the deal, Amy knew, that being married to Todd meant he would go off on climbing trips. "I kind of liked when he left for a month," she says, a little sheepishly. "That sounds kind of bad to say, but you know what I mean. He'd come home with these great stories, and we'd really want to be together."

Toward the end, before the accident, Todd didn't like being away from the family, Amy says. "He loved being home. All he wanted to do when he came home was sit in the backyard with the kids, doing dad stuff."

I STOOD ALONE ATOP a rock outcropping at the edge of the Mojave Desert near Palmdale early on October 22, 2006, looking out over the high-desert hills and valleys and waves of golden rocks stretching off to the horizon in all directions. At the summit of this little rock formation, I found a sun-faded knotted sling wedged in a fissure, an abandoned rappel or toprope anchor, and thought of Todd Skinner. Peering down over the edge, I could see a shallow flare one might almost call a crack angling up the overhanging wall. This scene reminded me of some other place, some other time—a shaded cove at the edge of Queen Mountain, a sunbaked cliff at the fringe of the Amargosa Desert, a golden dome towering over the South Platte, somewhere I had once been climbing with Todd or some obscure area where Todd had appeared out of nowhere.

In fact, I was standing on top of that sharp little fin of desert stone that I had driven past so many times before because of Todd. Every time I had driven past it, I thought, "I should climb that," but then I always continued on, thinking, "Next time." I had a plane to catch, a desk job to get back to, a lawn to mow. But every time I drove by I could almost hear Todd scolding me for procrastinating. He'd say, with that smirk, "You don't want to be lying on your deathbed sixty years from now thinking, 'Jesus! If only I had climbed that godforsaken rock.'" He was right: I would probably never come back this way; I might never again have this chance. I pulled off the freeway and drove up a canyon road and scrambled up to the top, half expecting to find a weathered note under a rock at the summit: "Smoot! What took you so long?"

From the summit, I scanned the horizon, wondering where Todd might be at this time of year. Joshua Tree? No, not in the fall; he might be there in the spring if he thought there was anything there still worth climbing, but in the fall he would be in Wyoming or Colorado or maybe even Yosemite. It was late, though. Winter was approaching. The big walls would be getting cold, the high mountains would be getting snow. Was he packing out of the Wind River Range? Sending a new desperate route at Wild Iris? Heading south to Urique to explore some as yet undiscovered canyon? I had no doubt he was preparing for or climbing some godforsaken rock somewhere. When I got back to work a couple days later and went online to find out what he was up to, maybe send him an email, I saw the news.

At the exact moment I was on that outcropping thinking of him, Todd was in Yosemite, working on the latest climb of the future, one of his new great projects: a free ascent of an old aid route on Leaning Tower. It was going to be hard, maybe even 5.14. It would be his last big climb in Yosemite, he had confided to others. After this, he was headed home to Lander, finished with Yosemite for good.

Todd had always had a love-hate relationship with Yosemite. He had established some of the hardest free climbs in Yosemite Valley over the past two decades, but free climbing big walls had taken a toll over the years, both physically and mentally. It wasn't all that much fun anymore, and this Leaning Tower route, *Jesus Built My Hotrod*, was just another long, hot, dusty, hard free climb that was taking too damn long to finish. At age forty-seven, Todd was just plain tired of Yosemite. But he was still at it, still pushing it harder than climbers half his age, this time on the verge of establishing a new free route up the most overhanging wall in the Valley—another last great problem that he could not resist if it was humanly possible for him to climb it. He could end his Yosemite climbing career on a high note with this route. And so, he kept at it.

At only 1,100 feet high, Leaning Tower was not such a big wall that you had to suffer too much to free climb it. You didn't have to commit to living on the wall for days or weeks to push a route through. You could rappel off at any point and be on the Valley floor in no time. Leaning Tower was convenient.

Todd was no stranger to the wall. A couple of years before, he and his latest climbing partner, Jim Hewett, had free climbed a variant of another aid route on Leaning Tower, *Wet Denim Daydream*. They renamed it *Wet Lycra Nightmare* (5.13d) for comic effect, even though self-respecting climbers had quit wearing Lycra a decade earlier. No doubt, over the days and weeks and months of effort on *Wet Lycra Nightmare*, Todd had looked over at *Jesus Built My Hotrod*, had perhaps swung over while rappelling down to grab holds here and there and had thought, "You know, this will go." I'm sure he admonished Hewett to tell no one under penalty of death, lest some other climber out there abandon both job and family to try—even though over the years only Todd and a small supporting cast had proven themselves crazy enough to spend that kind of time on a wall in the hope of free climbing what seemed to others to be an impossible line.

It was early afternoon on October 23, 2006, a Monday. Todd and Hewett were back on *Jesus Built My Hotrod*. They had been making progress, inch by inch, day by day, enough to keep them interested and coming back. But after a day of effort rewarded only with several airy leader falls, they decided to start down.

The descent from this high up on Leaning Tower involved a series of airy rappels down fixed ropes anchored at the top and bottom of each pitch—an hour or so of rappelling—then a short walk through the cooling air of Yosemite Valley. Todd and Hewett had already spent many days working on the route, not to mention their previous two years working on *Wet Lycra Nightmare*, so they were all too familiar with the routine, perhaps complacent even. They would rappel off, take a rest day or two, then jumar up the fixed ropes to their high point and continue working the route. Chances were good they might work out the moves and then hopefully complete the route on their next attempt from the ground. Just another couple of days of work and they would be rewarded. Certainly Todd, the eternal optimist, thought so.

Todd went first, sliding off the ledge and out of sight below, as he had done so many times before. Then Hewett heard a *pop*, and the rope, previously taut under the weight of the rappelling climber, went suddenly slack. Hewett looked down to see Todd plummeting into the shadows. After composing himself, and determining that the rope had not failed, Hewett slowly rappelled down. He found Todd's rappel device and a locking carabiner still attached to the rope. When he saw it, he knew exactly what had happened. He detached Todd's hardware from the rope and continued his agonizing descent to the Valley floor.

The belay loop on Todd's harness had failed. It had become frayed over the summer, and Hewett had even asked Todd whether he should get a new harness. "Yeah, yeah, I've got a new one coming," Hewett recalled Todd saying. Frayed or not, the belay loop was plenty strong as far as Todd was concerned, or else he wouldn't have continued to use it, or so one imagines. He had climbed on worse without incident, and had rappelled off Leaning Tower several times already with the frayed belay loop. Those things were bombproof. Even so, he had ordered a new harness, but for now the old one would have to do.

The thing that bothers me and a lot of others who knew him is that Todd's accident was preventable. Most climbers are taught early on to tie backup knots or place backup anchors. An extra overhand knot tied snug against a bowline or figure-eight knot can protect against the knot loosening and raveling. It may seem unlikely that such a knot could untie itself, but it doesn't take much effort to back up a knot, just to be sure. Likewise, anchoring to protection in a crack off to the side of the main anchor—even an old piton—can protect against a fatal fall if the main anchor should fail, as Todd well knew after his and Paul Piana's nearly fatal accident atop the *Salathé Wall*. They had used a large block as an anchor dozens of times, and so had every other climber on the route, and nothing had ever happened. It was bombproof, right? Even so, to be safe, Paul had backed it up, and had lived to tell the tale. Todd could have looped a backup sling through his harness or clipped a Prusik knot tied to the rope.

If he had backed up his frayed belay loop, he might be alive today. The loop may have failed, but the backup system would have stopped Todd's fall after a few inches. Todd's death, regrettably, was entirely his own fault.

Todd's longtime friend and climbing companion Paul Piana concurred. "I'm sad to say that it was equipment failure," Paul said during an NPR interview shortly after Todd's death, "but I have to say it was also Todd's failure in continuing to use it."

AMY FOUND OUT ABOUT THE ACCIDENT the afternoon of October 23, 2006. As usual, she was home in Lander with the kids while Todd was climbing, this time in Yosemite. She'd been running errands, picking up Hannah from ballet lessons, when she was summoned to her parents' home. There was a phone call. It was Jim Hewett, Todd's climbing partner. "There's been an accident," he said.

"Hannah was old enough to know what happened," Amy says. "The twins were too young to really understand. They kind of knew, but . . . " She is silent for a moment, then adds, "I'm kind of mad at him. He was heading home after that trip. He was planning to get in all the work he could on the wall, then get home for the twins' birthday."

The phone kept ringing. Steve Bechtel stepped in and took the calls—calls from friends wanting to express condolences Amy wasn't ready to handle. The town rallied around her. They planned Todd's memorial service, which was held at Sinks Canyon on a sunny October day, Todd's birthday. "It's such a beautiful day," Amy remembers Paul telling the assembled mourners. "You know Todd would be out climbing instead of being here."

TODD SKINNER'S DEATH WAS VERY HARD on Paul. They had climbed together for almost thirty years, all over the world. "He was the brother I never had, the brother I always wanted, and somehow got," Paul said during the NPR interview. "You gained so much more strength being around him, because his energy level was so high. And the joy for climbing is something we both shared, and that exuberance came through. It just bubbled through the rope as you were climbing; it made you climb harder and you could hang on longer. And he was just as happy to see somebody do even better than he would have done on that day, for example, delighted with that person's achievement."

Paul has returned to Newcastle, Wyoming, his childhood hometown. Newcastle is a postwar oil boomtown, "the Western Gateway to the Black Hills, home of the amazing hand-dug oil well," as Paul describes it, referencing aspects of the town's history that the current generation doesn't remember. "Newcastle has always been hard on itself," Paul says. "When they were going to put the interstate through town, the powers that be didn't want all that traffic, so they put it through Gillette. Gillette's a big, thriving town now. Newcastle is still struggling."

Paul's wife, Deb, is the current mayor of Newcastle, and she's trying to bring change, instill some youth into the town's fossilized culture. Paul laments the long, windy, cold winters and the long shifts driving a truck at a nearby coal mine, because he can't go climbing as much as he'd like to. But he still climbs when he can, on local cliffs and in the Needles, and he talks about climbing and his friendship with Todd Skinner with the same youthful enthusiasm he had three decades ago.

"I wasn't as good a climber as Todd," Paul admits. "He was traveling full-time and climbing almost every day. But I was determined. I had the doggedness to do those things. Not the hangdoggedness, though," he adds, laughing.

"The thing I remember most about Todd is he wasn't afraid to do things others were afraid to do," Paul says. "He wasn't afraid to approach people, to ask a dumb question. He wasn't afraid to fall. He kept asking, and he kept trying everything. If he couldn't do it, he kept at it until he succeeded, even if others said it was impossible."

Although Paul did a lot more climbs with Todd, all over the world ("which is why I'm driving a coal truck now," he says. "I spent all my money going on climbing trips with Todd and didn't save anything for retirement!"), he regards the *Salathé Wall* as the most meaningful. "The *Salathé* is such a beautiful route, especially the upper half," he says. "The sweeping corners and cracks, the big roof at the top of the headwall. Just beautiful. We did a lot of other walls after the *Salathé*, but that climb was the most important to us. Our eyes were opened up to what could be possible. It spurred us on to do bigger things. It opened a lot of doors.

"I'm amazed by some of the things that went free," he adds, "and how fast people are doing things now. Holy cow! People running up and down El Cap in just a few hours. I'm jealous of what these young guys and gals are doing now, but I'm also excited.

"I'm proud of the climbs I did with Todd. I also had a blast. I was living the lifestyle I had only dreamed about. Climbing, traveling, meeting people. I wish I could go back and do it all again."

THE SOUND OF A SLAMMING DOOR startles me awake. I sit up, blinking, trying to remember the vestiges of a rapidly fading dream. A desert landscape, a gentle breeze, a white cloud drifting west across an endless blue sky, Todd sitting on top of a granite dome, rope held in his chalked hands, ready to rappel. He looks out across the desert, a tuft of his thinning blond hair waving in the breeze, and smiles at the beauty of it all.

"Everything you ever wanted to do is still possible," he says. "It's only you who says it can't be done." He stands up, steps back, weights the rope, and begins to descend, and as he does he looks at me with that goofy grin of his. "If there is something you want to do in life, you'd better get on it," he says. And then, as he slips over the ledge and out of sight, he adds, "Time waits for no one."

I hear you, Pilgrim. I hear you.

AUTHOR'S NOTE

During the two decades I worked on this book, I tried to write a comprehensive historical narrative that covered every climber, hard climb, contentious issue, and humorous anecdote I could remember or track down. When I approached Kate Rogers at Mountaineers Books, she told me my manuscript was more than twice the length they would consider publishing. I did my best to edit it down to a manageable size, but could not quit adding material even as I deleted. Instead of a sweeping six-hundred-page saga covering the entire sport climbing movement, the story became sharper, focused on a few characters over a more condensed period. Because my original manuscript was cut by more than half, a few scenes ended up being compressed or listed out of order.

Some might complain that the history is incomplete, that I have left out or glossed over important events and characters. Given that an entire book's worth of material was cut, I can't disagree. Others will think I have written too much, that the controversies have been hashed out enough. Fair enough. I didn't set out to stir up old quarrels; I merely wanted to relate this tumultuous period in the sport in an unbiased and humorous manner.

John Long assures me that the story about Ron Fawcett and Peter Livesy on *The Stigma* isn't true. He climbed a lot with Fawcett during his visits to Yosemite, and would know. True or not, it's still a pretty good story, one that Todd seemed to earnestly believe. If so, for once the joke was on him.

I still have not climbed *Astroman*. It's at the top of my list. If somebody wants to climb it with me, we'd better get on it. I don't want to be lying on my deathbed thirty years from now thinking—well, you know.

ACKNOWLEDGMENTS

So much of this happened so long ago, it would be easy to say I don't remember everyone who contributed to this book in some way, but I think I do. Thanks to everyone who made the journey quite memorable. If I've omitted anyone, forgive me. It was a long time ago.

Without the catalysts of those early road trips, I might have melted away in the Seattle rain. My late friend Chris Gentry, who decided we would go to Joshua Tree in the spring of 1982; Mike Mirande, who insisted that I quit my job and come with him to Yosemite in the summer of 1982; and Bob Vinton and Tom Dolliver, for that magic bus ride back to Joshua Tree in the spring of 1983 where I met Todd Skinner and the whole strange journey truly began.

To the many climbers and others I met along the way who provided mentorship, inspiration, a slander session, a place to toss my sleeping bag, a letter or postcard here, a tall tale there, or something else that may have seemed unimportant at the time but stood out upon reflection so many years later especially: Fred Beckey, Erik Thixton, Russell Erickson, Pat Timson, John Stoddard, Jeff Kelley, Kirk Johnston, Rich Marshall, Mark Gunlogson, Brian Scott, Mark Scott, Reese Martin, Kjell Swedin, Dan Lepeska, Mikal Jakubal, Jim Yoder, Bob Kroese, Mark Kroese, Dick Cilley, Richard Ellison, Doug Weaver, Matt Arksey, Jeff Boucher, Kathy Phibbs, Rich Johnston, Dan Cauthorn, Greg Collum, Greg Child, Tom Hargis, Matt Kerns, Mark Twight, Jon Krakauer, Bryan Burdo, Jeff Baird, Ted Yakulic, Darryl Cramer, Terry Lien, Jon Nelson, Greg Olsen, Nicola Masciandaro, Tim Wilson, Scott Northey, Dave Sorrick, Dave Valenzuela, Jean Bonner, Russ Walling, Randy Vogel, Colin Day, Mike Barbitta, Robin Jones, Alison Osius, Steve Hong, Dan Goodwin, Hidetaka Suzuki, Mari Gingery, Lynn Hill, Russ Clune, Mike Freeman, Jonny Woodward, Mariah Cranor, H.B., Mike Paul, John Sherman, Randy Leavitt, Bob Horan, Jimmie Dunn, Neil Cannon,

Steve Schneider, John Middendorf, Charles Cole, Scott Cosgrove, Kurt Smith, Walt Shipley, Perry Beckham, Warren Harding, Jeff Achey, Milt Stickler, Pat Ament, Jim Erickson, Mick Johnston, Chris Hill, Jim Donini, Jim Nelson, Kit Lewis, Jim Purdy, Drew Williams, Ernest M. Burgess, Al Rappoport, Riley Caton, Mary Chambers, Lisa Schassberger, Beth Wald, Diane French, Linda Davis, Patty O'Dea, and Valley Girl Jenny.

To fellow authors, outdoor adventure journalists, authors of those innumerable spirited letters to the editors, and obsessive message board trolls, your writings helped refresh my memory of some of the crazy things that went on back in the day, and I'm sure you will correct any factual errors we didn't catch in your usual thoughtful way.

To the editors of *Climbing*, *Rock & Ice*, and *Mountain* magazines, Michael Kennedy, George Bracksieck, Bernard Newman, and John Steiger, thank you for encouraging me to talk to people I'd never have otherwise talked to, take photos, and write things down. Thank you for paying me for my scribbling or second-rate photos and for sometimes going climbing with me and allowing me to sleep on your couch or in your basement.

To the Smith Rock crew of Alan Watts, Chris Groves, Brooke Sandahl, and Kent Benesch, the toughest editorial board I have ever faced: you taught me how to face rejection with humility, humor, and resilience. And to Mike Volk, for providing a welcoming home base for my many visits there.

To Mark Hudon, Max Jones, John Long, John Sherman, Alan Watts, Paul Piana, Bill Hatcher, Rich Johnston, Amy Skinner, Drew Ruana, Rudy Ruana, Chris Ruana, and Brittany Goris for consenting to interviews and enduring my endless follow-up questions, and to Hudon and Hatcher for providing photos for use in the book.

To Kerwin Klein for helping to weed out any unintended bias and inflammatory rhetoric that may have seeped into the original manuscript, and for saying the story didn't suck too much, which boosted my confidence enough to keep going.

To Chris Miller for keeping me sane enough to finish the project; Nick O'Connell for his mentorship and persuading me to finally seek a publisher; Kate Rogers, Ellen Wheat, Laura Case Larson, Laura Shauger, Jen Grable, and everyone else at Mountaineers Books who helped turn my wordy manuscript into something I hope is worth reading, and Beth Harman for her encouragement and for putting up with me during the final stages.

Of course to Todd Skinner, Paul Piana, John Bachar, Jerry Moffatt, Peter Croft, Kim Carrigan, Geoff Weigand, Alan Watts, and Hugh Herr for letting me ride along and share in so many unforgettable adventures.

And as always, to my parents for allowing me to run wild in the mountains in my youth, and to my brothers for joining me on my early climbing misadventures. It is a wonder we survived.

SELECT REFERENCES

Achey, Jeff, Dudley Chelton, and Bob Godfrey. *Climb! The History of Rock Climbing in Colorado*. Mountaineers Books, 2002.

Bachar, John. "Bachar-Yerian." *Alpinist,* 2009.

Bingham, Dave. "Yaniro Speaks." *Climbing*, 1986.

Cannon, Neil. "The Smoot Syndrome." *Climbing*, 1986.

Chouinard, Yvon. "Are Bolts Being Placed by Too Many Unqualified Climbers?" *Summit Magazine*, 1961.

Colaptino, John. "The Day Todd Skinner Fell to Earth." *Men's Journal*, 2013.

"El Cap: The Free Revolution." *Rock & Ice*, 2018.

Frost, Tom. "Preserving the Cracks!" *American Alpine Journal*, 1972.

Griffith, Christian. "Manifesto." *Climbing*, 1986.

Harding, Warren. *Downward Bound: A Mad! Guide to Rock Climbing*. Prentice-Hall, 1975.

Higgins, Tom. "Tricksters and Traditionalists: A Look at Conflicting Climbing Styles." *Ascent*, Sierra Club, 1984.

Hill, Lynn. *Climbing Free: My Life in the Vertical World*. W. W. Norton & Co., 2003.

———. "El Capitan's Nose Climbed Free." *American Alpine Journal*, 1994.

Hudon, Mark. "Almost Free on the Salathe Wall in 1979." *Climbing* online, 2012.

———. "Astroman." *Climbing*, 1979.

———. "Long, Hard and Free." *Mountain*, 1981.

Hudon, Mark, and Max Jones. "States of the Art." *Mountain* (UK), 1979.

"John Bachar's Last Interview." *Rock & Ice* online, 2012.

Kennedy, Michael, and John Steiger. "The Great Debate." *Climbing*, 1987.

———. "Same Board, Different Rules." *American Alpine Journal*, 1987.

Long, John. *The Stonemasters: California Rock Climbers in the Seventies*. T. Adler Books/Stonemaster Press, 2009.

McNeely, Ammon. "El Cap's Hardest: Wings of Steel." *Rock & Ice*, 2013.

Osius, Alison. *Second Ascent: The Story of Hugh Herr*. Stackpole Books, 1991.

Perlman, Eric. "A Friend in Need." *Mountain*, 1979.

Piana, Paul. *Big Walls: Breakthroughs on the Free-Climbing Frontier*. Sierra Club Books, 1998.

———. "The Free Salathe." *American Alpine Journal,* 1989.

———. "The Free Salathe." *Climbing,* 1988.

———. "The Future Is Now: A Conversation with Todd Skinner." *Rock & Ice,* 1985.

"Profiles (of Women Climbers)." *Climbing,* 1987.

"Remembering John Bachar." *Alpinist,* 2009.

Robbins, Royal. "The El Capitan Climb." *Summit,* 1970.

———. "Yosemite Renaissance." *Summit,* 1971.

Roberts, David. "The Mechanical Boy Comes Back." *Moments of Doubt*. Mountaineers Books, 1986.

Robinson, Bestor. "Shiprock." *American Alpine Journal,* 1940.

Robinson, Rob. "Pox in Vulgaria: The Profit of Impurism." *Climbing,* 1979.

Rowell, Galen. "Climbing Half Dome the Hard Way." *National Geographic,* 1974.

Samet, Matt. "Todd Skinner: Loss of a Legend." *Climbing* online, 2006.

Scott, Chic. *Pushing the Limits: The Story of Canadian Mountaineering*. Rocky Mountain Books, 2002.

Sherman, John. "Down to Earth with Ron Kauk." *Climbing,* 1986.

Skinner, Todd. "Storming the Tower." *National Geographic,* 1996.

———. "Half Dome Free Climbed." *American Alpine Journal,* 1994.

Smoot, Jeff. "Alan Watts (Profile)." *Rock & Ice,* 1986.

———. "A Conversation with Jerry Moffatt." *Climbing,* 1985.

———. "Kim Carrigan: A Conversation with Australia's Leading Rock Climber." *Climbing,* 1985.

———. "The Valley Syndrome." *Climbing,* 1986.

———. "Altered States: Hard Climbing in America in the 1980s." *Climbing,* 1986.

———. "Peter Croft (Profile)." *Climbing,* 1986.

———. *Pumping Concrete: A Guide to Seattle-Area Climbing Walls*. Fourth Hill Publishing, 2018.

———. *Schurman Rock: A History & Guide*. Fourth Hill Publishing, 2018.

Steiger, John. "Johnny Rock." *Climbing,* 1986.

———. "Lynn Hill (interview)." *Climbing,* 1987.

Taylor, Joseph E., III. *Pilgrims of the Vertical: Yosemite Rock Climbers and Nature at Risk*. Harvard University Press, 2010.

Watts, Alan. *Climber's Guide to Smith Rock*. Chockstone Press, 1992.

———. "Eurotrends." *Climbing,* 1987.

"Who's Your Friend? Alec Sharp Interviews Ray Jardine." *Mountain,* 1979.

ABOUT THE AUTHOR

Jeff Smoot is a lawyer, writer, and photographer primarily known for his hiking and climbing guidebooks. He was a frequent contributor to *Climbing*, *Rock & Ice*, and *Mountain* magazines during the 1980s, and has also written for *Backpacker* and *Outside* magazines, the *Western American Literature* journal, and *The Writer's Workshop Review*. He lives in Seattle.

MOUNTAINEERS BOOKS

SKIPSTONE   BRAIDED RIVER

recreation • lifestyle • conservation

MOUNTAINEERS BOOKS, including its two imprints, Skipstone and Braided River, is a leading publisher of quality outdoor recreation, sustainability, and conservation titles. As a 501(c)(3) nonprofit, we are committed to supporting the environmental and educational goals of our organization by providing expert information on human-powered adventure, sustainable practices at home and on the trail, and preservation of wilderness.

Our publications are made possible through the generosity of donors, and through sales of more than 800 titles on outdoor recreation, sustainable lifestyle, and conservation. To donate, purchase books, or learn more, visit us online:

MOUNTAINEERS BOOKS

1001 SW Klickitat Way, Suite 201 • Seattle, WA 98134
800-553-4453 • mbooks@mountaineersbooks.org • www.mountaineersbooks.org

An independent nonprofit publisher since 1960

OTHER MOUNTAINEERS BOOKS TITLES YOU MAY ENJOY

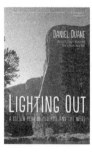